力争 5 分：AP 中文考试模拟练习题

CHENG & TSUI STRIVE FOR A 5

AP* Chinese Practice Tests

Weiman Xu 徐未曼
Han Qu 瞿菡
Sara Gu 顾新
So Mui Chang 张素梅
Lisha Kang 康丽莎

CHENG & TSUI
USA

27 26 25 24 23 11 12 13 14 15

11th Printing

Published by
Cheng & Tsui Company, Inc.
25 West Street
Boston, MA 02111-1213 USA
Fax (617) 426-3669
www.cheng-tsui.com
"Bringing Asia to the World"™

Traditional and Simplified Characters
ISBN 978-0-88727-764-1

Library of Congress Cataloging-in-Publication Data

Cheng & Tsui Strive for a 5 : AP Chinese practice tests / Weiman Xu ... [et al.] = [Li zheng 5 fen: AP Zhong wen kao shi mo ni lian xi ti / Xu Weiman ... et al.]
p. cm.
Parallel title in Chinese characters.
Includes bibliographical references and index.
ISBN 978-0-88727-764-1
1. Chinese language--Examinations, questions, etc. 2. Advanced placement programs (Education) I. Xu, Weiman. II. Title: AP Chinese practice tests. III. Title: Li zheng 5 fen : AP Zhong wen kao shi mo ni lian xi ti.

PL1119.C45 2009
495.1'82421076--dc22

2009075169

Audio production by Jiawei Guo, Han Qu, Weiman Xu, and Jasmine Guo
Artwork by Sara Gu and Sheridan Moehle
Chinese text editor: Dali Tan
English text editor: Laurel Damashek

Printed in the United States of America

Publisher's Note

The Cheng & Tsui AP Preparation Series is designed to publish and widely distribute quality language learning materials created by leading instructors from around the world. We welcome readers' comments and suggestions concerning the publications in this series. Please contact the following members of our Editorial Board, in care of our Editorial Department (e-mail: **editor@cheng-tsui.com**).

Audio Information

Readers have access to free audio files that correspond to the listening and speaking sections of the practice tests. The sections that have corresponding audio files are marked with this icon: ▶

To access the audio, simply visit **www.cheng-tsui.com/resources** and follow the instructions.

For technical support, please contact **support@cheng-tsui.com** or call 1-800-554-1963 (toll-free) or 617-988-2400.

We owe our heartfelt gratitude to our families for their unwavering support.

This book is dedicated to our families.

ABOUT THE AUTHORS

Weiman Xu earned her Ph.D. in Sociology from the State University of New York at Albany, her M.A. in Economics from Chinese Academy of Social Sciences in Beijing, and her B.A. in Economics from Peking University. Her research articles have been published in various professional journals. Dr. Xu has been actively involved in teaching and promoting Chinese cultural heritage in her community. She lives with her family in California.

Han Qu earned her post-graduate degrees from the University of Illinois at Urbana-Champaign and Jiao Tong University in Shanghai. She was born and raised in China and has been working in the United States for many years. She lives in California and travels to China every year.

Sara Xin Gu earned her M.S. in Library and Information Science from the University of California at Berkeley and her B.S. in Computer Science from Jiao Tong University in Shanghai. She has been a principal and an academic dean in a local Chinese school for many years. She is now a business owner promoting technology exchanges between Western countries and China.

So Mui Chang earned her M.S. in Computer Science at Union College, New York, and her B.S. in Computer Science and Applied Mathematics at the State University of New York at Stony Brook. She has been Children's Mandarin Class Program Coordinator in Alameda, California since 2000.

Lisha Kang obtained her Graduate Diploma in Computer Science from Concordia University in Canada and her Bachelor of Science from Liaoning University in China. She has been the Director and Vice Principal of local Chinese schools in California for many years. In 2007, she led 53 students from California in a Chinese instrumental performance in Beijing for the 2008 Olympics one year countdown celebrations, which aired on China's CCTV television station. She has been a Chinese teacher since 2003.

CONTENTS

PREFACE

AP Chinese Language and Culture: Practice Tests has been written primarily as a resource for the high school Advanced Placement Chinese Language and Culture (hereafter AP Chinese) course and exam preparation. The tests in this book will provide you with extensive language skills practice and broad culture exposure to help you prepare for the AP Chinese Exam and reinforce your Chinese language skills. The practice tests in this book use the format and themes specified by the College Board for the AP Chinese Examination in 2009–2011.

This book is organized in eight units by cultural theme: customs, daily life, economics, education, entertainment, family, geography, and mixed theme. Each unit is an independent full-length practice test that comes with answer keys for the multiple-choice section. Depending on your preferences and needs, the units can be completed in order, or rearranged to focus on areas that may need more review. This book provides practice questions for all four language skills tested on the exam: listening, reading, writing, and speaking.

How to Use This Book

- This book is designed to be used within the timeline of a typical AP class. Normally, an AP class runs for eight months from September to April, given that the AP Chinese Exam takes place in early May every year. We suggest covering one practice exam per month during the school year.

- If you are seeking a self-paced resource for extra exam preparation, we hope you will also find this book to be a useful supplement.

- The first seven units of the book are organized around cultural themes that are widely used in AP courses, covered in AP-level textbooks, and tested on the AP exam. Each unit provides a full practice exam covering listening, reading, writing, and speaking sections.

- Teachers and students may choose to use the units in this book in any order to fit the needs of their curriculum. The eighth unit has a mixed theme, which can be used at the end of the course or for intensive review before the AP Exam.

Unique Features

- This book adheres closely to the testing format specified in the latest *AP Chinese Language and Culture Course Description, 2009–2011*. The book simulates all aspects of the actual AP exam, such as the length of the test, number of questions, response time restrictions, types of materials, and level of difficulty.

- This book provides eight full-length practice tests, enough to use in a year-long AP Chinese course.

- This book presents Chinese in both simplified and traditional characters, as in the actual AP Chinese examination. In this book, we present simplified characters on the left and traditional characters on the right wherever the two character sets appear side by side; we present simplified characters followed by traditional characters wherever the two character sets appear one after another.

- This book offers valuable suggestions for effective test preparation and test-taking skills, based on the authors' extensive experience as teachers and parents, and their research on College Board's AP exam scoring guidelines.

Supplementary Materials

- Free downloadable audio files for the listening and speaking exercises may be downloaded from www.cheng-tsui.com/downloads.
- Text scripts for all audio materials used in the tests, in both simplified and traditional Chinese characters, are included in this book's appendix.
- This book provides a vocabulary index as a convenient reference and study tool.

Acknowledgments

We thank Kristen Wanner, acquisitions editor at Cheng & Tsui Company, for her guidance and support throughout the process. We thank managing editor Penny Stratton at Cheng & Tsui Company for her diligent work. We thank the Chinese text editor Dali Tan and the English text editor Laurel Damashek for their valuable input. We thank all the members of the Cheng & Tsui editorial team for their reviews and suggestions.

We thank Mr. Ruping Xu for his valuable advice.

We also thank following people for their contributions: Angelica Pan, Annie Wang, Austin Moehle, Eric Tu, Jiawei Guo, Neil Tu, Rebecca Pan, Sheridan Moehle, and Tracy Guo.

Strive for a 5

AP Chinese Practice Tests

An Introduction to AP Chinese Language and Culture

About the AP Exam

The Advanced Placement (AP hereafter) Program offered by the College Board provides high school students an opportunity to take college-level courses. As of 2009, the AP Program offers more than 30 exams.[1] There are 10 AP exams for foreign languages, such as French, Spanish, Japanese, and Chinese.

The AP exam is scored on a 5-point scale:

5 = extremely well qualified
4 = well qualified
3 = qualified
2 = possibly qualified
1 = no recommendation

According to College Board, "AP Exam grades of 5 are equivalent to A grades in the corresponding college course. AP Exam grades of 4 are equivalent to grades of A–, B+, and B in college. AP Exam grades of 3 are equivalent to grades of B–, C+, and C in college."[2] Although scores of 3 or above are considered qualifying AP Exam Scores for college credit, each college or university has its own policy on granting credits or placement for AP exams.

Currently, colleges and universities in more than 55 countries accept AP exam scores for college credit. Taking AP courses is neither a high school graduation requirement nor a college admission requirement; however, many colleges use AP scores and course experience to measure students' readiness for college.

The AP exams are held annually during the first two weeks of May. The College Board announces the exam calendar at the beginning of each school year. Students must register through their school or school district for AP courses and exams. The test center is usually at the students' own school. Please refer to the College Board website (www.collegeboard.com) for further details.

---

1 The College Board. "About AP." http://www.collegeboard.com/student/testing/ap/about.html (accessed September 24, 2009). All statistics and information regarding the AP exam in this Introduction are from the College Board website.

2 The College Board. "AP Chinese Language and Culture Course Description 2009-2011" http://apcentral.collegeboard.com/apc/public/repository/ap08_chinese_coursedesc.pdf (accessed September 24, 2009).

There are typically two exam sessions per day. In most states, the first session starts at 8 a.m. and the second session begins at noon. If a student has two AP exams scheduled at the same time, one of the exams will be moved to a later testing date. Students should take the possible time conflict into consideration when selecting AP classes and student who are enrolled in multiple AP classes should try to avoid having to take two exams on the same day.

About AP Chinese

The AP Chinese Exam was first held in 2007 with 3,261 participants, and has become more and more popular every year. In 2008 there were 4,311 students participated in the exam and in 2009 the number of participants increased to 5,100[3]. The initial AP Chinese Exam lasted about 3 hours. Beginning in 2009, the testing format was adjusted and the testing time has now been shortened to 2 hours and 15 minutes.

According to the *Chinese Language and Culture Course Description 2009-2011*[4], the AP Chinese course is comparable to a fourth-semester or equivalent college course in Mandarin Chinese. The AP Chinese exam is designed for students who have taken either the AP Chinese course or an equivalent Chinese course. However, students who are not able to take an AP course (for example, students whose schools do not offer an AP Chinese course, or homeschooled students) can also take the AP exam through a participating school (contact the College Board for more details).

The AP Chinese Exam tests both language skills and cultural knowledge. Each section of the exam tests interpretive, interpersonal, and presentational language skills. The exam does not explicitly test grammatical knowledge, but rather integrates grammatical knowledge into the language skills that are tested. The AP exam not only assesses your communication skills, but also evaluates your knowledge of Chinese customs, history, literature, art, and society.

The Testing Environment

The entire AP Chinese Exam is administered on the computer. You will be given time to test the computer and its peripherals at the beginning of the exam.

You will have an opportunity to set up your Chinese typing preferences before the exam begins. Microsoft IME is the designated software for Chinese input. You may choose

---

3 The College Board. "Program Summary Report 2009." http://professionals.collegeboard.com/profdownload/program-summary-report-09.pdf (accessed September 24, 2009).

4 The College Board. "AP Chinese Language and Culture Course Description 2009-2011." http://apcentral.collegeboard.com/apc/public/repository/ap08_chinese_coursedesc.pdf

between two input methods: *Pinyin* and *Zhuyin Fuhao (Bopomofo)*. If you choose Zhuyin Fuhao as an input method, traditional characters will be displayed. If you intend to use Pinyin for input, you need to further choose the display method by selecting either simplified (简) or traditional (繁) characters on the IME toolbar.

For Chinese text display, you may choose between traditional or simplified characters by using a toggle button. This toggle button will be shown on the toolbar, whenever Chinese text is displayed for you to read during the exam.

Test-related instructions and directions are pre-recorded. They will appear on the screen while the sound recordings are played on the computer. There is a countdown clock on screen to help you keep track of the time in the reading, writing, and speaking sections.

Scrap paper will be provided for those who want to take notes. Any notes you write will be collected by the proctor at the end of the exam, but the notes will not be graded.

The Four Exam Sections

The AP Chinese Exam is divided into two major sections. The first section consists of multiple-choice listening and reading questions. The second section consists of free-response to writing and speaking questions. Although the allotted testing times for listening, reading, writing, and speaking sections are different, each section counts for 25 percent of the final score.

- **Listening:** Only those questions and choices that are in English will be displayed on screen. On the other hand, any questions and choices that are in Chinese will not be displayed on screen, but you will hear the Chinese through headphones. You will select the answers on screen.

- **Reading:** All reading materials and corresponding questions will be displayed on screen. You will also mark your answers on screen.

- **Writing:** The writing prompt is displayed on screen. In this part of the exam, you will be given the opportunity to choose your desired input method by selecting "Pinyin" or "Bopomofo" from a dropdown list.

- **Speaking:** The prompts for the Conversation and Cultural Presentation sections are read out by the computer and are also displayed on screen. You will use the microphone provided to record your verbal reply and presentation.

For detailed explanations and examples of each part of the exam, please refer to the College Board's AP Chinese Language and Culture Exam Overview.[5]

---

[5] The College Board. "AP Chinese Language and Culture Exam Overview." http://professionals.collegeboard.com/profdownload/AP-Chinese-Exam-Overview.pdf (accessed September 24, 2009).

AP CHINESE EXAM SECTION I: MULTIPLE CHOICE

Section I of the AP Chinese Exam is multiple choices, and it primarily assesses your interpersonal and interpretive communication skills. This section is further divided into Part A: Listening and Part B: Reading. Answers for this section are graded by computer. A correct answer receives 1 point; a blank answer receives 0 points, and a wrong answer deducts 1/3 points. In other words, for multiple choice sections:

	Correct answer	Blank	Incorrect answer
raw score	+1	0	−1/3

Total raw score = # of correct answers – # of incorrect answers * 1 / 3

For example, if there are 36 multiple choice questions in reading, a student gets 26 right, 4 unanswered and 6 incorrect, then the total raw score of the section for the student is 24 (26 – 6 * 1/3 = 24).

Suggestions

1. Do not guess randomly

The AP Chinese Exam is a four-option multiple-choice test. If you guess at random on four questions in a row, you should get one of these four correct and three of them wrong by random chance. Since you will get one point for the one correct answer, and lose one-third of a point for each of the three wrong answers, your net raw score will be zero. Therefore, random guessing should not help or hurt you on the exam. This means that you should not waste your time by randomly guessing on questions that you do not have time to answer. It is better to leave it blank than to guess randomly.

You should not use a set pattern to guess at answers, such as marking all Bs. It is a myth that some letters (such as C) are used for correct answers more frequently than others (A, B, and D).

2. Use "process of elimination" aggressively and frequently

While completely random guessing is neutralized by one-third of a point deduction for every incorrect answer, educated or informed guessing will increase your score. "Process of elimination" is a commonly used strategy for educated guessing in multiple-choice test. In many cases, identifying the wrong answers is easier than identifying the right ones, especially for more difficult problems. On most problems that you have time to think over carefully, you will be able to eliminate something. If you can eliminate even one choice and make informed guesses, then you will improve your odds to get it right. Even if you cannot definitively identify the correct answer, you should eliminate the choices that you know are impossible or unreasonable, guess from the remaining choices, and move on to the next problem.

Part A: Listening

The listening part of the exam is further subdivided into Rejoinders and Listening Selections. The topics on this part of the exam are often related to everyday life, travel, entertainment, education, daily life routines, etc.

	Time (in Minutes)	% of Final Score	Number of Questions	Response Time Per Question
Rejoinders	10	10%	10–15	5 seconds
Listening Selections	10	15%	15–20	12 seconds

I. Rejoinders

You will select an answer from the four choices provided to best complete or continue a given conversation segment in Chinese. The answer choices will be read out loud on the recording, but will not be shown on the screen. You will only see the question number and four choices: (A), (B), (C), and (D) on screen.

Example:

[You will hear this recording]

甲： 今天的天气真热！

乙： (A) 是啊，要多穿些衣服。
(B) 那就开冷气吧。
(C) 昨天下雨了？
(D) 热狗真好吃。

[Screen display]

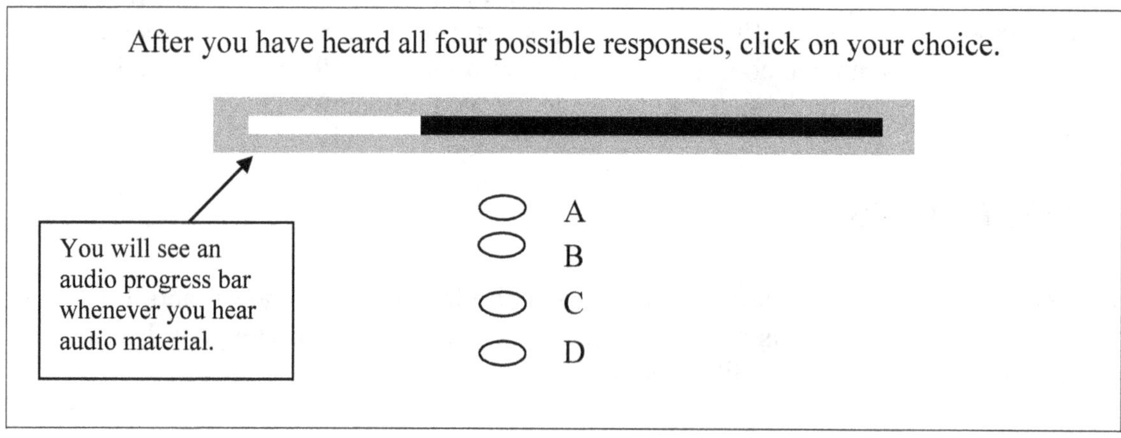
After you have heard all four possible responses, click on your choice.
You will see an audio progress bar whenever you hear audio material.
A
B
C
D

Correct Answer: (B)

II. Listening Selections

You will listen to many types of stimuli such as notices, announcements, instructions, advertisements, conversations, etc. You will answer one to five questions based on each listening selection. The recordings for some selections will be played more than once.

The Listening Selections portion of the exam will display the questions and the multiple choices in English on the screen; however, the recordings are in Chinese only.

Example:

[You will hear this recording]

<身份证检查>

自 2008 年 6 月 21 日起，年满十八岁的乘客必须出示美国联邦或州政府发行的有效身份证通过检查站后，才能搭乘航班。身份证上必须有乘客的照片、姓名、出生日期、性别和有效日期。未能出示有效证件的乘客将被拒绝搭乘航班。

[Screen display]

AP Chinese Language and Culture - Listening		VOLUME
	Question 6 of 20	HIDE TIME 00 : 00 : 12

What is the point of this announcement?

- ○ Children under 18 must travel with an adult guardian.
- ○ Adult passengers must present a valid identification card at the airport checkpoint.
- ○ The identification card must show name, birth date, gender, and date of issue.
- ○ All passengers must show a valid identification card at the airport

Correct Answer: The second choice

The multiple choice answer options for each question, for both Rejoinders and Listening Selections, only appear once on the screen. You must answer the question in the given order and within the time limit; otherwise, you forfeit the question. It is not possible to go back and answer a question later.

Suggestions

1. **Practice within the time limits**
   In the listening section, you may not have time at all to jot down any notes, because the time to respond to each question is very short. We recommend that you take the practice test at home with a time limit when you use this book. In all of our audio recordings, we leave you a response time after each question that matches the response time given in a real exam. The recordings are available at Cheng & Tsui's website (www.cheng-tsui.com); please see page iv for information about how to download audio files. Please take advantage of those recordings to practice. Timed practice will give you a feel of the test in real time, help you pace yourself, and in turn increase your speed of response.

2. **Become familiar with different types of questions**
   Through repeated practice, you will become familiar with different types of questions; knowing how to respond to each type of question will save you a second or two of reaction time per question, which is to your advantage when there are only five seconds to answer some of the questions. This familiarity will not only improve speed but also the accuracy. Note that this listening section accounts for 25% of the total score.

My study notes and useful tips:

Part B: Reading

The reading selections include a wide range of stimulus types such as advertisements, notes, posters, articles, signs, e-mails, etc. The reading selections vary in length and level of difficulty. Each reading selection is followed by 1–5 questions.

In this part of the exam, you do not have to read the selections or answer the questions in sequential order. You can move back and forth among the selections and questions. There will be no time limit set for each passage or each question. Rather, the time limit is for the entire reading section, which is 60 minutes.

	Time (In Minutes)	% of Final Score	Number of Questions	Number of Reading Selections
Reading	60	25%	35–40	7–10

Example:

AP Chinese Language and Culture – Reading | SWITCH TO TRADITIONAL | REVIEW MARK HELP BACK NEXT

Question 3 of 40 | HIDE TIME 00 : 55 : 00

Read this essay

在美国学中文

周末，许多在美国生活的华人孩子大概都要做同样的一件事，那就是上中文学校。

从小我父母就跟我说，我们是华人，必须要学会中文，才能传承中国文化。每逢周日，邻家的孩子们高高兴兴地到公园里玩，我却要背着书包到中文学校学中文。

起先，我不明白我为什么一定要学中文，很不愿意去中文学校。年复一年，我慢慢地找到了学中文的乐趣，在中文学校里，我不但学中文，还学中国画，武术等才艺。去年夏天，我到中国看望爷爷奶奶，大家都夸我的中文讲得好呢。

3. Which day does the author have to go to Chinese school?

(A) Monday

(B) Friday

(C) Saturday

(D) Sunday

Correct Answer: (D)

There is a toggle button that you can use to switch between simplified characters and traditional characters.

AP Chinese Language and Culture – Reading	SWITCH TO SIMPLIFIED	REVIEW MARK HELP BACK NEXT
	Question 3 of 40	HIDE TIME 00 : 55 : 00

Read this essay

在美國學中文

週末，許多在美國生活的華人孩子大概都要做同樣的一件事，那就是上中文學校。

從小我父母就跟我說，我們是華人，必須要學會中文，才能傳承中國文化。每逢週日，鄰家的孩子們高高興興地到公園裡玩，我卻要背著書包到中文學校學中文。

起先，我不明白我為什麼一定要學中文，很不願意去中文學校。年復一年，我慢慢地找到了學中文的樂趣，在中文學校裡，我不但學中文，還學中國畫，武術等才藝。去年夏天，我到中國看望爺爺奶奶，大家都誇我的中文講得好呢。

3. Which day does the author have to go to Chinese school?

(A) Monday

(B) Friday

(C) Saturday

(D) Sunday

Correct Answer: (D)

Notes

During this part of the exam, there are several functional buttons on screen, such as REVIEW, MARK, HELP, BACK, NEXT, and also a countdown clock onscreen that shows the amount of time remaining in the section.

- **REVIEW：** When you click the "REVIEW" button, the screen will display all questions in numerical order with corresponded passages, a flag if a question is marked, and whether the question has been answered. You can simply click the question number and the "GO TO QUESTION" button to move to a specific question, instead of wasting valuable time by moving one question at a time.

- **MARK:** Clicking the MARK button flags a question for later review. Click MARK again to unmark.

- **HELP：** Provides test-related information and instructions. There you can get information on direct topics by clicking on one of the following buttons:

Testing Tools	How to Answer	How to Scroll	General Directions	Part Directions

  For example, during reading exam, if you click on **Testing Tools**, the HELP screen will display information on how to use the buttons on top of the screen, such as REVIEW, MARK, HELP, BACK, and NEXT.

- **BACK:** BACK returns the screen to the previous question or the previous selection.

- **NEXT:** Use NEXT to move to the next question or screen.

Suggestions

1. Before the exam officially starts, you will be given a few minutes to test the computer setup and try out the function buttons. You should familiarize yourself with these buttons, so you can use them efficiently during the exam.

2. It is not possible to highlight or make notes on the reading selections or questions on the computer. You may use the scrap paper provided to take simple notes on key words or facts such as time, place, direction, number, etc.

3. It's a good idea to browse the questions that go with the reading selection before reading the passage in detail. By doing this, you can focus your attention on the relevant information in a passage. Remember, there is only one BEST answer.

4. The length and level of difficulty of each reading selection varies. If you have trouble comprehending a selection, you may want to skip it and go on to the next one. You can always return later to that particular passage if time permits.

5. The level of difficulty of the questions may vary even within the same reading selection. Since each question is worth the same point value whether it is easy or hard, do not spend too much time on any one question. Instead, you may use the "MARK" button to mark a question if you are unsure of the answer before moving on to other questions. One strategy that many people find useful is to answer the easier questions first and then come back to tackle the marked questions later.

There is a 10-minute break between the multiple-choice and free-response sections. After the break, you must wait for the proctor's instructions before resuming the exam. You should take advantage of this time to rest. Try not to think about the parat of the test that you have just finished. Clear your mind and get ready for the next part of the test.

My study notes and useful tips:

AP CHINESE EXAM SECTION II: FREE RESPONSE

The free-response section includes writing and speaking parts. The writing and speaking sections each count for 25 percent of the final score. AP Exam readers (college professors of Chinese and experienced AP teachers from all over the country) will score your answers following the College Board's *AP Chinese Language and Culture Scoring Guidelines.*[6] The grading rubrics for writing and speaking take into account three general aspects: Task Completion, Delivery, and Language Usage. The score for each of these aspects ranges from 0 (Unacceptable) to 6 (Excellent). The total score is the sum of the three composite scores.

While the writing and speaking test formats are different, the scoring criteria are similar.

The Task Completion aspect considers:

- Are all parts of the question answered? Does the answer stay on topic?
- Is the answer complete and thorough? For example, does the story narration have a beginning, middle, and an end?
- Is the content well organized and coherent with a clear progression of ideas?
- Are there relevant details and examples? Is the topic explored in detail?
- Are the sentences and ideas well connected? Does the answer use appropriate transitional elements and cohesive devices?

The Delivery aspect is about the consistent use of language register[7] appropriate to situation. For example, you would use more formal language for a story narration than for an e-mail response. Similarly, the delivery of a conversation is less formal than that of a cultural presentation.

The Language Usage aspect evaluates your use of appropriate vocabulary words, phrases, and idioms to enhance the vividness of the writing or speech. It is desirable to use a wide range of grammatical structures with minimal errors; however, accuracy is also important, so you should make sure you are familiar with the grammatical structures you

---

6 The College Board. "AP Chinese Language and Culture 2008 Scoring Guidelines." 01 Oct. 2008. http://www.collegeboard.com/prod_downloads/ap/students/china/ap08_chinese_sgs.pdf (accessed September 24, 2009).

7 *Register* in this context means the level of formality. We all use different levels of language formality in written and spoken English. For instance, the register of a formal history paper differs from an informal e-mail to a friend. The language register used should be appropriate to the intended audience.

use. In the writing part, make sure to select the correct words from the list of homophones that come up in the Chinese input software. If you have time, taking a moment to review your answer after you finish can help you to spot any errors. As trivial as it may seem, proper punctuation marks are also noted and contribute to the overall grade. For example, you should make sure to use the Chinese period "。" in place of an English "." at the end of a Chinese sentence.

Part A: Writing

The writing part of the exam assesses interpersonal and presentational communication skills. The exam tests your ability to interpret the problem(s) presented in the prompt, analyze the problem(s), and come up with solutions or suggestions. It also tests whether you can write in Chinese in a logical and coherent way.

The writing part of the exam is divided into Story Narration and E-mail Response. In Story Narration, you interpret and narrate a story from a series of four pictures. In E-mail Response, you analyze the problems presented in the e-mail and respond with solutions or suggestions.

	Time (in Minutes)	% of Final Score	Number of Questions
Story Narration	15	15%	1
E-mail Response	15	10%	1

I. Story Narration

In this part of the exam, you are asked to write a story narration based on a set of four pictures. The story should be presented in a well-organized, logical, and coherent format to demonstrate excellence in presentational writing. It should have a beginning, middle, and an end; it should also include details that are relevant to the topic. Furthermore, for the highest possible score, it is crucial to use transitional phrases, cohesive devices, and time phrases to show a clear progression of ideas.

Example:

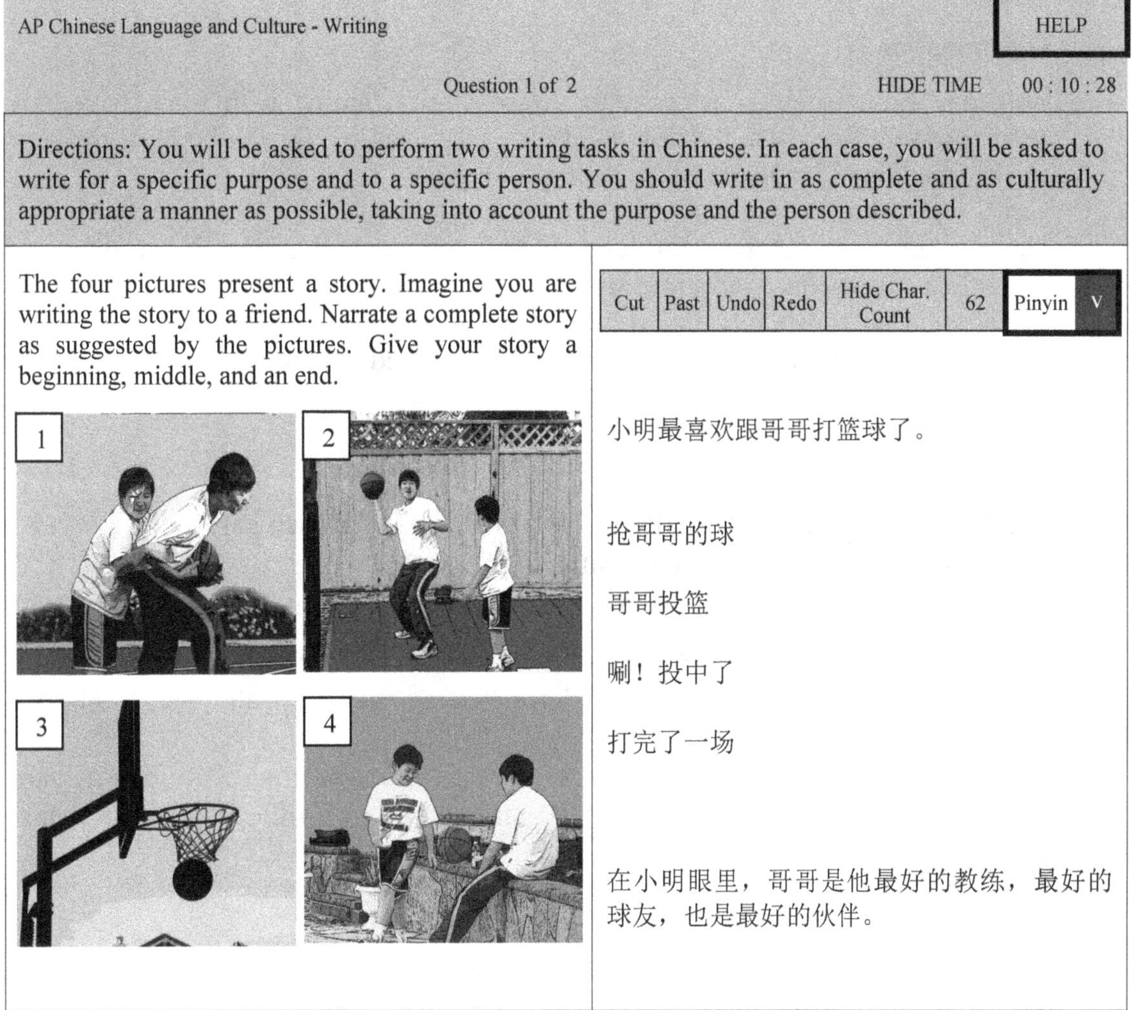

Notes

A clock at the top of the screen will show you how much time is remaining to write your response. When the response time has ended, you will automatically go on to the next question. You cannot return to previous questions.

You can choose between two input methods by selecting “Pinyin” or “Bopomofo” from the drop-down list.

As in the reading part of the exam, you may also access the Help screens in this section. For instance, by clicking **How to Answer** button on the **Help** screen during the writing exam, you will find help on editing tools, such as how to cut, paste, undo, redo, character count, input method, and keyboard keys (tab, backspace, and delete).

Suggestions

1. Organization

You may find it helpful to first jot down a brief outline with three parts: 1) a beginning sentence, 2) a few key points from the pictures for the body of the story, and 3) an ending sentence. See the example above.

This can help you organize your thoughts and come up with a storyline. Having such an outline also helps you come up with a complete story that has a beginning, middle, and an end before time runs out. To save time, you can write the outline directly on the computer instead of on scrap paper, and then replace it with the actual story as you write it.

2. Coherence

After you write your outline, fill in supporting details for each part of the story. It is essential to use the appropriate transitional phrases and cohesive devices, such as 然后，于是，当...的时候，一...就..., and so on to connect sentences and details. This will ensure that the story flows smoothly. Using our example, you may add“从小”，“每天”，or“哥哥一进家门...小明就...” to the opening paragraph.

With a clear progression of ideas, readers can follow the writing easily, and the story will no longer sound like an outline. Do make sure to vary the transitional phrases you use, in order to avoid repetition.

3. Narration

The pictures are in sequence. You should follow the order of the pictures to tell a story, and use the information given in each and every picture. Be sure to add supporting details to your outline. For example, in the above example add "his older brother is the basketball team captain at his high school." Use descriptive words and phrases to paint a vivid picture for your readers and to bring your characters to life. For example, you may use words like“身材高大”,“动作敏捷”,“球艺高超”,“大汗淋漓”,“气喘吁吁”,“紧紧地”，or“佩服”etc.

Although different students may interpret the pictures differently and there is no one right answer or storyline, you do need to keep the story consistent with the theme you choose and stay on topic. In other words, you should tell a consistent story and avoid drifting away from the topic.

4. **Level of formality**

The narration should use a level of formality that is appropriate to the situation. A good rule of thumb is to write it as if you were telling the story to a friend. The point of view should be consistent throughout the narration. Using the third person, or giving a name to the characters, is often a great idea. In our example, we call the younger boy 小明 instead of "that boy" or "the younger boy".

5. **Time management**

It is a good idea to keep an eye on the clock so you can balance the amount of time you spend on each picture. If you take too much time on one picture, you may not have enough time left for others. You should also save a few minutes at the end to proofread and revise or edit your story. Even if you do not have enough time to edit in depth, it helps to do a quick scan for any mistyped characters or punctuation.

My study notes and useful tips:

II. E-mail Response

In this part of the test, you will be asked to read an e-mail in Chinese and then write a reply in Chinese to address the issues raised. The goal of this part is to assess your ability to express opinions and/or make suggestions cohesively in writing. You will not be judged on whether your suggestions or opinions are right or wrong, only on how well you express them. Again, task completion, delivery, and usage are three important aspects of your answers in this part.

Example:

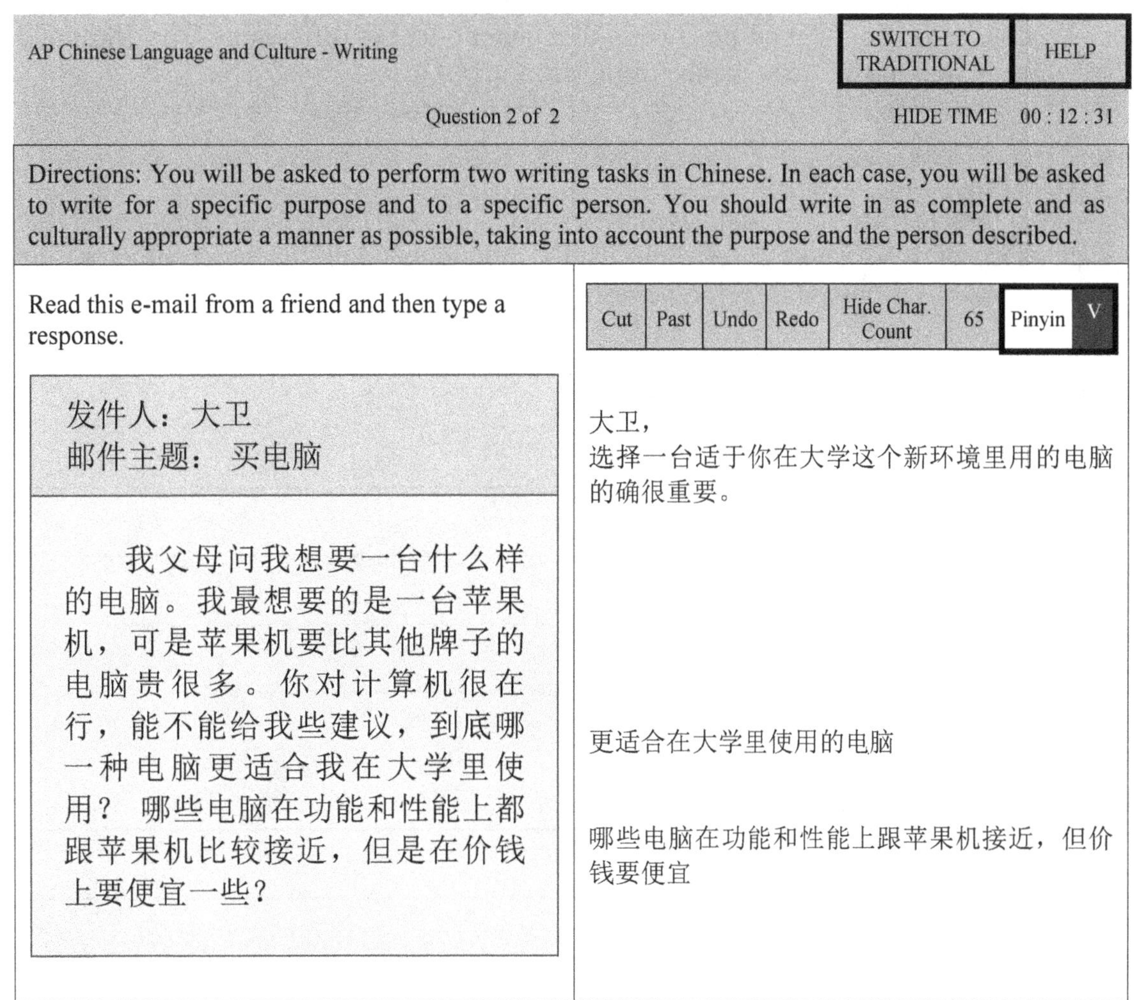

AP Chinese Language and Culture - Writing

SWITCH TO TRADITIONAL | HELP

Question 2 of 2

HIDE TIME 00 : 12 : 31

Directions: You will be asked to perform two writing tasks in Chinese. In each case, you will be asked to write for a specific purpose and to a specific person. You should write in as complete and as culturally appropriate a manner as possible, taking into account the purpose and the person described.

Read this e-mail from a friend and then type a response.

发件人：大卫
邮件主题： 买电脑

我父母问我想要一台什么样的电脑。我最想要的是一台苹果机，可是苹果机要比其他牌子的电脑贵很多。你对计算机很在行，能不能给我些建议，到底哪一种电脑更适合我在大学里使用？ 哪些电脑在功能和性能上都跟苹果机比较接近，但是在价钱上要便宜一些？

Cut | Past | Undo | Redo | Hide Char. Count | 65 | Pinyin | V

大卫，
选择一台适于你在大学这个新环境里用的电脑的确很重要。

更适合在大学里使用的电脑

哪些电脑在功能和性能上跟苹果机接近，但价钱要便宜

Suggestions

1. Address all the questions

Make sure to address all the questions posed in the e-mail. One way to do this is to list all the questions or issues with a few words or phrases in the input window, and then use these keywords as a response outline (See the example above). Before writing the e-mail response in detail, make sure that your outline covers all of the questions posed in the e-mail. Write an opening statement to reiterate the main idea or key issue; in our example, it would be "buying a computer for college."

2. **Focus on relevant information**

   Make sure to focus on providing only relevant information, to the best of your knowledge and ability. Remember, you will be graded on the quality of your writing, not whether the specific information in your answer is correct or incorrect; if you do not know the answer to a question, you can use your imagination to come up with a plausible response. A good practice is to elaborate on the differences, specifics, and details of your answer to make the response more vivid.

3. **Pace yourself**

   Make sure to plan your time wisely so that you will be able to answer all the questions with sufficient supporting details. Avoid spending too much time on one question and leaving no time for the rest.

My study notes and useful tips:

___

___

___

___

___

___

___

___

___

___

___

___

Part B: Speaking

The speaking part of the exam is divided into Simulated Conversation and Cultural Presentation. You will listen to the prompts on headphones and record your responses in Chinese using the microphone that is connected to the computer. It is ideal to provide a complete answer with the appropriate register, suitable grammatical structures, and correct pronunciation. You should also make sure to speak clearly in a natural tone of voice.

Before starting this part, you will perform another headset and microphone check. During the response time, a clock will show you how much time is remaining on screen.

	Time (in Minutes)	% of Final Score	Number of Questions	Response Time Per Question
Simulated Conversation	4	10%	6	20 seconds
Cultural Presentation	7	15%	1	4 minutes to prepare 2 minutes to answer

I. Simulated Conversation

This part of the exam consists of 6 sets of questions. Each set contains 1–3 sub-questions. You will have 20 seconds to answer each set of questions.

Because of the 20-second time limit, you will not have time to prepare in advance for an answer; you will only have to make a spontaneous reply. If you are not accustomed to impromptu speaking, you should practice often. Having frequent conversations with your classmates and teacher is a great way to develop your ability to express your thoughts verbally without advance preparation.

Example:

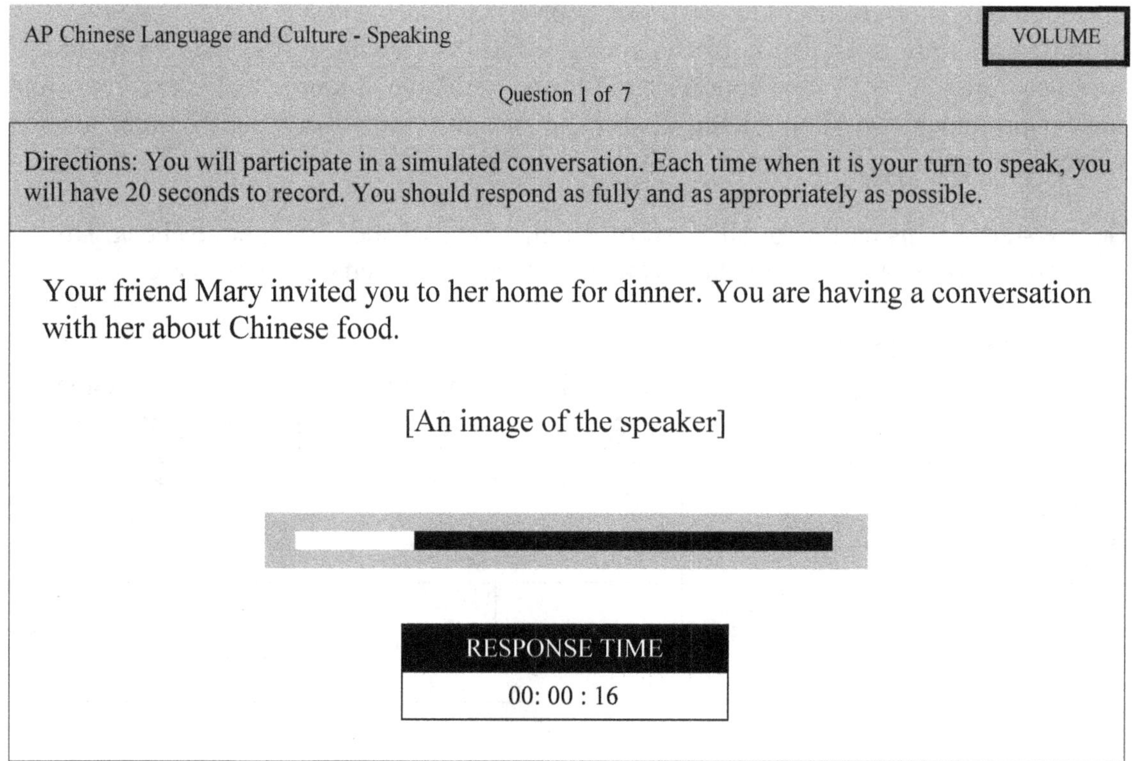

Two example questions(student can only hear the following):

Mary: 我今天给你做上海菜，不知道你以前尝过没有？你都知道哪些风味的中国菜？
[You have 20 seconds to record the response]

Mary: 你最喜欢哪个风味的中国菜？为什么？这个风味的菜都有哪些特色？
[You have 20 seconds to record the response]

Suggestions

1. Support your answer

You may encounter a question that leads to a yes or no answer. In this situation, do not stop with yes or no. Even though the questioner may not ask directly, you should expand on, elaborate, explain, or justify your answer. Giving an example or providing descriptions will be quite effective. The 20 seconds may seem very long otherwise.

Let's use the above conversation as an example. Suppose that you do not know the answer to the question "你都知道哪些风味的中国菜?" Instead of merely replying with "I don't know," you may use the information that you do know about China to address the question. For example, you may say that Chinese is a large country with diverse ethnic and regional subcultures. Each region or province in China has its own unique and rich customs. Therefore, cuisines are often very different from region to region. "For instance, Shanghai style food that you (Mary) are preparing for me may be very different from Beijing style food that I accustomed to. I can't wait to try it." Of course, you will answer all those questions in Chinese.

To answer the question about which style of Chinese food that you like the most, you should pick a cuisine that you are familiar with, even though it may not be your favorite. For instance, you may know Sichuan cuisine very well, although it is not your favorite.

You may tell Mary that Sichuan cuisine is one of eight main regional cuisines (八大菜系): Anhui, Cantonese, Fujian, Hunan, Jiangsu, Shandong, Sichuan and Zhejiang. If you are not able to cite the names of these cuisines, then you may simply say "one of the main cuisines."

Next, you will explain why. There is no right or wrong answer. You may say that it is the unique tingly-numbing taste of peppercorns used in Sichuan cuisine. Or you may draw on personal experience to say that it brings back fond memories of your grandmother, who used to cook authentic Sichuan food for the family.

Then, you should mention at least one of the distinctive characteristics of Sichuan cuisine, such as its spiciness. To be even more specific, you may name a couple of your grandmother's specialties (拿手好菜), such as Mapo Tofu (麻婆豆腐), Dan Dan Noodles (担担面), or Twice-cooked Pork (回锅肉).

2. Avoid repetition and hesitation

Do not use the same words, sentences, or points repetitively. Be concise. Repetition or hesitation may be interpreted as a sign of insufficient knowledge or poor language skills, so it is best to use a variety of vocabulary and grammar structures, and to speak confidently. It may feel unnatural at first to record your answers to the questions. If you can practice recording yourself when you do the practice tests in this book, you will sound much more comfortable and confident when you take the exam.

My study notes and useful tips:

II. Cultural Presentation

The general rules for the other free response sections of the exam also apply to the Cultural Presentation. In addition, the Cultural Presentation evaluates your presentational skills and cultural knowledge. The presentation must address all aspects of the prompt, and provide accurate and detailed information to demonstrate your cultural knowledge about the given topic.

You will have four minutes to prepare and then two minutes to record your presentation.

Example:

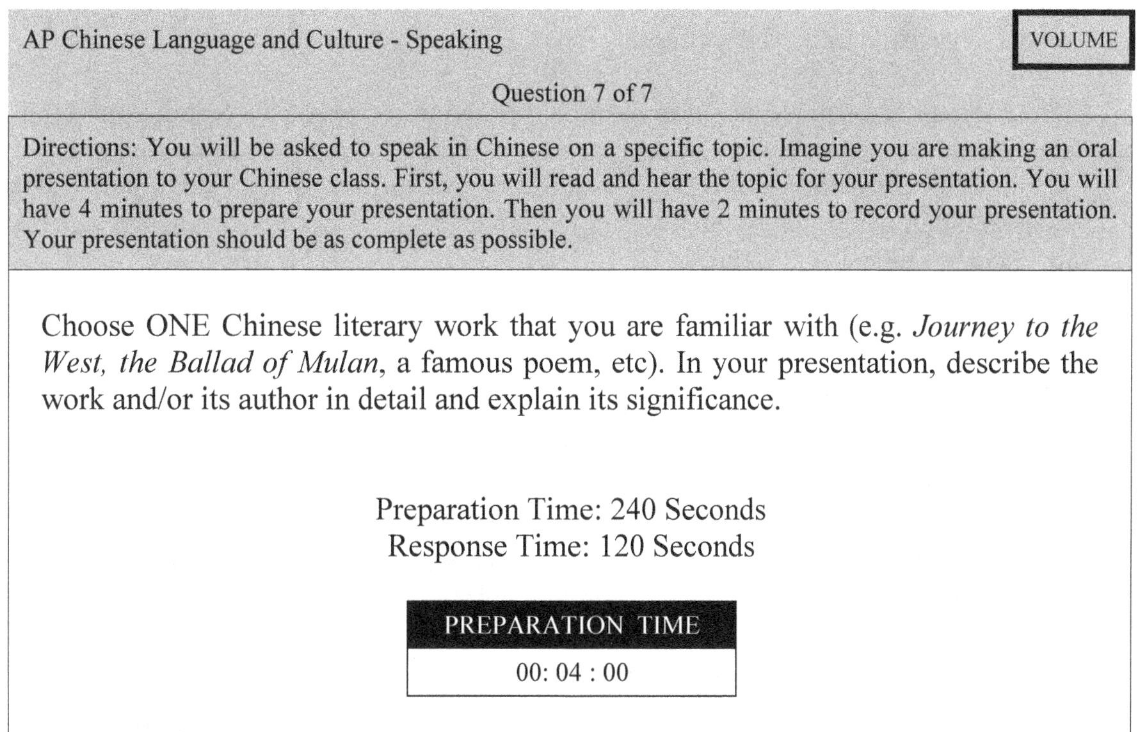

Suggestions

1. **Stay on Topic**

   To conduct a coherent oral presentation, you should first understand the topic and the questions correctly and thoroughly. Read the prompt carefully and jot down notes if you need to. You must address all aspects of the prompt and stay on topic.

2. **Create an outline**

   During the preparation time, it is a good idea to use an outline to organize your thoughts. An outline may include the main ideas, key words, supporting details, or examples. Outlines and notes will not be graded. You may use your outline as a guide during the recording, but it is best not to read from it line by line.

3. **Be accurate and detailed**

   It is better to deliver a concise and complete presentation than to have a long and unfocused talk; writing an outline will help you organize your presentation and include all the information you need to. The presentation should provide accurate and detailed information. Where relevant to the topic, personal experiences often add richness to the presentation.

4. **Avoid repetition and pace yourself**

   Use a steady and calm voice with minimal hesitation or repetition. Speak confidently and clearly. Keep track of the recording time using the countdown timer displayed on screen. When the time is almost up, it is better to wrap up your presentation than to squeeze in an incomplete sentence. On the other hand, do not repeat the same points just because there is extra time.

General Study Tips

Practice makes perfect. Using this book, you can familiarize yourself with the AP test and sharpen your skills through practice.

In addition to the test preparation suggestions that we provided above, there are some general study tips that are important for you to know.

1. **Practice taking notes and typing in Chinese**

   Although listening, reading, writing, and speaking are the four language skills tested on AP Chinese exam, two other critical skills may also affect the outcome of you test performance: note-taking and Chinese typing skills. We strongly recommend that you practice these skills on a regular basis.

   To practice note-taking, for example, you may try to jot down key information while you watch a TV show or answer a phone call from a friend of yours. Then, you can turn these key words into full sentences and paragraphs. You may also use your notes to retell the story that you saw on TV or write an e-mail response to a telephone call.

   To practice typing, try to use Microsoft IME for Chinese input as frequently as possible. For example, when you write an e-mail or send a text message to your Chinese teacher or your Chinese friends, try to type it in Chinese instead of English. It is also an excellent way to practice your Chinese writing and develop overall language fluency by expressing your thoughts and ideas in Chinese.

Find something that interests you, and keep a journal or start a blog in Chinese; it will be a fun and effective way of practicing both Chinese writing and typing.

2. **Look for authentic Chinese materials**

   Rome was not built in one day. In order to gain knowledge about Chinese culture and language, there is no better way than learning and practicing daily. You should take advantage of the rich resources available all around you, such as Chinese newspapers, magazines, movies, and books, etc., in your local community, library, or on the Internet.

   You may find these original materials more difficult to understand than the materials used in this book and in your textbook. Do not be discouraged. Again, it takes practice.

   It is a good idea to save those newspaper clippings, printouts from the Internet, or copies of magazine articles that you have read. Put them in a binder. From time to time, you may revisit them or write a summary or outline. If you have any questions, bring your binder to your teacher or people who know Chinese well for help.

   Be sure to look for a variety of materials to read, such as news stories, significant events, commercials, job postings, public announcements, movies, TV shows, poems, novels, and so on. Most importantly, try to start with something that you are interested in or passionate about.

3. **Be consistent and persistent**

   To prepare for the exam, it is much more effective if you spend a little bit of time on Chinese every day than if you spend a lot of time all in one day, once a week or month. For example, you could set aside 15 minutes per day to watch a TV news broadcast in Chinese, read a Chinese newspaper, read a Chinese magazine, visit a Chinese website, or chat in Chinese with your Chinese friends. Please see Appendix II for a list of resources for studying Chinese.

   This book has eight full-length practice tests. We recommend that you take one of them first as a diagnostic test to figure out your strengths and weaknesses. Make sure that you study Chinese daily or as often as you can. By the end of each month, take a practice test. Keep track of your progress with the progress chart provided on the next page.

Preparing for the AP exam includes reviewing, practicing, understanding the testing procedure and content, and becoming familiar with the testing format and medium. This book will help you get to know the exam and understand how to use all your knowledge of Chinese language and culture to do well on it. With practice and preparation, we hope this practice book will help you reach your full potential on the AP Chinese exam.

Student Progress Chart for Multiple Choice Sections

Answers	Listening	Reading	Total Points
Customs			
# of correct answers			
# of blank x 0			
– (# of incorrect answers / 3)			
= Subtotal			
Daily Life			
# of correct answers			
# of blank x 0			
– (# of incorrect answers / 3			
= Subtotal			
Economics			
# of correct answers			
# of blank x 0			
– (# of incorrect answers / 3)			
= Subtotal			
Education			
# of correct answers			
# of blank x 0			
– (# of incorrect answers / 3)			
= Subtotal			
Entertainment			
# of correct answers			
# of blank x 0			
– (# of incorrect answers / 3)			
= Subtotal			
Family			
# of correct answers			
# of blank x 0			
– (# of incorrect answers / 3)			
= Subtotal			
Geography			
# of correct answers			
# of blank x 0			
– (# of incorrect answers / 3)			
= Subtotal			
Mixed Theme			
# of correct answers			
# of blank x 0			
– (# of incorrect answers / 3)			
= Subtotal			

AP 中文考试简介

AP 考试概述

Advanced Placement (AP®) 是大学先修课程, 也就是学生在高中期间提前选修的大学课程。AP 课程和考试由大学理事会 (College Board) 统一管理。AP 现有 30 多门考试[1]，其中有 10 门是外语考试，其中包括法文、西班牙文、日文和中文。

AP 考试评分为 5 分制：
5 ＝ 非常优秀
4 ＝ 优秀
3 ＝ 合格
2 ＝ 可能合格
1 ＝ 不推荐

一般来说，考生的 AP 考试成绩达 3 分以上，就有可能获取大学相关科目的学分，但具体什么样的 AP 成绩、哪些科目能转换大学学分则由各大学根据自己的学分政策自行决定。参照大学理事会的标准，得五分的 AP 考试成绩相当于大学同等课程的 A，四分大致为 A-，B+ 或是 B，而三分差不多就是 B-，C+ 或是 C 的水平[2]。

到目前为止，世界上至少有五十五个国家的大学承认 AP 学分。虽然 AP 课并不是高中的必修课，AP 考试也不是所有大学的入学要求，但许多大学会把 AP 考试成绩作为学生是否能够胜任大学学习的参考尺度之一。

AP 考试每年一次，集中在五月的前两周举行，大学理事会在学年开始前公布具体的考试日期及时间，考试地点则通常在学生就读的学校。参加 AP 考试的学生需要在就读的学校或校区统一报名。所有相关信息可到大学理事会的网站(www.collegeboard.com)上查询。

考试的安排通常为每天两场，美国大多数的州都采用早场 8 点，午场中午 12 点的开考时间。需要注意的是不同的科目有时会被安排在同一时间里进行，考生应及时了解考试信息，在选课时尽量避免考试时间的冲突。在时间冲突不可避免的情况下，其中一门考试时间可以另作安排。

---

1 The College Board. "About AP." http://www.collegeboard.com/student/testing/ap/about.html (accessed September 24, 2009). All statistics and information regarding the AP exam in this Introduction are from the College Board website.

2 The College Board. "AP Chinese Language and Culture Course Description 2009-2011" http://apcentral.collegeboard.com/apc/public/repository/ap08_chinese_coursedesc.pdf (accessed September 24, 2009).

AP 中国语言和文化考试

“**AP 中文: 语言和文化**”考试是目前唯一的中文 AP 考试，以下简称为“AP 中文”。AP 中文考试在 2007 年首次举行，考试时间约 3 个小时，2007 年度有 3,261 人参加了考试。2008 (4,311 人)，2009 (5,100 人) 年参加考试的人数稳步增长[3]。2008 年，大学理事会对 2009 至 2011 年度的 AP 中文考试形式和流程做了进一步的调整，考试时间缩短到 2 小时 15 分。

根据大学理事会的说明[4]，AP 中文考试的难度相当于修完四个学期大学中文课的程度。 虽然 AP 中文考试是为了选修 AP 中文或同等水平的中文课程的学生而设立的，但并不是只对这些学生开放。那些由于各种原因（例如，所在学校没有设立 AP 中文课，或是自修中文）而没有选修或无法选修 AP 中文课的学生，如果希望参加考试，可以与大学理事会联系，查找主办 AP 中文考试的高中，就近报名参加。

在内容上，考试将语言能力和文化知识的测试融为一体。AP 中文考试並不专设语法考题。至于文化部分，AP 中文考试不但考核传统、历史、文学、艺术等各方面的知识，而且测验学生们在日常生活中语言沟通和文化知识运用的能力。

考试环境

AP 中文考试从头至尾都在电脑上进行。考生到达考场后的其中一项准备工作就是熟悉电脑和其它相关的考试用具、软件。

在计时考试正式开始之前，考生需要选择中文输入方式以及写作时是使用简体还是繁体来显示中文写作内容。可供选择的输入方式为拼音或注音符号。如果选用注音符号来输入，写作内容的显示就是繁体。要是考生采用拼音输入，还需要在 IME 工具栏上用鼠标点击“简”（选择简体），或点击“繁”（选择繁体）来进一步指定显示方式。

整个考试中，每当有供考生阅读的中文在屏幕上出现，就会有一个转换按钮同时显现让考生选择简体或繁体显示。

---

3 The College Board. “Program Summary Report 2009,” http://professionals.collegeboard.com/profdownload/program-summary-report-09.pdf (accessed September 24, 2009)

4 The College Board. “AP Chinese Language and Culture Course Description 2009-2011.” http://apcentral.collegeboard.com/apc/public/repository/ap08_chinese_coursedesc.pdf.

与考试相关的所有说明都会在屏幕上显示，同时还会由电脑读出。在听力、阅读、写作和口语各个部分的考试过程中，电脑屏幕上都会显示倒计时器，帮助考生掌握时间。

为方便考生的需要，考场内备有草稿纸，在考试完毕时，监考员会收回所有纸张，纸张上的内容都不予计分。

四项考试

在题目形式上，AP 中文考试分为两大部分，第一部分是选择题，其中包括听、读两项考试。第二部分是问答题，其中包括写、说两项考试。虽然，听、说、读、写四项考试的时间长短不一，但每一项都占总分的 25%。

- **听力部分：** 听力部分的所有中文内容都不在电脑上显示，只由电脑播放录音，考生用耳机收听，然后在屏幕上选择答案。英文部分的可选答案则只显示在电脑上，没有录音播放。
- **阅读部分：** 阅读材料、考题和可选答案都在电脑屏幕上显示，考生在屏幕上选择答案。
- **写作部分：** 写作部分的提示由电脑显示。在此考生们可以更改中文的输入方式，或用拼音或用注音符号，但输入的文字显示则延用考试开始时考生自己设定的字体，或简或繁不能更改。
- **口语部分：** 文化介绍和模拟对话的提示也都由电脑读出并显示，考生用电脑上的话筒录下自己的回答。

欲知每项考试的详细说明和具体例子，请参阅大学理事会的《AP 中文考试概述》[5]。

[5] The College Board. “AP Chinese Language and Culture Exam Overview.” http://professionals.collegeboard.com/profdownload/AP-Chinese-Exam-Overview.pdf (accessed September 24, 2009).

AP 中文考试第一部分：选择题

AP 中文考试的第一部分是选择题，它包括听力和阅读两部分，主要是考察考生的人际沟通和理解能力。这部分的答案由机器评判，正确答案得 1 分，空白答案得 0 分，错误答案则倒扣 1/3 分。每道题的得分根据答案的正确与否计算如下：

	正确	未答	不正确
得分	+1	0	–1/3

总分的计算为：总分 ＝ 正确答题总数 － 不正确答题总数 * 1/3

例如，阅读理解有 36 道题，如果一位学生答对了 26 道，答错了 6 道，还有 4 道没答，那他阅读比分的得分就是 26 – 6 * 1/3 = 24。

建议

1. 切忌盲目猜测

AP 中文考试选择题部分的题目都是四项选择题。如果一个考生全盲目地猜题，一连猜测了四道题，按概率算，他很可能猜对一道，猜错三道。每一道答对的题得一分，答错的题扣掉的三分之一分，因此，三道答错的题目抵消一道答对的题，净得零分。按这样的算法，任意瞎猜对考生既无利也无害。也就是说，如果没有时间去细看题目或细想答案的话，劝他们最好不要浪费时间去盲目地猜测答案，与其毫无根据地瞎猜，不如空过去不答。

有人误以为如果有规律地选择答案, 比如固定地选择某一个答案，可以增加猜对的可能性，其实，那仍然是在瞎猜。另外，认为某一个选择（例如 C）是正确答案的机会比其他选择要大，也是没有根据的。

2. 积极运用“排除法 ”

如前所述，完全随意地猜题，于事无补。但如果是有根据的推断却能够增加得分的机会。“排除法”就是在选择题考试中常用的一种技巧之一。运用排除法，考生可以有效地提高猜到正确答案的可能性。

所谓“排除法”就是在做选择题的过程中，将不符合主题或逻辑的选择排除掉，而获得正确答案的方法。有很多时候，发现错误答案会比直接找到正确答案要来得容易。尤其是面对比较复杂或困难的问题，而又对如何解决这个问题束手无策的时候，“排除法”有时能收到柳暗花明的效果。即使是面对很难的题目，如果考生能静下心来，有效利用时间，仔细分析问题，多数情况下都可以排除一些错误的选择。在考试中能够排除掉哪怕一个选择都比毫无根据地猜测要好，因为这增加了他们选择正确答案的可能性。即使猜不出哪个是正确答案，考生也应该排除掉他们知道是不可能或不合情理的选择，然后，在剩余的选择里猜测答案。不过，我们在这里还是要提醒考生们不要在一道题上滞留过久。

Part A: 听力考试

听力部分又细分为对话连接和听力理解两小部分。题材涉及日常生活、旅游、娱乐、教育和起居饮食等等。

	时间	占总分的百分比	题目数量	每题回答时限
对话连接	10 分钟	10%	10–15	5 秒
听力理解	10 分钟	15%	15–20	12 秒

I. 对话连接

对话连接测检考生在简单对话环境中，对中文的理解和回应能力。考生需要根据听到的中文对话片断，在四个选择中挑选一个最恰当的句子来完成对话。对话连接部分的题目及可选答案都是中文，全由录音播出，选择内容不在屏幕上显示。考生在屏幕上只看到题目号码和 (A)、 (B)、(C)、 (D) 四个选择。

例子：

[考生听到的录音]

甲： 今天的天气真热！

乙： (A) 是啊, 要多穿些衣服。
(B) 那就开冷气吧。
(C) 昨天下雨了？
(D) 热狗真好吃。

[屏幕上显示的可选答案]

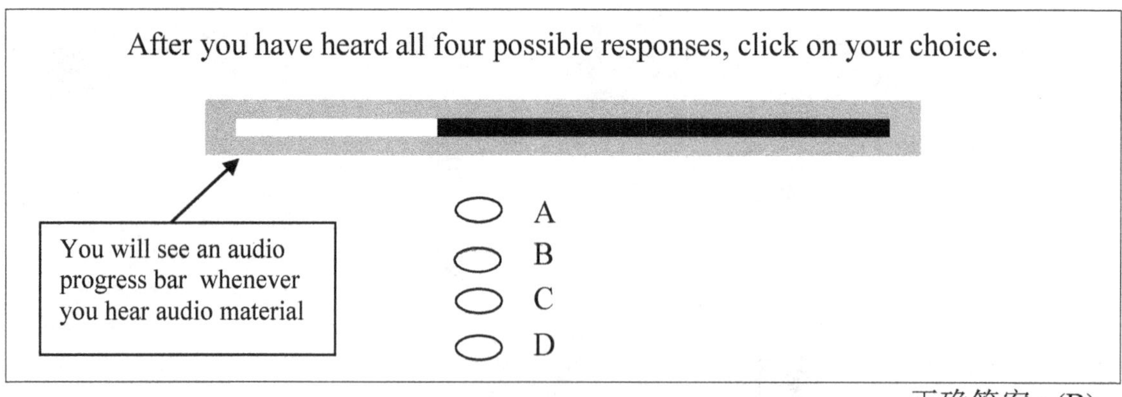
After you have heard all four possible responses, click on your choice.
You will see an audio progress bar whenever you hear audio material
A
B
C
D

正确答案: (B)

II. 听力理解

顾名思义，听力理解考查学生的理解诠释能力。这部分包括多种听力形式，如通告、报导、指令、广告及谈话等等。在听完一段中文录音后，考生需要回答 1 至 5 道有关该录音的英文问题。有些录音会重播一次。

听力理解部分，考生在屏幕上可以看到英文提问和可选答案，录音只播放中文听力选段。

例子：

[考生听到的录音]

<身份证检查>

自 2008 年 6 月 21 日起，年满十八岁的乘客必须出示美国联邦或州政府发行的有效身份证通过检查站后，才能搭乘航班。身份证上必须有乘客的照片、姓名、出生日期、性别和有效日期。未能出示有效证件的乘客将被拒绝搭乘航班。

[屏幕上显示的问题和可选答案]

AP Chinese Language and Culture - Listening | VOLUME

Question 6 of 20 | HIDE TIME 00 : 00 : 12

What is the point of this announcement?

- ○ Children under 18 must travel with an adult guardian.
- ○ Adult passengers must present a valid identification card at the airport checkpoint.
- ○ The identification card must show name, birth date, gender, and date of issue.
- ○ All passengers must show a valid identification card at the airport

正确答案: 第二个选择

对话连接和听力理解的题目全部按顺序限时回答。每道题在屏幕上独立显示，并且只出现一次，时间一到，屏幕内容立即被刷新。因此，时间的掌握非常重要，即使听懂了，但如果不能在时限内及时回答的话，就会造成不必要的失分。

建议

1. 速度练习

听力考试部分每道题的答题时间都非常短，考生基本上没有时间作笔记。我们建议，当考生们用这本书在家做练习的时候，最好能象真正的考试那样限定时间。我们提供的所有听力练习都留有回答时间，回答时间的长短与真正的AP中文考试相同。考生们应该充分利用这些录音、限时练习，从而帮助他们缩短反应时间、提高回答问题的速度。这些听力练习的录音可在剑桥出版社的网站上（www.cheng-tsui.com）下载，具体操作方法请查阅本书 iv 页上的下载说明。

2. 熟悉题型

通过反复练习，熟悉各种题目类型，了解回答这些类型题目的规则，不但能帮助学生增强语感，也有助于他们提高答题的速度和正确率。在真正的AP考场上，回答听力问题的时间不过五秒或十二秒钟而已，如果考生有回答这类题型的经验，就能省下一、两秒钟的反应时间，这对他们非常有利。

Part B: 阅读考试

阅读部分的取材广泛、内容丰富。选文形式包括广告、短讯、海报、故事、公共标志和电子邮件等等。选文的篇幅有长有短，难易程度也不尽相同。通常每篇选文会有一至五道问题不等。

阅读考试的时限为 60 分钟，这部分不要求考生按顺序阅读或回答问题，所以每一道题没有答题的时间限制，考生可以依据自己的情况，决定阅读顺序，分配答题时间。

	时间	占总分的百分比	题目数量	选文数量
阅读	60 分钟	25%	35–40	7–10

例子：

AP Chinese Language and Culture – Reading | SWITCH TO TRADITIONAL | REVIEW MARK HELP BACK NEXT

Question 3 of 40 | HIDE TIME 00 : 55 : 00

Read this essay

在美国学中文

周末，许多在美国生活的华人孩子大概都要做同样的一件事，那就是上中文学校。

从小我父母就跟我说，我们是华人，必须要学会中文，才能传承中国文化。每逢周日，邻家的孩子们高高兴兴地到公园里玩，我却要背着书包到中文学校学中文。

起先，我不明白我为什么一定要学中文，很不愿意去中文学校。年复一年，我慢慢地找到了学中文的乐趣，在中文学校里，我不但学中文，还学中国画，武术等才艺。去年夏天，我到中国看望爷爷奶奶，大家都夸我的中文讲得好呢。

3. Which day does the author have to go to Chinese school?

   (A) Monday

   (B) Friday

   (C) Saturday

   (D) Sunday

正确答案 (D)

屏幕正上方正中的按钮用于转换阅读显示的字体。当阅读文章用简体显示时，按钮会显示“Switch to Traditional”，点击按钮，阅读文章的显示就会转换成繁体，按钮也会相应变为“Switch to Simplified”，这时如果再次点击按钮又可将文章显示变回简体。

AP Chinese Language and Culture – Reading | SWITCH TO SIMPLIFIED | REVIEW MARK HELP BACK NEXT

Question 3 of 40 | HIDE TIME 00 : 55 : 00

Read this essay

在美國學中文

周末，許多在美國生活的華人孩子大概都要做同樣的一件事，那就是上中文學校。

從小我父母就跟我說，我們是華人，必須要學會中文，才能傳承中國文化。每逢周日，鄰家的孩子們高高興興地到公園裡玩，我卻要背著書包到中文學校學中文。

起先，我不明白我為什麼一定要學中文，很不願意去中文學校。年復一年，我慢慢地找到了學中文的樂趣，在中文學校裡，我不但學中文，還學中國畫，武術等才藝。去年夏天，我到中國看望爺爺奶奶，大家都夸我的中文講得好呢。

3. Which day does the author have to go to Chinese school?

(A) Monday

(B) Friday

(C) Saturday

(D) Sunday

正确答案 (D)

注意事项

阅读考试部分，有几项屏幕设置与其他部分不同，例如，“REVIEW”，“MARK”，“HELP”，“BACK”，“NEXT”等按钮。另外右上角的倒计时器是从60分钟算起，显示整个阅读考试的剩余时间。下面是对上面这些功能按钮的一些简单说明：

- **REVIEW：** "REVIEW" 用来显示阅读部分的答题情况总表，显示内容包括阅读题目的题号、问题、标记和答题状况。考生作了标记的题目都会显示在标记栏内，当需要从总表回到某一个题目时，先点击该题目的号码，然后点击"GO TO QUESTION"就可以直接回到该题目，不必浪费时间用"NEXT"或"BACK"一道题一道题地去翻。答题状况则记载每一道题目是否已经回答的情况。
- **MARK：** "MARK"可用来给需要的题目做标记，这是一个转换按钮，点击一次设置标记，再次点击取消标记。当遇到比较困难的题目或对答案不确定，需要暂时跳过去时，就可用"MARK"来做记号，等有时间再回头推敲。
- **HELP：** "HELP"为考生提供一些与考试相关的基本指南。点击"HELP"，屏幕上会出现以下几个按钮：

Testing Tools	How to Answer	How to Scroll	General Directions	Part Directions

例如在阅读考试部分，如果点击"Testing Tools"，屏幕上会以英文列出"REVIEW"，"MARK"，"HELP"，"BACK"和"NEXT"等按钮的功能和使用说明。

- **BACK：** 点击"BACK"来返回前一题或上一页。
- **NEXT：** 点击"NEXT"进入下一道题或翻到下一页。

建议

1. 在开始考试之前，有一段特定的时间拨给考生测试和熟悉有关软件及设备。考生最好能充分利用这段时间，熟悉考试软件及其功能，调试耳机及话筒的音量。这样在考试时，才能做到游刃有余，避免因为不熟悉考试软件或设备的使用而浪费过多的时间。

2. 鉴于考试全部使用电脑，无法直接在选文上做记号，考生如发现关键部分或词语，除了用 "MARK" 按钮以外，还可以利用考场提供的草稿纸做些简要笔记。笔记不拘形式，以简单有效为宜，比如，可以用关键字或者草图记下時间、地点、方向、数字等等。

3. 先浏览一下有关选文的所有问题和可选答案，再仔细阅读与问题相关的段落，这样可以帮助考生更好地理解选文、而又不失重点地寻找最好答案。记住，"最好答案"只有一个。

4. 选文的长短难易各异。如果有困难理解某段选文，不妨暂时跳过去，读下一篇选文，有时间再回來斟酌。

5. 就是针对同一篇选文的题目，难易程度 也往往不同。但无论难易，每道题都占一样的分数比例，因此，遇到困难的题目，不要滞留过久，最好先做容易的题目，有时间再细细琢磨较难的题目。

考试在第一部分选择题和第二部分问答题之间，有10分钟的休息时间。考生应利用这段时间好好休息，尽量不要想刚刚完成的考试，而要想办法把精力集中到接下来的考試上。另外，考生需要注意的是第二部分的考试要在得到监考员的认可之后才能开始。

AP 中文考试第二部分：问答题

第二部分的问答题又分为写作和口语两项，各占总分的 25%。这部分是由评分人员根据大学理事会的《AP 中文考试评分准则》[6] 来评分。评分时考虑以下三个主要方面：答题的完整程度、语域选择、和语言运用。每一方面从最低 0 分 (不合格) 到最高 6 分 (优秀)，总分是三个方面所得分数的总和。尽管每一项考试需要考虑的具体因素会有所不同，但是总的评分原则大同小异。

在评估作文的完整程度时，通常又要考虑以下一些因素：

- 是否按照要求回答了所有的问题、有没有扣题（或跑题）
- 答题的结构是否完整，例如，叙述文是否有开头、中间、结尾
- 内容（句子、观点等）是否清楚明了、协调一致地组织在一起
- 是否提供相关的细节或实例，是否围绕主题进一步做了阐述、说明、或解释
- 是否运用过渡词、转换词、连接词等等

语域[7]选择是否得体，主要是看语气或措词是不是与使用的场合或文体一致。例如，讲故事与回复电邮，无论是在措辞上还是语气上，都会有所不同。同样，模拟对话与文化介绍也会有类似的区别：文化介绍要用比较正式的语体，而模拟对话的形式就不如文化介绍那么正式。

语言运用方面，要尽量用丰富而又贴切的词汇和成语、以及多种多样的语法结构和句型，让文章更生动。不过，考生应该选用自己熟悉的词汇、成语和句型，这样可以避免错误。其次，要特别注意同音异义的字、词。在输入拼音或注音符号后，字单上往往会显示一系列的同音字，考生要小心地选择自己想要用的字词。最后，标点符号听起来似乎不足轻重，但也是要考察的写作知识之一，考生应该知道如何使用恰当的中文标点符号。例如，写作时要用中文句号 “。”，而不要使用英文的句号 “.”。

---

[6] The College Board. “AP Chinese Language and Culture 2008 Scoring Guidelines.” 01 Oct. 2008. http://www.collegeboard.com/prod_downloads/ap/students/china/ap08_chinese_sgs.pdf (accessed September 24, 2009).

[7] *Register* in this context means the level of formality. We all use different levels of language formality in written and spoken English. For instance, the register of a formal history paper differs from an informal e-mail to a friend. The language register used should be appropriate to the intended audience.

Part A：写作考试

写作部分测试考生对人际沟通和书面表达的能力。写作部分又分看图叙述故事和回复电子邮件两小部分。学生们要根据提示，理解问题、分析情况、找出解决方法，然后有条有理地叙述事件、提供建议、阐述原因。

	时间	占总分的百分比	题目数量
看图叙述故事	15 分钟	15%	1
回复电子邮件	15 分钟	10%	1

I. 看图叙述故事

看图叙述故事要求考生根据一组提示图用中文写一篇叙述文。一篇优秀的叙述文应该结构完整，合乎情理，文字通顺。整篇作文要有开头、中间和结尾，不但要叙事清楚，有细节，有扩展，而且要始终紧扣主题。同时，还要恰当地运用过渡词、连接词、以及时间词组把句子段落串联成章，让全文溶为一体。

例子:

AP Chinese Language and Culture - Writing

HELP

Question 1 of 2

HIDE TIME 00 : 10 : 28

Directions: You will be asked to perform two writing tasks in Chinese. In each case, you will be asked to write for a specific purpose and to a specific person. You should write in as complete and as culturally appropriate a manner as p
ossible, taking into account the purpose and the person described.

The four pictures present a story. Imagine you are writing the story to a friend. Narrate a complete story as suggested by the pictures. Give your story a beginning, middle, and an end.

小明最喜欢跟哥哥打篮球了。

抢哥哥的球

哥哥投篮

唰！投中了

打完了一场

在小明眼里，哥哥是他最好的教练，最好的球友，也是最好的伙伴。

注意事项

倒计时器依然出现在屏幕上的右上角，显示回答这道题目的剩余时间。当回答限时一到，题目就自动更新，不能返回再次返回了。

如有需要，考生可以随时利用写作区右上角的列表更改中文输入方式，或用拼音或用注音符号。

与阅读部分一样，写作部分也提供“HELP”功能。例如，在使用“HELP”以后再点击“How to Answer”，屏幕上会用英文显示“Cut”，“Paste”，“Undo”，“Redo”，“Character Count”，“Input Method”和“Keyboard Keys”等按钮的功能和使用说明。

建议

1. 提纲挈领

在开始写叙述文之前，最好起草一个大纲。虽然考生可以用草稿纸写大纲，但是直接在电脑上輸入大纲，可以省些时间。例子参阅上页。

大纲最好包括一个简要的开头，根据每幅提示图列一些关键词、句作为中间，再写一个完整的句子作为结尾。这样的大纲不但可以帮助学生组织主题思想和故事情节，还可以在时间不够用的情况下，保证作文有头有尾。

2. 连贯流畅

大纲一旦列出，就如同搭下了一个完整的骨架，接下来考生要把关键词变成完整的句子、再把句子连成段落。这时，运用适当的过渡词、连接词、以及时间词组是非常重要的，例如“然后”、“于是”、“可是”、“当…的时候”、“ 一…就…”等等。这些词起着承上启下的作用，把句子和细节串联起来，使故事读起来连贯流畅、清晰易懂。如果能够恰当地运用这些词，加上详情细节，例如在前面这个例子中，考生可以在第一段落加入“从小”，“每天”，或“哥哥一进家门…小明就…”，故事读起来就不再象一个大纲了。不过，要注意避免反复使用同一样的词语。

3. 循序描述

不同的学生对提示图也许会有不同的理解或解释。但是一旦确定了主题，考生就应该围绕这个主题来叙述故事在要避免文不对题或者离题。

考生最好按提示图的顺序逐一描述细节，不要错过任何一张图，要充分利用每一张提示图上提供的信息把故事写得有血有肉，不妨发挥自己的想象力来添加些细节，譬如，在上面这个例子中，加上“哥哥可是高中篮球队的队长呢！”，再用一些生动的词语，象“身材高大”，“动作敏捷”，“球艺高超”，等来描述小明的哥哥，使人物更真实饱满，又比如用诸如“大汗淋漓”、“气喘吁吁”、“紧紧地”、“佩服”等形容词让整个场景更加栩栩如生。这时，已经写好大纲，写明结尾的考生，就显出优势来了，他们可以从从容容地扩充内容，不用担心来不及写故事的结尾了。

4. 语域恰当

考生应该由始至终使用得体的语域。换句话说，作文读起来应该象是在给朋友讲述一个故事、或者告诉朋友一件事情发生的前前后后。作文中使用的人称要一致，可以考虑使用第三人称，例如给故事中的人物起名字。我们的例子中就给那个小男孩起了个名字，叫“小明”。

5. 掌握时间

最好能在四张图之间均匀地分布写作时间，避免在一张图上花费过多时间，否则，故事很可能写得虎头蛇尾，头重脚轻。如果时间允许，可以进一步修饰文字，校正全文。

II. 回复电子邮件

这里考生要先阅读一封中文电子邮件(简称电邮)，然后根据电邮的内容用中文写回信，回信要针对来信中提出的问题发表意见或建议。这是一个对考生中文能力的综合测试，考生要读懂来信，再用中文来表达自己的观点。根据大学理事会给出的参考评判标准，回信是否完整性，是否连贯流畅，使用的语域恰当依然是评分的三大要素，而回信中考生阐述的观点、发表的意见是否正确目前并没有被列入考试的评分范畴。

例子:

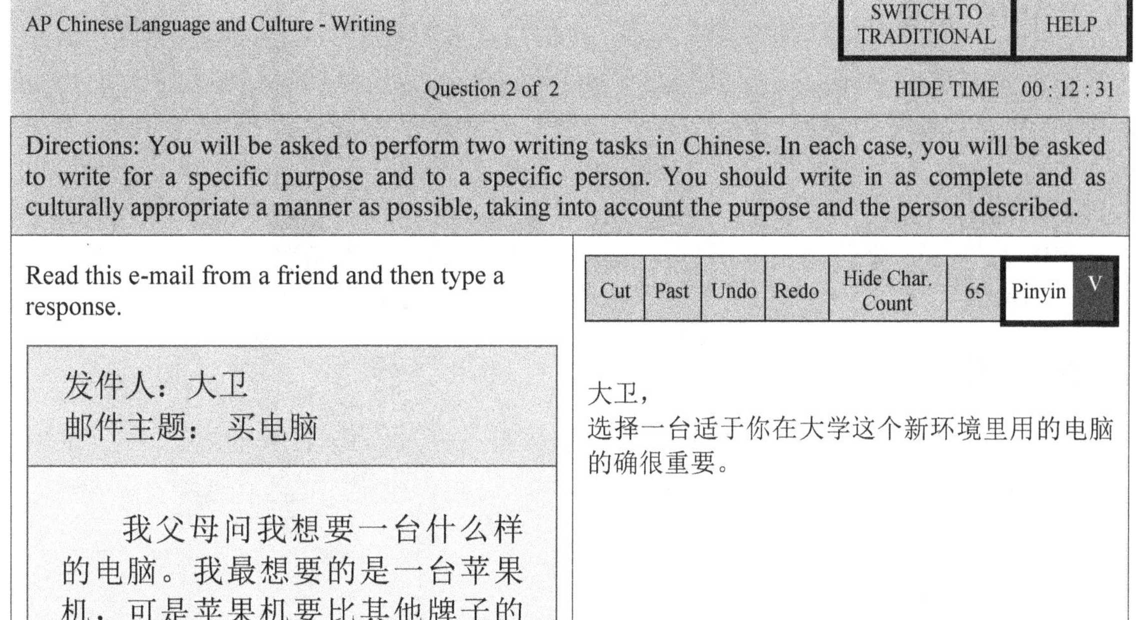

建议

1. 找出所有问题

来信中提及的所有问题，考生都应该逐一回答。为了避免不必要的遗漏，不妨先把来信中提到的问题，用简练的关键字逐一放到回信里（参阅例子），以此作为答复的大纲。确认没有遗漏任何问题后，再开始书写回执。不妨用来信的主题开篇，上面的例子中，以“买一台计算机上大学”这个主题做文章，“选择一台适于你在大学这个新环境里用的电脑的确很重要。”就成了一句不错的开场白。

2. 运用相关信息

考试时尽量使用精准详尽的资料，列举实例、提供细节、或者对比异同，都有助于考生们把回信写得有声有色。不过，作文的评分着重考虑的是文章的写作质量，而不是追究具体信息正确与否，因此，如果实在不知道该怎样直接回答来信提出的问题，不妨换个角度，比如说提一些反问，诸如“你为什么会这么想呢？”，“我从来没经历过这种情况，你能不能给我介绍一下你的经历和体会”等等。

3. 合理安排时间

要想充分发挥水平，考试时间的合理安排至关重要，考生要学会在限定的时间里回答每一个问题，不要在前面的问题上花过多的时间反复陈述，而让后面的问题因为时间不足而草草了结。

Part B: 口语考试

口语考试再分为模拟对话和文化介绍两项，测試考生的口语表达能力。考试时，考生将使用耳机收听提问，再用话筒录下自己的回答。回答问题时，要尽量做到完整切题、用词恰当、发音准确和语调自然。

在这部分开始前，考生们有时间再一次检查耳机和话筒。答题时，屏幕上的倒计时器显示考生答题的剩余时间。

	时间	占总分的百分比	题目数量	每题回答时限
模拟对话	4 分钟	10%	6	20 秒
文化介绍	7 分钟	15%	1	4 分钟准备 2 分钟回答

I. 模拟对话

模拟对话部分一共有六组问题。每组有一到三个提问不等。每组提问后，留给考生20秒的时间来回答。

模拟对话，顾名思义，就是模拟日常谈话，对听到的问题即席回答，没有另行准备答案的时间。但因为是考试，又与平常对话不同，回答问题有时间限制。不习惯这种考试方式的考生，平日要多多练习，提高回答问题的速度，训练即席表达的能力。

例子：

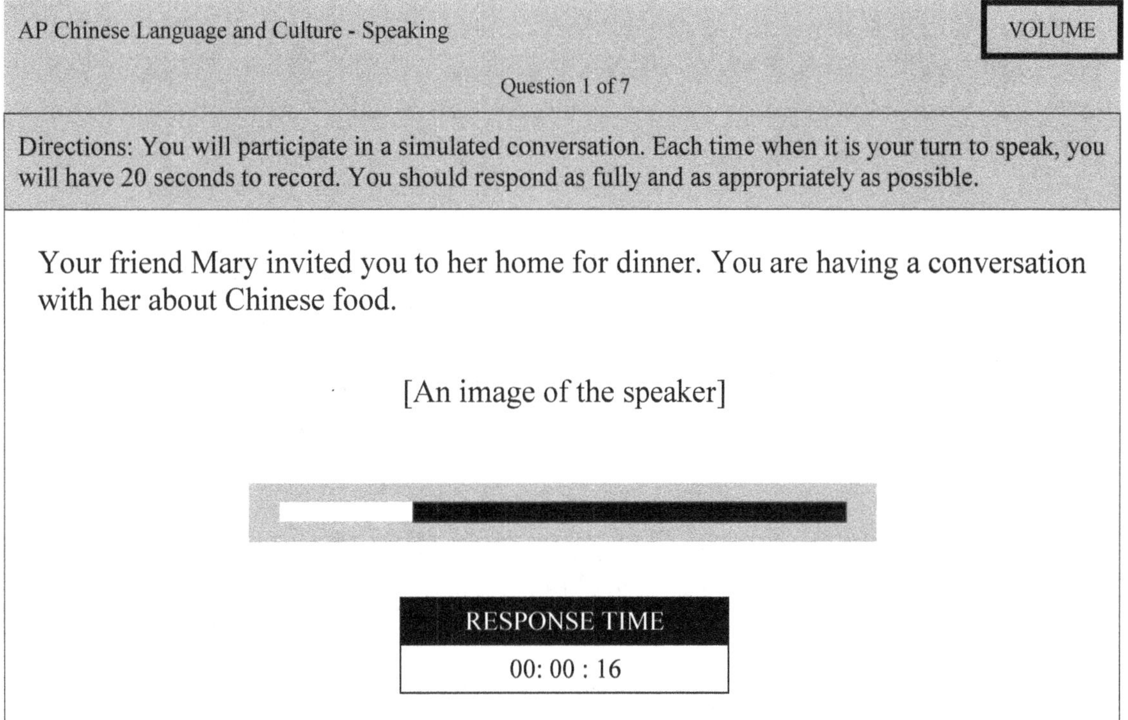

以下是两组对话的例子（注：考生只听得到录音，但看不到以下文字）：

Mary: 我今天给你做上海菜， 不知道你以前尝过没有？ 你都知道哪些风味的中国菜？
[You have 20 seconds to record the response]

Mary: 你最喜欢哪个风味的中国菜？ 为什么？这个风味的菜都有哪些特色？
[You have 20 seconds to record the response]

建议

1. 详细阐述

对于有些可以简单地用“是”或“不是”来回答的问题，即使发问者没有直接要求细说，考生们也最好不要只简单地回答“是”或“否”，而要尽量讲出一些道理，对自己的回答给予一定的解释或对自己的观点做些进一步的阐述，比如说举个例子等等，否则，20 秒会显得非常漫长。

以上面的对话题材为例，假如考生不知道如何回答“你都知道哪些风味的中国菜?”，不要简单地回答“我不知道”，而是要想办法借用相关的知识来回答。比如，考生可以说，中国是一个多民族的大国，拥有丰富多彩的民族文化和风俗习惯。因此，不难想象，各地的美食也都各有特色。然后，利用对话里提供的信息说：“你为我准备的上海菜可能跟我所熟悉的北京菜很不一样。这么香，忍不住要赶紧尝尝...。”

回答“你最喜欢哪个风味的中国菜？”时，考生应挑选自己比较熟悉并知道一些特点的风味美食来讲，但不一定非要是真正喜欢。比如，考生比较熟悉四川菜的特色，能够讲出内容，是否喜欢就可暂且不究。

考生可以说川菜是中国的八大菜系之一，再试着从中列举几个自己知道的菜系，安徽菜、广东菜、福建菜、湖南菜、江苏菜、山东菜、四川菜和浙江菜等等，不全也没有关系。

要回答关于为什么这个问题，因为无关对错，所以可以自由发挥，讲川菜麻辣的口感，可以讲些自己的感受，比如说，“它让我想起了外婆，她的拿手好菜就是川菜。”

既然问到了菜系的特点，就不能避免地要讲，哪怕是只讲一个特点也比不讲好。试着说说四川菜以麻辣著名，要想讲得更详细，还可以说些名菜，“麻婆豆腐”，“担担面”，“回锅肉”等等。

2. 避免重复停顿

回答要简明切题，不要反来复去的说同一句话或同一个观点，避免犹犹豫豫、吞吞吐吐，否则，很容易被认为缺乏文化知识或者语言表达能力。刚开始对着电脑录音、回答问题觉得不自然是正常现象。我们建议考生按部就班地利用这本书提供的多套习题，经常练习，目的就是为了帮助考生在正式考试的时候，做到放松自如。

II. 文化介绍

这部分除了测试考生的语言表达能力外，也考查考生对相应的文化知识的了解程度。因此，题目不但要求考生准确地、详细地介绍相关的文化知识，还会要求考生进一步阐述这个主题的文化意义。

在正式录音回答问题之前，考生有四分钟的准备时间，录音时间限定为两分钟。

例子：

AP Chinese Language and Culture - Speaking — VOLUME

Question 7 of 7

Directions: You will be asked to speak in Chinese on a specific topic. Imagine you are making an oral presentation to your Chinese class. First, you will read and hear the topic for your presentation. You will have 4 minutes to prepare your presentation. Then you will have 2 minutes to record your presentation. Your presentation should be as complete as possible.

Choose ONE Chinese literary work that you are familiar with (e.g. *Journey to the West, the Ballad of Mulan*, a famous poem, etc). In your presentation, describe the work and/or its author in detail and explain its significance.

Preparation Time: 240 Seconds
Response Time: 120 Seconds

PREPARATION TIME
00: 04 : 00

建议

1. 主题明确

学生们在作文化介绍时，首先应该搞清楚题目的主题和需要回答的问题，仔细读懂提示内容，做一些必要的笔记，这样才能避免答非所问。急急忙忙地回答问题，很容易文不对题。

2. 大纲简洁

在做准备时，学生最好写个简要的大纲；在大纲中，列一下想说的要点、细节或者实例。列大纲时用关键字词即可，不必写出完整的句子。 这些笔记或大纲都不会用来计分的。大纲是作参考或提示用的，录音时不要一条一条地读大纲。

3. 内容充实

说得多不如说得全、说得准。与其匆匆忙忙地堆砌很多句子，不如作一个简洁而又有头有尾，有血有肉的完整介绍。不妨引用一些实际例子、亲身经历、或者个人体会，使得介绍的内容更加充实。

4. 节奏平稳

用平稳的节奏和轻松的语调，从容地进行。在录音时，要注意屏幕上显示的倒计时器，掌握好时间。千万不要在最后一刻，为了赶着多录一些，结果最后一句话没有录全。另一方面，即使有多余的时间，如果问题已经回答完整，与其重复已经讲过的内容，不如就此打住。

考试技巧概述

勤能补拙！为了帮助学生们更好地熟悉考试环境、提高考试水平，除了以上针对各部分考试的具体建议外，在这里我们再讲一些比较通用的经验之谈，希望能对学生们有所帮助。

1. 虽然 AP 中文考试只分听说读写四部分，但其他方面的能力也会直接影响学生的考试成绩，譬如中文输入的熟练程度、记笔记的能力等等。因此我们建议学生们平时就要对这些技能多加练习，这样才能在考试时做到临阵不乱。

   如何能把笔记做得又快又准呢？又该如何练习呢？其实日常生活中可以用来练习的机会还是不少的，例如看电视、接电话都是机会。学生们可以练习先记下一些重要的词，然后再把这些关键词扩展成完整的句子、段落，再进一步写成一篇故事或一封短信。

   中文打字也要多练，每当需要和中文老师或者懂中文的朋友进行书面交流时，不妨用中文来试试。这样的练习，不仅能够帮助学生熟练掌握中文打字输入，更是增进中文写作能力，锻炼用中文进行思考的好办法。

   另外，用中文写日记、写博客，这些都是既新鲜有趣，又能提高中文水平，练习中文打字的事，如果有机会大家何不尝试一下？！

2. 语言文化的学习绝不是一朝一夕的事，要学会利周边的资源，例如中文报章、杂志、电影和书籍等等，日复一日，多多练习。俗话说得好，只要功夫深，铁棒也能磨成针。勤学苦练一定能带来丰硕的成果。

不要被书报上的内容难倒，实际生活中用到的内容和词汇都要比课本上的更丰富多彩，也会更难些。多用多练就能熟能生巧。

把读过的文章剪报收集起来，有空时拿出来复习一下，写个评论、做个总结，老师和家长也一定会乐意帮助解决学习中可能遇到的问题。

学习中文时要注意选择涵盖面丰富的题材，新闻报道，商业动向，职场信息，公共告示，电影，电视，诗歌，小说都应该尽量涉及。万事开头难，不妨从自己最感兴趣的题材开始，循序渐进。

3. 持之以恒是学习语言的关键。争取每天安排看几分钟的中文电视，读一篇中文报刊或是浏览一下中文网站，日积月累，经常练习要比临时突击的效果要更持久更有效。本书附录里我们还收集了一些有价值的网站供学生参考。

   我们建议考生将平时的中文学习与这本书结合起来。本书包括八套完整的模拟考题。考生们可以考虑先挑一套题对自己进行水平测定，用以发现自己的长处和不足，然后每月一套。每次测试的得分情况可用第 28 页上的表格记录在案，做进展分析。另外，学生们还可利用书中留有的空白，及时记下自己在各个部分的学习心得。

考试前的准备工作是非常重要的。学生们不但在考前要温故知新、多做练习，而且还应该充分了解考试的过程和内容，熟悉考试的形式和方式。希望本书能帮助考生做好考试前的准备，在考场上充分发挥他们的潜力。

AP 中文考試簡介

AP 考試概述

Advanced Placement (AP®) 是大學先修課程,也就是學生在高中期間提前選修的大學課程。AP 課程和考試由大學理事會 (College Board) 統一管理。AP 現有 30 多門考試[1]，其中有 10 門是外語考試，其中包括法文、西班牙文、日文和中文。

AP 考試評分為 5 分制：
5 ＝非常優秀
4 ＝優秀
3 ＝合格
2 ＝可能合格
1 ＝不推薦

一般來說，考生的 AP 考試成績達 3 分以上，就有可能獲取大學相關科目的學分，但具體什麼樣的 AP 成績、哪些科目能轉換大學學分則由各大學根據自己的學分政策自行決定。參照大學理事會的標準，得五分的 AP 考試成績相當於大學同等課程的 A，四分大致為 A-，B+ 或是 B，而三分差不多就是 B-，C+ 或是 C 的水平[2]。

到目前為止，世界上至少有五十五個國家的大學承認 AP 學分。雖然 AP 課並不是高中的必修課，AP 考試也不是所有大學的入學要求，但許多大學會把 AP 考試成績作為學生是否能夠勝任大學學習的參考尺度之一。

AP 考試每年一次，集中在五月的前兩周舉行，大學理事會在學年開始前公佈具體的考試日期及時間，考試地點則通常在學生就讀的學校。參加 AP 考試的學生需要在就讀的學校或校區統一報名。所有相關信息可到大學理事會的網站 (www.collegeboard.com)上查詢。

考試的安排通常為每天兩場，美國大多數的州都採用早場 8 點，午場中午 12 點的開考時間。需要注意的是不同的科目有時會被安排在同一時間裡進行，考生應及時瞭解考試信息，在選課時儘量避免考試時間的沖突。在時間沖突不可避免的情況下，其中一門考試時間可以另作安排。

1 The College Board. “About AP.” http://www.collegeboard.com/student/testing/ap/about.html (accessed September 24, 2009). All statistics and information regarding the AP exam in this Introduction are from the College Board website.

2 The College Board. “AP Chinese Language and Culture Course Description 2009-2011” http://apcentral.collegeboard.com/apc/public/repository/ap08_chinese_coursedesc.pdf (accessed September 24, 2009).

AP 中國語言和文化考試

"AP 中文：語言和文化" 考試是目前唯一的中文 AP 考試，以下簡稱為"AP 中文"。AP 中文考試在 2007 年首次舉行，考試時間約 3 個小時，2007 年度有 3,261 人參加了考試。2008 (4,311 人)，2009 (5,100 人) 年參加考試的人數穩步增長[3]。2008 年，大學理事會對 2009 至 2011 年度的 AP 中文考試形式和流程做了進一步的調整，考試時間縮短到 2 小時 15 分。

根據大學理事會的說明[4]，AP 中文考試的難度相當於修完四個學期大學中文課的程度。雖然 AP 中文考試是為了選修 AP 中文或同等水平的中文課程的學生而設立的，但並不是只對這些學生開放。那些由於各種原因（例如，所在學校沒有設立 AP 中文課，或是自修中文）而沒有選修或無法選修 AP 中文課的學生，如果希望參加考試，可以與大學理事會聯系，查找主辦 AP 中文考試的高中，就近報名參加。

在內容上，考試將語言能力和文化知識的測試融為一體。AP 中文考試並不專設語法考題。至於文化部分，AP 中文考試不但考核傳統、歷史、文學、藝術等各方面的知識，而且測驗學生們在日常生活中語言溝通和文化知識運用的能力。

考試環境

AP 中文考試從頭至尾都在電腦上進行。考生到達考場後的其中一項準備工作就是熟悉電腦和其他相關的考試用具、軟件。

在計時考試正式開始之前，考生需要選擇中文輸入方式以及寫作時是使用簡體還是繁體來顯示中文寫作內容。可供選擇的輸入方式為拼音或注音符號。如果選用注音符號來輸入，寫作內容的顯示就是繁體。要是考生採用拼音輸入，還需要在 IME 工具欄上用鼠標點擊"簡"（選擇簡體），或點擊"繁"（選擇繁體）來進一步指定顯示方式。

整個考試中，每當有供考生閱讀的中文在屏幕上出現 ，就會有一個轉換按鈕同時顯現讓考生選擇簡體或繁體顯示。

---

3 The College Board. "Program Summary Report 2009," http://professionals.collegeboard.com/profdownload/program-summary-report-09.pdf (accessed September 24, 2009)

4 The College Board. "AP Chinese Language and Culture Course Description 2009-2011." http://apcentral.collegeboard.com/apc/public/repository/ap08_chinese_coursedesc.pdf

與考試相關的所有說明都會在屏幕上顯示，同時還會由電腦讀出。在聽力、閱讀、寫作和口語各個部分的考試過程中，電腦屏幕上都會顯示倒計時器，幫助考生掌握時間。

為方便考生的需要，考場內備有草稿紙，在考試完畢時，監考員會收回所有紙張，紙張上的內容都不予計分。

四項考試

在題目形式上，AP 中文考試分為兩大部分，第一部分是選擇題，其中包括聽、讀兩項考試。第二部分是問答題，其中包括寫、說兩項考試。雖然，聽、說、讀、寫四項考試的時間長短不一，但每一項都佔總分的 25%。

- **聽力部分：**聽力部分的所有中文內容都不在電腦上顯示，只由電腦播放錄音，考生用耳機收聽，然後在屏幕上選擇答案。英文部分的可選答案則只顯示在電腦上，沒有錄音播放。
- **閱讀部分：**閱讀材料、考題和可選答案都在電腦屏幕上顯示，考生在屏幕上選擇答案。
- **寫作部分：**寫作部分的提示由電腦顯示。在此考生們可以更改中文的輸入方式，或用拼音或用注音符號，但輸入的文字顯示則延用考試開始時考生自己設定的字體，或簡或繁不能更改。
- **口語部分：**文化介紹和模擬對話的提示也都由電腦讀出並顯示，考生用電腦上的話筒錄下自己的回答。

欲知每項考試的詳細說明和具體例子，請參閱大學理事會的《AP 中文考試概述》[5]。

[5] The College Board. "AP Chinese Language and Culture Exam Overview." http://professionals.collegeboard.com/profdownload/AP-Chinese-Exam-Overview.pdf (accessed September 24, 2009).

AP 中文考試第一部分：選擇題

AP 中文考試的第一部分是選擇題，它包括聽力和閱讀兩部分，主要是考察考生的人際溝通和理解能力。這部分的答案由機器評判，正確答案得 1 分，空白答案得 0 分，錯誤答案則倒扣 1/3 分。每道題的得分根據答案的正確與否計算如下：

	正確	未答	不正確
得分	+1	0	—1/3

總分的計算為：總分 ＝ 正確答題總數 － 不正確答題總數 * 1/3

例如，閱讀理解有 36 道題，如果一位學生答對了 26 道，答錯了 6 道，還有 4 道沒答，那他閱讀比分的得分就是 26 – 6 * 1/3 = 24。

建議

1. 切忌盲目猜測

AP 中文考試選擇題部分的題目都是四項選擇題。如果一個考生全盲目地猜題，一連猜測了四道題，按概率算，他很可能猜對一道，猜錯三道。每一道答對的題得一分，答錯的題扣掉的三分之一分，因此，三道答錯的題目抵消一道答對的題，淨得零分。按這樣的算法，任意瞎猜對考生既無利也無害。也就是說，如果沒有時間去細看題目或細想答案的話，勸他們最好不要浪費時間去盲目地猜測答案，與其毫無根據地瞎猜，不如空過去不答。

有人誤以為如果有規律地選擇答案, 比如固定地選擇某一個答案，可以增加猜對的可能性，其實，那仍然是在瞎猜。另外，認為某一個選擇（例如 C）是正確答案的機會比其他選擇要大，也是沒有根據的。

2. 積極運用“排除法”

如前所述，完全隨意地猜題，於事無補。但如果是有根據的推斷卻能夠增加得分的機會。“排除法”就是在選擇題考試中常用的一種技巧之一。運用排除法，考生可以有效地提高猜到正確答案的可能性。

所謂“排除法”就是在做選擇題的過程中，將不符合主題或邏輯的選擇排除掉，而獲得正確答案的方法。有很多時候，發現錯誤答案會比直接找到正確答案要來得容易。尤其是面對比較複雜或困難的問題，而又對如何解決這個問題束手無策的時候，“排除法”有時能收到柳暗花明的效果。即使是面對很難的題目，如果考生能靜下心來，有效利用時間，仔細分析問題，多數情況下都可以排除一些錯誤的選擇。在考試中能夠排除掉哪怕一個選擇都比毫無根據地猜測要好，因為這增加了他們選擇正確答案的可能性。即使猜不出哪個是正確答案，考生也應該排除掉他們知道是不可能或不合情理的選擇，然後，在剩餘的選擇裡猜測答案。不過，我們在這裡還是要提醒考生們不要在一道題上滯留過久。

Part A: 聽力考試

聽力部分又細分為對話連接和聽力理解兩小部分。題材涉及日常生活、旅遊、娛樂、教育和起居飲食等等。

	時間	佔總分的百分比	題目數量	每題回答時限
對話連接	10 分鐘	10%	10–15	5 秒
聽力理解	10 分鐘	15%	15–20	12 秒

I. 對話連接

對話連接測檢考生在簡單對話環境中，對中文的理解和回應能力。考生需要根據聽到的中文對話片斷，在四個選擇中挑選一個最恰當的句子來完成對話。對話連接部分的題目及可選答案都是中文，全由錄音播出，選擇內容不在屏幕上顯示。考生在屏幕上只看到題目號碼和 (A)、(B)、(C)、(D) 四個選擇。

例子：

[考生聽到的錄音]

甲：　今天的天氣真熱！

乙：　(A) 是啊，要多穿些衣服。
　　　(B) 那就開冷氣吧。
　　　(C) 昨天下雨了？
　　　(D) 熱狗真好吃。

[屏幕上顯示的可選答案]

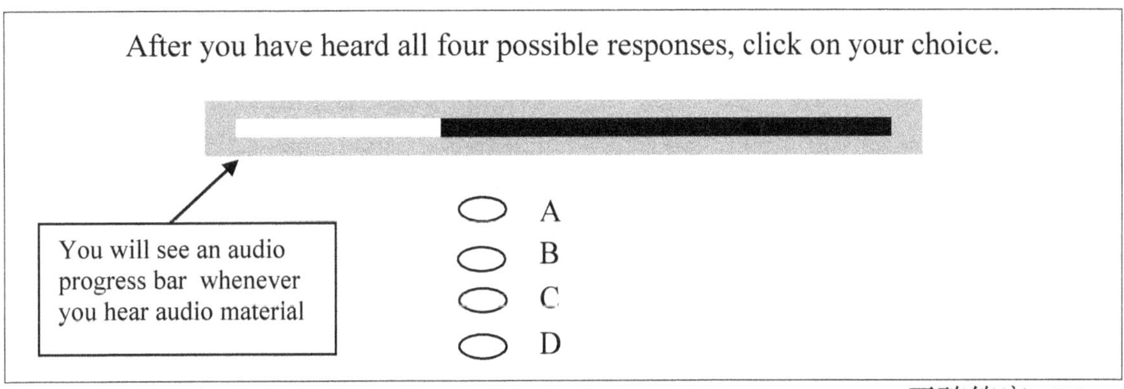
After you have heard all four possible responses, click on your choice.
You will see an audio progress bar whenever you hear audio material
A
B
C
D

正確答案: (B)

II. 聽力理解

顧名思義，聽力理解考查學生的理解詮釋能力。這部分包括多種聽力形式，如通告、報導、指令、廣告及談話等等。在聽完一段中文錄音後，考生需要回答 1 至 5 道有關該錄音的英文問題。有些錄音會重播一次。

聽力理解部分，考生在屏幕上可以看到英文提問和可選答案，錄音只播放中文聽力選段。

例子：

[考生聽到的錄音]

<身份証檢查>

自 2008 年 6 月 21 日起，年滿十八歲的乘客必須出示美國聯邦或州政府發行的有效身份証通過檢查站後，才能搭乘航班。身份証上必須有乘客的照片、姓名、出生日期、性別和有效日期。未能出示有效証件的乘客將被拒絕搭乘航班。

[屏幕上顯示的問題和可選答案]

AP Chinese Language and Culture - Listening   VOLUME

Question 6 of 20   HIDE TIME   00 : 00 : 12

What is the point of this announcement?

- ⬭ Children under 18 must travel with an adult guardian.
- ⬭ Adult passengers must present a valid identification card at the airport checkpoint.
- ⬭ The identification card must show name, birth date, gender, and date of issue.
- ⬭ All passengers must show a valid identification card at the airport

正確答案: 第二個選擇

對話連接和聽力理解的題目全部按順序限時回答。每道題在屏幕上獨立顯示，並且只出現一次，時間一到，屏幕內容立即被刷新。因此，時間的掌握非常重要，即使聽懂了，但如果不能在時限內及時回答的話，就會造成不必要的失分。

建議

1. 速度練習

聽力考試部分每道題的答題時間都非常短，考生基本上沒有時間作筆記。我們建議，當考生們用這本書在家做練習的時候，最好能像真正的考試那樣限定時間。我們提供的所有聽力練習都留有回答時間，回答時間的長短與真正的AP中文考試相同。考生們應該充分利用這些錄音、限時練習，從而幫助他們縮短反應時間、提高回答問題的速度。這些聽力練習的錄音可在劍橋出版社的網站上（www.cheng-tsui.com）下載，具體操作方法請查閱本書 iv 頁上的下載說明。

2. 熟悉題型

通過反復練習，熟悉各種題目類型，瞭解回答這些類型題目的規則，不但能幫助學生增強語感，也有助於他們提高答題的速度和正確率。在真正的AP考場上，回答聽力問題的時間不過五秒或十二秒鐘而已，如果考生有回答這類題型的經驗，就能省下一、兩秒鐘的反應時間，這對他們非常有利。

Part B: 閱讀考試

閱讀部分的取材廣泛、內容豐富。選文形式包括廣告、短訊、海報、故事、公共標誌和電子郵件等等。選文的篇幅有長有短，難易程度也不盡相同。通常每篇選文會有一至五道問題不等。

閱讀考試的時限為 60 分鐘，這部分不要求考生按順序閱讀或回答問題，所以每一道題沒有答題的時間限制，考生可以依據自己的情況，決定閱讀順序，分配答題時間。

	時間	佔總分的百分比	題目數量	選文數量
閱讀	60 分鐘	25%	35–40	7–10

例子：

AP Chinese Language and Culture – Reading | SWITCH TO TRADITIONAL | REVIEW MARK HELP BACK NEXT

Question 3 of 40 | HIDE TIME 00 : 55 : 00

Read this essay

在美国学中文

周末，许多在美国生活的华人孩子大概都要做同样的一件事，那就是上中文学校。

从小我父母就跟我说，我们是华人，必须要学会中文，才能传承中国文化。每逢周日，邻家的孩子们高高兴兴地到公园里玩，我却要背着书包到中文学校学中文。

起先，我不明白我为什么一定要学中文，很不愿意去中文学校。年复一年，我慢慢地找到了学中文的乐趣，在中文学校里，我不但学中文，还学中国画，武术等才艺。去年夏天，我到中国看望爷爷奶奶，大家都夸我的中文讲得好呢。

3. Which day does the author have to go to Chinese school?
   (A) Monday
   (B) Friday
   (C) Saturday
   (D) Sunday

正確答案 (D)

屏幕正上方正中的按鈕用於轉換閱讀顯示的字體。當閱讀文章用簡體顯示時，按鈕會顯示"Switch to Traditional"，點擊按鈕，閱讀文章的顯示就會轉換成繁體，按鈕也會相應變為"Switch to Simplified"，這時如果再次點擊按鈕又可將文章顯示變回簡體。

AP Chinese Language and Culture – Reading | SWITCH TO SIMPLIFIED | REVIEW MARK HELP BACK NEXT

Question 3 of 40 HIDE TIME 00 : 55 : 00

Read this essay

在美國學中文

周末，許多在美國生活的華人孩子大概都要做同樣的一件事，那就是上中文學校。

從小我父母就跟我說，我們是華人，必須要學會中文，才能傳承中國文化。每逢周日，鄰家的孩子們高高興興地到公園裡玩，我卻要背著書包到中文學校學中文。

起先，我不明白我為什麼一定要學中文，很不願意去中文學校。年復一年，我慢慢地找到了學中文的樂趣，在中文學校裡，我不但學中文，還學中國畫，武術等才藝。去年夏天，我到中國看望爺爺奶奶，大家都夸我的中文講得好呢。

3. Which day does the author have to go to Chinese school?

(A) Monday

(B) Friday

(C) Saturday

(D) Sunday

正確答案 (D)

注意事項

閱讀考試部分，有幾項屏幕設置與其他部分不同，例如，"REVIEW"，"MARK"，"HELP"，"BACK"，"NEXT"等按鈕。另外右上角的倒計時器是從60分鐘算起，顯示整個閱讀考試的剩餘時間。下面是對上面這些功能按鈕的一些簡單說明：

- **REVIEW：** "REVIEW" 用來顯示閱讀部分的答題情況總表，顯示內容包括閱讀題目的題號、問題、標記和答題狀況。考生作了標記的題目都會顯示在標記欄內，當需要從總表回到某一個題目時，先點擊該題目的號碼，然後點擊“GO TO QUESTION”就可以直接回到該題目，不必浪費時間用“NEXT”或“BACK”一道題一道題地去翻。答題狀況則記載每一道題目是否已經回答的情況。

- **MARK：**“MARK”可用來給需要的題目做標記，這是一個轉換按鈕，點擊一次設置標記，再次點擊取消標記。當遇到比較困難的題目或對答案不確定，需要暫時跳過去時，就可用“MARK”來做記號，等有時間再回頭推敲。
- **HELP：**“HELP”為考生提供一些與考試相關的基本指南。點擊“HELP”，屏幕上會出現以下幾個按鈕：

Testing Tools	How to Answer	How to Scroll	General Directions	Part Directions

例如在閱讀考試部分，如果點擊“Testing Tools”，屏幕上會以英文列出“REVIEW”,“MARK”,“HELP”,“BACK”和“NEXT”等按鈕的功能和使用說明。

- **BACK：**點擊“BACK”來返回前一題或上一頁。
- **NEXT：**點擊“NEXT”進入下一道題或翻到下一頁。

建議

1. 在開始考試之前，有一段特定的時間撥給考生測試和熟悉有關軟件及設備。考生最好能充分利用這段時間，熟悉考試軟件及其功能，調試耳機及話筒的音量。這樣在考試時，才能做到游刃有餘，避免因為不熟悉考試軟件或設備的使用而浪費過多的時間。

2. 鑒於考試全部使用電腦，無法直接在選文上做記號，考生如發現關鍵部分或詞語，除了用 “MARK” 按鈕以外，還可以利用考場提供的草稿紙做些簡要筆記。筆記不拘形式，以簡單有效為宜，比如，可以用關鍵字或者草圖記下時間、地點、方向、數字等等。

3. 先瀏覽一下有關選文的所有問題和可選答案，再仔細閱讀與問題相關的段落，這樣可以幫助考生更好地理解選文、而又不失重點地尋找最好答案。記住，“最好答案” 只有一個。

4. 選文的長短難易各異。如果有困難理解某段選文，不妨暫時跳過去，讀下一篇選文，有時間再回來斟酌。

5. 就是針對同一篇選文的題目，難易程度 也往往不同。但無論難易，每道題都佔一樣的分數比例，因此，遇到困難的題目，不要滯留過久，最好先做容易的題目，有時間再細細琢磨較難的題目。

考試在第一部分選擇題和第二部分問答題之間，有10分鐘的休息時間。考生應利用這段時間好好休息，儘量不要想剛剛完成的考試，而要想辦法把精力集中到接下來的考試上。另外，考生需要注意的是第二部分的考試要在得到監考員的認可之後才能開始。

AP 中文考試第二部分：問答題

第二部分的問答題又分為寫作和口語兩項，各佔總分的 25%。這部分是由評分人員根據大學理事會的《AP 中文考試評分準則》[6] 來評分。評分時考慮以下三個主要方面：答題的完整程度、語域選擇、和語言運用。每一方面從最低 0 分 (不合格) 到最高 6 分 (優秀)，總分是三個方面所得分數的總和。儘管每一項考試需要考慮的具體因素會有所不同，但是總的評分原則大同小異。

在評估作文的完整程度時，通常又要考慮以下一些因素：

- 是否按照要求回答了所有的問題、有沒有扣題（或跑題）
- 答題的結構是否完整，例如，敘述文是否有開頭、中間、結尾
- 內容（句子、觀點等）是否清楚明瞭、協調一致地組織在一起
- 是否提供相關的細節或實例，是否圍繞主題進一步做了闡述、說明、或解釋
- 是否運用過渡詞、轉換詞、連接詞等等

語域[7] 選擇是否得體，主要是看語氣或措詞是不是與使用的場合或文體一致。例如，講故事與回覆電郵，無論是在措辭上還是語氣上，都會有所不同。同樣，模擬對話與文化介紹也會有類似的區別：文化介紹要用比較正式的語體，而模擬對話的形式就不如文化介紹那麼正式。

語言運用方面，要儘量用豐富而又貼切的詞匯和成語、以及多種多樣的語法結構和句型，讓文章更生動。不過，考生應該選用自己熟悉的詞匯、成語和句型，這樣可以避免錯誤。其次，要特別注意同音異義的字、詞。在輸入拼音或注音符號後，字單上往往會顯示一系列的同音字，考生要小心地選擇自己想要用的字詞。最後，標點符號聽起來似乎不足輕重，但也是要考察的寫作知識之一，考生應該知道如何使用恰當的中文標點符號。例如，寫作時要用中文句號 “。”，而不要使用英文的句號 “.” 。

---

6 The College Board. “AP Chinese Language and Culture 2008 Scoring Guidelines.” 01 Oct. 2008. http://www.collegeboard.com/prod_downloads/ap/students/china/ap08_chinese_sgs.pdf (accessed September 24, 2009).

7 *Register* in this context means the level of formality. We all use different levels of language formality in written and spoken English. For instance, the register of a formal history paper differs from an informal e-mail to a friend. The language register used should be appropriate to the intended audience.

PART A：寫作考試

寫作部分測試考生對人際溝通和書面表達的能力。寫作部分又分看圖敘述故事和回覆電子郵件兩小部分。學生們要根據提示，理解問題、分析情況、找出解決方法，然後有條有理地敘述事件、提供建議、闡述原因。

	時間	佔總分的百分比	題目數量
看圖敘述故事	15 分鐘	15%	1
回覆電子郵件	15 分鐘	10%	1

I. 看圖敘述故事

看圖敘述故事要求考生根據一組提示圖用中文寫一篇敘述文。一篇優秀的敘述文應該結構完整，合乎情理，文字通順。整篇作文要有開頭、中間和結尾，不但要敘事清楚，有細節，有擴展，而且要始終緊扣主題。同時，還要恰當地運用過渡詞、連接詞、以及時間詞組把句子段落串聯成章，讓全文溶為一體。

例子:

AP Chinese Language and Culture - Writing

HELP

Question 1 of 2

HIDE TIME 00 : 10 : 28

Directions: You will be asked to perform two writing tasks in Chinese. In each case, you will be asked to write for a specific purpose and to a specific person. You should write in as complete and as culturally appropriate a manner as possible, taking into account the purpose and the person described.

The four pictures present a story. Imagine you are writing the story to a friend. Narrate a complete story as suggested by the pictures. Give your story a beginning, middle, and an end.

小明最喜歡跟哥哥打籃球了。

搶哥哥的球

哥哥投籃

唰！投中了

打完了一場

在小明眼裡，哥哥是他最好的教練，最好的球友，也是最好的伙伴。

注意事項

倒計時器依然出現在屏幕上的右上角，顯示回答這道題目的剩餘時間。當回答限時一到，題目就自動更新，不能返回再次返回了。

如有需要，考生可以隨時利用寫作區右上角的列表更改中文輸入方式，或用拼音或用注音符號。

與閱讀部分一樣，寫作部分也提供“HELP”功能。例如，在使用“HELP”以後再點擊“How to Answer”，屏幕上會用英文顯示“Cut”，“Paste”，“Undo”，“Redo”，“Character Count”，“Input Method”和“Keyboard Keys”等按鈕的功能和使用說明。

建議

1. 提綱挈領

在開始寫敘述文之前，最好起草一個大綱。雖然考生可以用草稿紙寫大綱，但是直接在電腦上輸入大綱，可以省些時間。例子參閱上頁。

大綱最好包括一個簡要的開頭，根據每幅提示圖列一些關鍵詞、句作為中間，再寫一個完整的句子作為結尾。這樣的大綱不但可以幫助學生組織主題思想和故事情節，還可以在時間不夠用的情況下，保証作文有頭有尾。

2. 連貫流暢

大綱一旦列出，就如同搭下了一個完整的骨架，接下來考生要把關鍵詞變成完整的句子、再把句子連成段落。這時，運用適當的過渡詞、連接詞、以及時間詞組是非常重要的，例如“然後”、“於是”、“可是”、“當…的時候”、“ 一…就…”等等。這些詞起著承上啟下的作用，把句子和細節串聯起來，使故事讀起來連貫流暢、清晰易懂。如果能夠恰當地運用這些詞，加上詳情細節，例如在前面這個例子中，考生可以在第一段落加入“從小”，“每天”，或“哥哥一進家門…小明就…”，故事讀起來就不再像一個大綱了。不過，要注意避免反復使用同一樣的詞語。

3. 循序描述

不同的學生對提示圖也許會有不同的理解或解釋。但是一旦確定了主題，考生就應該圍繞這個主題來敘述故事在要避免文不對題或者離題。

考生最好按提示圖的順序逐一描述細節，不要錯過任何一張圖，要充分利用每一張提示圖上提供的信息把故事寫得有血有肉，不妨發揮自己的想像力來添加些細節，譬如，在上面這個例子中，加上“哥哥可是高中籃球隊的隊長呢！”，再用一些生動的詞語，像“身材高大”，“動作敏捷”，“球藝高超”，等來描述小明的哥哥，使人物更真實飽滿，又比如用諸如“大汗淋漓”、“氣喘吁吁”、“緊緊地”、“佩服”等形容詞讓整個場景更加栩栩如生。這時，已經寫好大綱，寫明結尾的考生，就顯出優勢來了，他們可以從從容容地擴充內容，不用擔心來不及寫故事的結尾了。

4. 語域恰當

考生應該由始至終使用得體的語域。換句話說，作文讀起來應該像是在給朋友講述一個故事、或者告訴朋友一件事情發生的前前後後。作文中使用的人稱要一致，可以考慮使用第三人稱，例如給故事中的人物起名字。我們的例子中就給那個小男孩起了個名字，叫“小明”。

5. 掌握時間

最好能在四張圖之間均勻地分佈寫作時間，避免在一張圖上花費過多時間，否則，故事很可能寫得虎頭蛇尾，頭重腳輕。如果時間允許，可以進一步修飾文字，校正全文。

II. 回覆電子郵件

這裡考生要先閱讀一封中文電子郵件(簡稱電郵)，然後根據電郵的內容用中文寫回信，回信要針對來信中提出的問題發表意見或建議。這是一個對考生中文能力的綜合測試，考生要讀懂來信，再用中文來表達自己的觀點。根據大學理事會給出的參考評判標準，回信是否完整性，是否連貫流暢，使用的語域恰當依然是評分的三大要素，而回信中考生闡述的觀點、發表的意見是否正確目前並沒有被列入考試的評分範疇。

例子:

AP Chinese Language and Culture - Writing

SWITCH TO SIMPLIFIED | HELP

Question 2 of 2 | HIDE TIME 00 : 12 : 31

Directions: You will be asked to perform two writing tasks in Chinese. In each case, you will be asked to write for a specific purpose and to a specific person. You should write in as complete and as culturally appropriate a manner as possible, taking into account the purpose and the person described.

Read this e-mail from a friend and then type a response.

發件人：大衛
郵件主題： 買電腦

我父母問我想要一台什麼樣的電腦。我最想要的是一台蘋果機，可是蘋果機要比其他牌子的電腦貴很多。你對計算機很在行，能不能給我些建議，到底哪一種電腦更適合我在大學裡使用？ 哪些電腦在功能和性能上都跟蘋果機比較接近，但是在價錢上要便宜一些？

大衛，

選擇一台適於你在大學這個新環境裡用的電腦的確很重要。

更適合在大學裡使用的電腦

哪些電腦在功能和性能上跟蘋果機接近，但價錢要便宜

建議

1. 找出所有問題

來信中提及的所有問題，考生都應該逐一回答。為了避免不必要的遺漏，不妨先把來信中提到的問題，用簡練的關鍵字逐一放到回信裡（參閱例子），以此作為答覆的大綱。確認沒有遺漏任何問題後，再開始書寫回執。不妨用來信的主題開篇，上面的例子中，以“買一台計算機上大學”這個主題做文章，“選擇一台適於你在大學這個新環境裡用的電腦的確很重要。”就成了一句不錯的開場白。

2. 運用相關信息

考試時儘量使用精準詳盡的資料，列舉實例、提供細節、或者對比異同，都有助於考生們把回信寫得有聲有色。不過，作文的評分著重考慮的是文章的寫作質量，而不是追究具體信息正確與否，因此，如果實在不知道該怎樣直接回答來信提出的問題，不妨換個角度，比如說提一些反問，諸如“你為什麼會這麼想呢？”，“我從來沒經歷過這種情況，你能不能給我介紹一下你的經歷和體會”等等。

3. 合理安排時間

要想充分發揮水平，考試時間的合理安排至關重要，考生要學會在限定的時間裡回答每一個問題，不要在前面的問題上花過多的時間反復陳述，而讓後面的問題因為時間不足而草草了結。

Part B: 口語考試

口語考試再分為模擬對話和文化介紹兩項，測試考生的口語表達能力。考試時，考生將使用耳機收聽提問，再用話筒錄下自己的回答。回答問題時，要儘量做到完整切題、用詞恰當、發音準確和語調自然。

在這部分開始前，考生們有時間再一次檢查耳機和話筒。答題時，屏幕上的倒計時器顯示考生答題的剩餘時間。

	時間	佔總分的百分比	題目數量	每題回答時限
模擬對話	4 分鐘	10%	6	20 秒
文化介紹	7 分鐘	15%	1	4 分鐘準備 2 分鐘回答

I. 模擬對話

模擬對話部分一共有六組問題。每組有一到三個提問不等。每組提問後，留給考生20秒的時間來回答。

模擬對話，顧名思義，就是模擬日常談話，對聽到的問題即席回答，沒有另行準備答案的時間。但因為是考試，又與平常對話不同，回答問題有時間限制。不習慣這種考試方式的考生，平日要多多練習，提高回答問題的速度，訓練即席表達的能力。

例子：

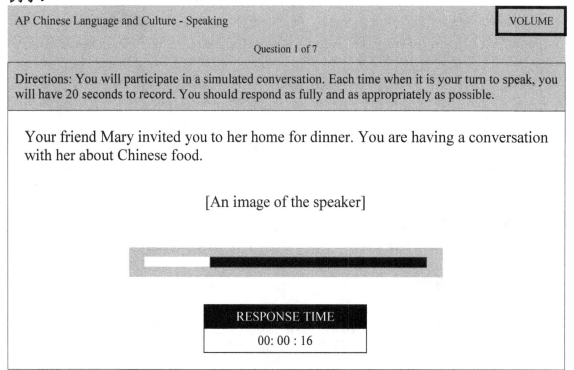

AP Chinese Language and Culture - Speaking

VOLUME

Question 1 of 7

Directions: You will participate in a simulated conversation. Each time when it is your turn to speak, you will have 20 seconds to record. You should respond as fully and as appropriately as possible.

Your friend Mary invited you to her home for dinner. You are having a conversation with her about Chinese food.

[An image of the speaker]

RESPONSE TIME

00: 00 : 16

以下是兩組對話的例子（注：考生只聽得到錄音，但看不到以下文字）：

Mary: 我今天給你做上海菜， 不知道你以前嚐過沒有？ 你都知道哪些風味的中國菜？
[You have 20 seconds to record the response]

Mary: 你最喜歡哪個風味的中國菜？ 為什麼？這個風味的菜都有哪些特色？
[You have 20 seconds to record the response]

建議

1. 詳細闡述

對於有些可以簡單地用“ 是”或“不是”來回答的問題，即使發問者沒有直接要求細說，考生們也最好不要只簡單地回答“ 是”或“ 否”，而要儘量講出一些道理，對自己的回答給予一定的解釋或對自己的觀點做些進一步的闡述，比如說舉個例子等等，否則，20秒會顯得非常漫長。

以上面的對話題材為例，假如考生不知道如何回答“你都知道哪些風味的中國菜?”，不要簡單地回答“我不知道”，而是要想辦法借用相關的知識來回答。比如，考生可以說，中國是一個多民族的大國，擁有豐富多彩的民族文化和風俗習慣。因此，不難想像，各地的美食也都各有特色。然後，利用對話裡提供的信息說：“你為我準備的上海菜可能跟我所熟悉的北京菜很不一樣。這麼香，忍不住要趕緊嚐嚐…。”

回答“你最喜歡哪個風味的中國菜？”時，考生應挑選自己比較熟悉並知道一些特點的風味美食來講，但不一定非要是真正喜歡。比如，考生比較熟悉四川菜的特色，能夠講出內容，是否喜歡就可暫且不究。

考生可以說川菜是中國的八大菜系之一，再試著從中列舉幾個自己知道的菜系，安徽菜、廣東菜、福建菜、湖南菜、江蘇菜、山東菜、四川菜和浙江菜等等，不全也沒有關系。

要回答關於為什麼這個問題，因為無關對錯，所以可以自由發揮，講川菜麻辣的口感，可以講些自己的感受，比如說，“它讓我想起了外婆，她的拿手好菜就是川菜。”

既然問到了菜系的特點，就不能避免地要講，哪怕是只講一個特點也比不講好。試著說說四川菜以麻辣著名，要想講得更詳細，還可以說些名菜，“麻婆豆腐”，“擔擔面”，“回鍋肉”等等。

2. 避免重複停頓

回答要簡明切題，不要反來復去的說同一句話或同一個觀點，避免猶猶豫豫、吞吞吐吐，否則，很容易被認為缺乏文化知識或者語言表達能力。剛開始對著電腦錄音、回答問題覺得不自然是正常現像。我們建議考生按部就班地利用這本書提供的多套習題，經常練習，目的就是為了幫助考生在正式考試的時候，做到放鬆自如。

II. 文化介紹

這部分除了測試考生的語言表達能力外，也考查考生對相應的文化知識的瞭解程度。因此，題目不但要求考生準確地、詳細地介紹相關的文化知識，還會要求考生進一步闡述這個主題的文化意義。

在正式錄音回答問題之前，考生有四分鐘的準備時間，錄音時間限定為兩分鐘。

例子：

AP Chinese Language and Culture - Speaking

VOLUME

Question 7 of 7

Directions: You will be asked to speak in Chinese on a specific topic. Imagine you are making an oral presentation to your Chinese class. First, you will read and hear the topic for your presentation. You will have 4 minutes to prepare your presentation. Then you will have 2 minutes to record your presentation. Your presentation should be as complete as possible.

Choose ONE Chinese literary work that you are familiar with (e.g. *Journey to the West, the Ballad of Mulan*, a famous poem, etc). In your presentation, describe the work and/or its author in detail and explain its significance.

Preparation Time: 240 Seconds
Response Time: 120 Seconds

PREPARATION TIME

00: 04 : 00

建議

1. 主題明確

學生們在作文化介紹時，首先應該搞清楚題目的主題和需要回答的問題，仔細讀懂提示內容，做一些必要的筆記，這樣才能避免答非所問。急急忙忙地回答問題，很容易文不對題。

大綱簡潔

在做準備時，學生最好寫個簡要的大綱；在大綱中，列一下想說的要點、細節或者實例。列大綱時用關鍵字詞即可，不必寫出完整的句子。 這些筆記或大綱都不會用來計分的。大綱是作參考或提示用的，錄音時不要一條一條地讀大綱。

3. 內容充實

說得多不如說得全、說得準。與其匆匆忙忙地堆砌很多句子，不如作一個簡潔而又有頭有尾，有血有肉的完整介紹。不妨引用一些實際例子、親身經歷、或者個人體會，使得介紹的內容更加充實。

4. 節奏平穩

用平穩的節奏和輕鬆的語調，從容地進行。在錄音時，要注意屏幕上顯示的倒計時器，掌握好時間。千萬不要在最後一刻，為了趕著多錄一些，結果最後一句話沒有錄全。另一方面，即使有多餘的時間，如果問題已經回答完整，與其重複已經講過的內容，不如就此打住。

考試技巧概述

勤能補拙！為了幫助學生們更好地熟悉考試環境、提高考試水平，除了以上針對各部分考試的具體建議外，在這裡我們再講一些比較通用的經驗之談，希望能對學生們有所幫助。

1. 雖然 AP 中文考試只分聽說讀寫四部分，但其他方面的能力也會直接影響學生的考試成績，譬如中文輸入的熟練程度、記筆記的能力等等。因此我們建議學生們平時就要對這些技能多加練習，這樣才能在考試時做到臨陣不亂。

   如何能把筆記做得又快又準呢？又該如何練習呢？其實日常生活中可以用來練習的機會還是不少的，例如看電視、接電話都是機會。學生們可以練習先記下一些重要的詞，然後再把這些關鍵詞擴展成完整的句子、段落，再進一步寫成一篇故事或一封短信。

   中文打字也要多練，每當需要和中文老師或者懂中文的朋友進行書面交流時，不妨用中文來試試。這樣的練習，不僅能夠幫助學生熟練掌握中文打字輸入，更是增進中文寫作能力，鍛煉用中文進行思考的好辦法。

   另外，用中文寫日記、寫博客，這些都是既新鮮有趣，又能提高中文水平，練習中文打字的事，如果有機會大家何不嘗試一下？！

2. 語言文化的學習絕不是一朝一夕的事，要學會利周邊的資源，例如中文報章、雜誌、電影和書籍等等，日復一日，多多練習。俗話說得好，只要功夫深，鐵棒也能磨成針。勤學苦練一定能帶來豐碩的成果。

不要被書報上的內容難倒，實際生活中用到的內容和詞匯都要比課本上的更豐富多彩，也會更難些。多用多練就能熟能生巧。

把讀過的文章剪報收集起來，有空時拿出來複習一下，寫個評論、做個總結，老師和家長也一定會樂意幫助解決學習中可能遇到的問題。

學習中文時要注意選擇涵蓋面豐富的題材，新聞報道，商業動向，職場信息，公共告示，電影，電視，詩歌，小說都應該儘量涉及。萬事開頭難，不妨從自己最感興趣的題材開始，循序漸進。

3. 持之以恆是學習語言的關鍵。爭取每天安排看幾分鐘的中文電視，讀一篇中文報刊或是瀏覽一下中文網站，日積月累，經常練習要比臨時突擊的效果要更持久更有效。本書附錄裡我們還收集了一些有價值的網站供學生進一步參考。

   我們建議考生將平時的中文學習與這本書結合起來。本書包括八套完整的模擬考題。考生們可以考慮先挑一套題對自己進行水平測定，用以發現自己的長處和不足，然後每月一套。每次測試的得分情況可用第 28 頁上的表格記錄在案，做進展分析。另外，學生們還可利用書中留有的空白，及時記下自己在各個部分的學習心得。

考試前的準備工作是非常重要的。學生們不但在考前要溫故知新、多做練習，而且還應該充分瞭解考試的過程和內容，熟悉考試的形式和方式。希望本書能幫助考生做好考試前的準備，在考場上充分發揮他們的潛力。

UNIT 1 CUSTOMS

SECTION I: MULTIPLE CHOICE

PART A: LISTENING [20 minutes, 25% of final score]

[Listen to the audio track **Customs - Listening.**]

Note: In this part of the exam, you may NOT move back and forth among questions.

I. REJOINDERS [10 minutes, 10% of final score]

Directions: You will hear several short conversations or parts of conversations followed by 4 choices, designated (A), (B), (C), and (D). Choose the one that continues or completes the conversation in a logical and culturally appropriate manner. You will have 5 seconds to answer each question.

QUESTION NUMBER	STUDENT CHOICE			
1	(A)	(B)	(C)	(D)
2	(A)	(B)	(C)	(D)
3	(A)	(B)	(C)	(D)
4	(A)	(B)	(C)	(D)
5	(A)	(B)	(C)	(D)
6	(A)	(B)	(C)	(D)
7	(A)	(B)	(C)	(D)
8	(A)	(B)	(C)	(D)
9	(A)	(B)	(C)	(D)
10	(A)	(B)	(C)	(D)
11	(A)	(B)	(C)	(D)
12	(A)	(B)	(C)	(D)
13	(A)	(B)	(C)	(D)
14	(A)	(B)	(C)	(D)
15	(A)	(B)	(C)	(D)

II. Listening Selections [10 minutes, 15% of final score]

Directions: You will listen to several selections in Chinese. For each selection, you will be told whether it will be played once or twice. You may take notes as you listen. Your notes will not be graded. After listening to each selection, you will see questions in English. For each question, choose the response that is best according to the selection. You will have 12 seconds to answer each question.

SELECTION 1

16. What occasion is the announcement for?

    (A) An exhibition

    (B) An auction

    (C) A trade show

    (D) A conference

17. Which form of art is specifically mentioned in this announcement?

    (A) Paper cutting

    (B) Chinese painting

    (C) Jade carving

    (D) Chinese knotting

18. How is the display arranged?

    (A) By region

    (B) By chronological order

    (C) By artist

    (D) By category

19. According to the announcement, which of the following statements is true?

    (A) An exhibition map is available for purchase.

    (B) Paper cuttings are on display.

    (C) Pottery is the oldest Chinese art form.

    (D) Some of the exhibition items are for sale.

SELECTION 2

20. How many times has Lele been to China?
    (A) Never
    (B) Once
    (C) Twice
    (D) Not mentioned in this recording

21. What should Lele do when he dines with people in China?
    (A) He should help himself to the food.
    (B) He should ask for permission to eat.
    (C) He should use only chopsticks.
    (D) He should not eat until the elders start.

22. What is the proper way to greet the elders?
    (A) Greet them by their names politely
    (B) Do not greet people unless you know them
    (C) Say hello and follow up with a proper title
    (D) Nod your head and keep quiet

SELECTION 3

23. What is the main purpose of Annie's message?
    (A) To let Wendy know that she has arrived at the airport
    (B) To let Wendy know that she will be home tomorrow
    (C) To ask Wendy to pick up her dress
    (D) To tell Wendy that her mother made the dress for her

24. What kind of outfit did Wendy ask for?
    (A) A wedding gown
    (B) A business suit
    (C) A cocktail dress
    (D) A *qipao*

25. Why does Wendy need the dress?
    (A) For a culture festival
    (B) For a wedding
    (C) For a conference
    (D) For a company's year-end party

26. What role will Wendy play in the upcoming event?
    (A) Performer
    (B) Guest speaker
    (C) Bridesmaid
    (D) Master of ceremonies

SELECTION 4

27. What does the woman ask the man to do?
    (A) Help her with history homework
    (B) Help her to set up a party
    (C) Ask his mother to make some Chinese food
    (D) Go to a festival with her

28. According to the conversation, what occasion is coming up?
    (A) Chinese New Year
    (B) Duanwu Festival
    (C) The woman's birthday
    (D) A class party

29. What course is the woman taking?
    (A) Chinese culture and customs
    (B) Chinese cooking
    (C) Chinese language
    (D) Chinese history

SELECTION 5

30. What is the most likely location from which the journalist is reporting?
    (A) Train station
    (B) Airport
    (C) Bus terminal
    (D) Subway station

31. When is the report being conducted?
    (A) Right after Chinese New Year
    (B) On the day of Chinese New Year
    (C) A few weeks before Chinese New Year
    (D) A few days before Chinese New Year

32. What is the report about?
    (A) An unprecedented traffic jam caused by a snowstorm
    (B) Very heavy traffic on the day of Chinese New Year
    (C) A huge crowd of people celebrating Chinese New Year in a plaza
    (D) An unexpected crowd in a transportation hub before the holiday

[This marks the end of the audio track **Customs - Listening**.]

PART B: READING

[60 minutes, 25% of final score]

Note: In this part of the exam, you may move back and forth among all the questions.

Directions: You will read several selections in Chinese. Each selection is accompanied by a number of questions in English. For each question, choose the response that is best according to the selection.

Read this sign

(Simplified Characters)	(Traditional Characters)
盆景出售 三角梅、九里香、雀梅、罗汉松	**盆景出售** 三角梅、九里香、雀梅、羅漢松

1. What type of sign is this?
   (A) For hire
   (B) For free
   (C) For rent
   (D) For sale

2. This sign would most likely appear at
   (A) a grocery store
   (B) a garden center
   (C) a pet store
   (D) a department store

3. Which of the following items is listed on the sign?
   (A) Spices
   (B) Bird cages
   (C) Snacks
   (D) Bonsai trees

Read this sign

(Simplified Characters)	(Traditional Characters)
上海菜馆 本店经营各色上海美食，每周七天营业，二十四小时服务，节假日除外。从今日起，午餐特价，以下菜单，十元一份，任意挑选： 油爆虾，腌笃鲜，炒年糕，酱鸭，丝瓜毛豆，熏鱼，上海菜饭，南翔小笼包（每份六只） ＊应顾客要求，本店新增一道武汉风味小吃热干面，敬请品尝。	**上海菜館** 本店經營各色上海美食，每週七天營業，二十四小時服務，節假日除外。從今日起，午餐特價，以下菜單，十元一份，任意挑選： 油爆蝦，醃篤鮮，炒年糕，醬鴨，絲瓜毛豆，熏魚，上海菜飯，南翔小籠包（每份六隻） ＊應顧客要求，本店新增一道武漢風味小吃熱乾麵，敬請品嚐。

4. What type of business is this sign for?
   (A) Catering service
   (B) Bakery
   (C) Restaurant
   (D) Grocery store

5. Which of the following information is provided on this sign?
   (A) New business hours
   (B) A new ownership
   (C) A holiday promotion
   (D) A special lunch menu

6. Which of the following is listed on the sign?
   (A) Hot soup
   (B) Steamed buns
   (C) Moon cakes
   (D) Assorted sandwiches

Read this article

(Simplified Characters)

中国的长城闻名世界，北京的烤鸭人人皆知。到中国，一定登长城，到北京，一定吃烤鸭。俗话说：“不到长城非好汉，不吃烤鸭很遗憾”。

我这次利用去北京观看奥运会的机会，在去鸟巢体育场观看奥运开幕式的前一天，终于游览了我向往已久的万里长城。

长城真是名不虚传，险要雄伟，气派非凡。我在刻着“不到长城非好汉”的牌扁下留了影。

登完长城，我又饿又渴。朋友猜到了我在想什么，带我来到“全聚德”烤鸭店，喝上一瓶凉凉的啤酒，吃上一口香香的烤鸭，终于成为一个没有遗憾的好汉，我真是很得意！

(Traditional Characters)

中國的長城聞名世界，北京的烤鴨人人皆知。到中國，一定登長城，到北京，一定吃烤鴨。俗話說：“不到長城非好漢，不吃烤鴨很遺憾”。

我這次利用去北京觀看奧運會的機會，在去鳥巢體育場觀看奧運開幕式的前一天，終於遊覽了我嚮往已久的萬里長城。

長城真是名不虛傳，險要雄偉，氣派非凡。我在刻著“不到長城非好漢”的牌扁下留了影。

登完長城，我又餓又渴。朋友猜到了我在想什麼，帶我來到“全聚德”烤鴨店，喝上一瓶涼涼的啤酒，吃上一口香香的烤鴨，終於成為一個沒有遺憾的好漢，我真是很得意！

7. According to the saying in this passage, what must a visitor do when visiting Beijing?
   (A) Visit the Bird's Nest Stadium
   (B) Drink Chinese beer
   (C) Eat Beijing roast duck
   (D) Take pictures of the Great Wall

8. According to the passage, which of the following places did the author visit first?
   (A) The Great Wall
   (B) The Beijing Roast Duck Restaurant
   (C) The Bird's Nest Stadium
   (D) The Forbidden City

9. At what location did the author choose to take a picture?
   (A) Outside the Bird's Nest Stadium
   (B) At the Great Wall
   (C) Inside the Forbidden City
   (D) At the Beijing Olympic Village

Read this journal

(Simplified Characters)	(Traditional Characters)
日期：十月十三日 星期五 天气：多云 今天是奶奶的九十大寿，全家的子子孙孙全都到齐了，为奶奶祝寿，就连远在香港的大伯一家也来了。庆祝九十大寿可是件大事啊。 多年的老邻居们听到消息后，也都纷纷前来向奶奶道喜拜寿。这一方面说明奶奶的人缘好，另一方面也体现了中国人的敬老风尚。 奶奶讲起了她出嫁时的情景，我们做小辈的，个个竖起了耳朵，就象听传奇小说一样入迷。 奶奶说，那时候女孩子出嫁要穿红衣，披盖头，跨火盆，坐花轿。除了敲锣打鼓，放鞭炮，吹喇叭，还要行大礼，闹洞房，热闹极了。 一晃几十年过去了，奶奶有我们这么多的孝顺子孙，怎能不心情舒畅，健康长寿呢？	日期：十月十三日 星期五 天氣：多雲 今天是奶奶的九十大壽，全家的子子孫孫全都到齊了，為奶奶祝壽，就連遠在香港的大伯一家也來了。慶祝九十大壽可是件大事啊。 多年的老鄰居們聽到消息後，也都紛紛前來向奶奶道喜拜壽。這一方面說明奶奶的人緣好，另一方面也體現了中國人的敬老風尚。 奶奶講起了她出嫁時的情景，我們做小輩的，個個豎起了耳朵，就像聽傳奇小說一樣入迷。 奶奶說，那時候女孩子出嫁要穿紅衣，披蓋頭，跨火盆，坐花轎。除了敲鑼打鼓，放鞭炮，吹喇叭，還要行大禮，鬧洞房，熱鬧極了。 一晃幾十年過去了，奶奶有我們這麼多的孝順子孫，怎能不心情舒暢，健康長壽呢？

10. What occasion is the author writing about?
    (A) A traditional wedding
    (B) A birthday celebration
    (C) A family reunion
    (D) A housewarming party

11. What is mentioned about the wedding ceremony in the article?
    (A) Wine toasting
    (B) Trumpet playing
    (C) Red envelopes
    (D) Wedding candy

12. According to the author, many people show up for the occasion because
    (A) the author's grandmother is a popular story teller
    (B) the family made a public announcement for the occasion
    (C) people would like to pay respect to the oldest citizen in the area
    (D) the author's grandmother has good relationships with her neighbors

13. This occasion took place in
    (A) spring
    (B) summer
    (C) fall
    (D) winter

Read this recipe

(Simplified Characters)	(Traditional Characters)
粽子	**粽子**
原料：糯米，红枣，红豆沙，芦苇叶，细绳	原料：糯米，紅棗，紅豆沙，蘆葦葉，細繩
做法：	做法：
(1)将芦苇叶泡软洗净。	(1)將蘆葦葉泡軟洗淨。
(2)将糯米洗净，滤干水分。	(2)將糯米洗淨，濾乾水分。
(3)将芦苇叶折成漏斗形状。	(3)將蘆葦葉折成漏斗形狀。
(4)一只手握住芦苇叶以免散开，另一只手在漏斗底部放一粒红枣，这样米就不会漏出去了。	(4)一隻手握住蘆葦葉以免散開，另一隻手在漏斗底部放一粒紅棗，這樣米就不會漏出去了。
(5)然后放入糯米和红豆沙直到填满为止。	(5)然後放入糯米和紅豆沙直到填滿為止。
(6)用芦苇叶盖住漏斗上面，再用细绳子扎紧。	(6)用蘆葦葉蓋住漏斗上面，再用細繩子紮緊。
(7)粽子放入锅中，加水，水要没过粽子。	(7)粽子放入鍋中，加水，水要沒過粽子。
(8)大火煮开后，改小火，两小时后粽子就好了。	(8)大火煮開後，改小火，兩小時後粽子就好了。
祝大家端午节快乐！	祝大家端午節快樂！

14. Which of the following ingredients is mentioned in this recipe?
    (A) Pork
    (B) Peanuts
    (C) Soybeans
    (D) Red dates

15. For what festival is this food most likely to be served?
    (A) Chinese New Year
    (B) The Lantern Festival
    (C) Duanwu Festival
    (D) The Mid-Autumn Festival

16. Why put a red date at the bottom of the funnel?
    (A) To prevent leaking
    (B) To symbolize good luck
    (C) To add flavor
    (D) To anchor the string

17. How should the rice be prepared?
    (A) Cleaned and soaked
    (B) Cleaned and germinated
    (C) Cleaned and marinated
    (D) Cleaned and drained

18. How is this food cooked?
    (A) Steamed
    (B) Boiled
    (C) Baked
    (D) Sautéed

Read this rhyme

(Simplified Characters)	(Traditional Characters)
陕西八大怪	**陝西八大怪**
面条像腰带，碗盆难分开，	麵條像腰帶，碗盆難分開，
手帕头上戴，唱戏吼起来，	手帕頭上戴，唱戲吼起來，
辣子是道菜，大饼像锅盖，	辣子是道菜，大餅像鍋蓋，
房子半边盖，吃饭不坐蹲着来。	房子半邊蓋，吃飯不坐蹲著來。

19. What is this rhyme about?
    (A) Eight popular dishes in the Shanxi region
    (B) Eight strange customs in the Shanxi region
    (C) Eight famous landscapes in the Shanxi region
    (D) Eight types of folk art in the Shanxi region

20. According to the rhyme, which statement is true about the noodles in the Shanxi region?
    (A) The noodles are a main dish.
    (B) The noodles are very tasty.
    (C) The noodles are very thick.
    (D) The noodles are a symbol of wealth.

21. Which of the following is most likely to be true about the local opera?
    (A) It has a lot of arguing scenes.
    (B) It is characterized by roaring voices.
    (C) It begins with a thunderous opening.
    (D) It is always performed in duet.

22. What is special about the dining customs?
    (A) People squat instead of sitting.
    (B) People eat outside instead of inside.
    (C) People eat with spoons instead of chopsticks.
    (D) People dine by the stove instead of by the table.

23. What is an unusual accessory that local people wear on their heads?
    (A) Belt
    (B) Feather
    (C) Handkerchief
    (D) Scarf

Read this passage

(Simplified Characters)	(Traditional Characters)
造纸术、印刷、火药和指南针是中国古代的四大发明。	造紙術、印刷、火藥和指南針是中國古代的四大發明。
早在公元 105 年左右，汉朝的蔡伦发明了造纸术。他用树皮，加上破烂的鱼网、旧布和麻绳，制造了纸张。	早在公元 105 年左右，漢朝的蔡倫發明了造紙術。他用樹皮，加上破爛的魚網、舊布和麻繩，製造了紙張。
古代印刷术最早是用木刻版，也起源于中国。木刻版印刷起先是用来在丝绸上印图案，后来才用在纸张印刷上。据考证，早在公元 220 年之前，中国人就开始使用这种木刻版印刷术了。	古代印刷術最早是用木刻版，也起源於中國。木刻版印刷起先是用來在絲綢上印圖案，後來才用在紙張印刷上。據考證，早在公元 220 年之前，中國人就開始使用這種木刻版印刷術了。
据说，在九世纪期间，有位道士在研制让人长生不老的灵丹妙药时，意外地发明了制造火药的方法。到了十二世纪末，中国配制的火药已经能炸裂金属容器了。	據說，在九世紀期間，有位道士在研製讓人長生不老的靈丹妙藥時，意外地發明了製造火藥的方法。到了十二世紀末，中國配製的火藥已經能炸裂金屬容器了。
关于指南针的记载，最早可以追溯到中国的宋朝，也就是公元 1040 到 1044 年间。在古代中国，最常见的指南针是一根磁针漂浮在一碗水里，针头指向南方。这就成为最原始的导航工具。	關於指南針的記載，最早可以追溯到中國的宋朝，也就是公元 1040 到 1044 年間。在古代中國，最常見的指南針是一根磁針漂浮在一碗水裡，針頭指向南方。這就成為最原始的導航工具。
中华民族的发明和创造为人类文明做出了重要贡献。	中華民族的發明和創造為人類文明做出了重要貢獻。

24. According to the passage, who invented the gunpowder?
    (A) A royal chef
    (B) A war general
    (C) An herbalist
    (D) A Taoist

25. According to the passage, which of the following statements is true?
    (A) The printing technique was first used on textiles in ancient China.
    (B) Paper was primarily made of mulberry leaves and silkworms.
    (C) Gunpowder was invented in China by the end of the 11th century.
    (D) The technique of making silk was invented by the ancient Chinese.

26. Which of the following items is needed to make an ancient Chinese compass?
    (A) Magnetic stone
    (B) Liquid mercury
    (C) A bowl
    (D) A dial

Read this article

(Simplified Characters)	(Traditional Characters)
磨磨秋千起源于中国的贵州，是深受当地彝族人喜爱的一种传统娱乐活动。 制作这种秋千的方法是：在一根长长的横木中段刻出一个凹槽，另外，在地上固定一根半人高尖头向上木桩。然后，把横木的槽口放在木桩的尖头上，秋千就搭成了。 玩的时候，两组人要分别扶着横木的两边，像推磨一样，推着推着，秋千就越转越快，载着人快速旋转，这就是彝族的游戏“磨磨秋千”。	磨磨鞦韆起源於中國的貴州，是深受當地彝族人喜愛的一種傳統娛樂活動。 製作這種鞦韆的方法是：在一根長長的橫木中段刻出一個凹槽，另外，在地上固定一根半人高尖頭向上木樁。然後，把橫木的槽口放在木樁的尖頭上，鞦韆就搭成了。 玩的時候，兩組人要分別扶著橫木的兩邊，像推磨一樣，推著推著，鞦韆就越轉越快，載著人快速旋轉，這就是彝族的遊戲“磨磨鞦韆”。

27. According to this article, how do you play this game?
    (A) Spinning
    (B) Sliding
    (C) Bouncing
    (D) Flying

28. According to the article, which of the following is used to build this game?
    (A) Pebbles
    (B) Planks
    (C) Logs
    (D) Bamboos

29. Which of the following is true about this game?
    (A) It can swing high.
    (B) It must be played by at least two people.
    (C) It is a popular game in China.
    (D) It is a newly invented game.

Read this sign

(Simplified Characters)	(Traditional Characters)
欣赏中国传统红木家具之美， 请点击图库。	欣賞中國傳統紅木家俱之美， 請點擊圖庫。

30. This sign directs you to
    (A) an antique store
    (B) a product catalog
    (C) a photo gallery
    (D) a warehouse

31. What kind of merchandise is mentioned in the sign?
    (A) Designer wallpaper
    (B) Luxury draperies
    (C) Rosewood carvings
    (D) Traditional furniture

Read this story

(Simplified Characters)

钟先生的故乡情

九月的一个星期五，钟先生一下班，没有像往常那样，直奔书房，而是一头钻进了厨房，翻箱倒柜的，弄得乒乓作响。钟太太好奇地跟了进去。钟先生问："明天你能不能替我准备一条鱼？要新鲜的，最好是黄鱼，还要木棒槌。对了，还要葱和姜。"

第二天傍晚，一位陌生人来到钟先生家。钟先生介绍说："这位是新来的访问学者，郑先生，是浙江温州人，我的老乡！今天我下厨！"

钟先生进了厨房没两分钟，就出来小声地问太太："鱼怎么洗?"钟太太哭笑不得，旁边的郑先生哈哈一笑，卷起袖子说："想吃正宗的温州菜？还是我来做吧！"

不一会儿，一锅"敲鱼"上桌了，面对这美味佳肴，钟先生回忆起来："记得我八岁那年，我爸爸做过敲鱼给我们吃。他先把一块去了皮、骨的鱼肉，掺上薯粉，用木槌敲啊敲，鱼块慢慢地变得又薄又大。等锅里的水煮开后，把这薄薄的鱼片切成条，下进去。

那晶莹透亮，热气腾腾的敲鱼汤是我记忆中最鲜美的食品。"

(Traditional Characters)

鍾先生的故鄉情

九月的一個星期五，鍾先生一下班，沒有像往常那樣，直奔書房，而是一頭鑽進了廚房，翻箱倒櫃的，弄得乒乓作響。鍾太太好奇地跟了進去。鍾先生問："明天你能不能替我準備一條魚？要新鮮的，最好是黄魚，還要木棒槌。對了，還要蔥和姜。"

第二天傍晚，一位陌生人來到鍾先生家。鍾先生介紹說："這位是新來的訪問學者，鄭先生，是浙江温州人，我的老鄉！今天我下廚！"

鍾先生進了廚房沒兩分鐘，就出來小聲地問太太："魚怎麼洗?"鍾太太哭笑不得，旁邊的鄭先生哈哈一笑，捲起袖子說："想吃正宗的温州菜？還是我來做吧！"

不一會兒，一鍋"敲魚"上桌了，面對這美味佳餚，鍾先生回憶起來："記得我八歲那年，我爸爸做過敲魚給我們吃。他先把一塊去了皮、骨的魚肉，掺上薯粉，用木槌敲啊敲，魚塊慢慢地變得又薄又大。等鍋裡的水煮開後，把這薄薄的魚片切成條，下進去。

那晶瑩透亮，熱氣騰騰的敲魚湯是我記憶中最鮮美的食品。"

32. What does Mr. Zhong normally do after coming home from work?
    (A) He goes to his study.
    (B) He prepares dinner.
    (C) He plays Ping-Pong.
    (D) He talks to his wife.

33. Which of the following items did Mr. Zhong ask his wife to prepare for him?
    (A) Cooking wine
    (B) Chicken broth
    (C) Green onions
    (D) Fish patty

34. According to the story, which of the following statements is true about the guest?
    (A) He is a visiting scholar.
    (B) He is a new neighbor.
    (C) He is an old friend of Mr. Zhong.
    (D) He is a business partner of Mr. Zhong.

35. What is Mrs. Zhong's reaction to Mr. Zhong's question when he comes out from the kitchen?
    (A) She is puzzled by the ambiguity of his question.
    (B) She is surprised by her husband's secretive tone.
    (C) She is stunned by the way he talks to her in front of a guest.
    (D) She is amused by his incompetence.

36. Which statement is true about the dish mentioned in the story?
    (A) It was the first dish made by Mr. Zhong's father.
    (B) It is the only dish that Mr. Zhong can make.
    (C) The dish was prepared by Mr. Zhong.
    (D) The dish brings back Mr. Zhong's sweet memories of childhood.

SECTION II: FREE RESPONSE

PART A: WRITING [30 minutes, 25% of final score]

Note: In this part of the exam, you may NOT move back and forth among questions.

Directions: You will be asked to perform two writing tasks in Chinese. In each case, you will be asked to write for a specific purpose and to a specific person. You should write in as complete and as culturally appropriate a manner as possible, taking into account the purpose and the person described.

I. Story Narration [15 minutes, 15% of final score]

The four pictures present a story. Imagine you are writing the story to a friend. Narrate a complete story as suggested by the pictures. Give your story a beginning, middle, and an end.

II. E-MAIL RESPONSE [15 minutes, 10% of total score]

Read this e-mail from a friend and then type your response.

(Simplified Characters)

发件人：珍妮

邮件主题：请帮助我了解中国风俗习惯

今年暑假我要去中国旅游，听说中国的风俗习惯和我们的有很多不同之处，你正在修AP中文课，对中国的文化习俗一定有不少了解，我想问问你，我去中国以前在这些方面要做些什么准备？到了中国又有些什么事情是应该特别注意的？我相信你的建议对我一定会有很大的帮助。谢谢！

(Traditional Characters)

發件人：珍妮

郵件主題：請幫助我瞭解中國風俗習慣

今年暑假我要去中國旅遊，聽說中國的風俗習慣和我們的有很多不同之處，你正在修AP中文課，對中國的文化習俗一定有不少瞭解，我想問問你，我去中國以前在這些方面要做些什麼準備？到了中國又有些什麼事情是應該特別注意的？我相信你的建議對我一定會有很大的幫助。謝謝！

PART B: SPEAKING [15 minutes, 25% of final score]

[Listen to the audio track **Customs - Speaking**.]

Note: In this part of the exam, you may NOT move back and forth among questions.

I. CONVERSATION [4 minutes, 10% of final score]

Directions: You will participate in a simulated conversation. Each time it is your turn to speak, you will have 20 seconds to record. You should respond as fully and as appropriately as possible.

You have a conversation with David, a friend that you have just met, about the Chinese zodiac at a Chinese New Year party.

David: [Audio]
[TONE]
[Student records the response] (20 seconds)

David: [Audio]
[TONE]
[Student records the response] (20 seconds)

David: [Audio]
[TONE]
[Student records the response] (20 seconds)

David: [Audio]
[TONE]
[Student records the response] (20 seconds)

David: [Audio]
[TONE]
[Student records the response] (20 seconds)

David: [Audio]
[TONE]
[Student records the response] (20 seconds)

II. CULTURAL PRESENTATION [7 minutes, 15% of final score]

Directions: You will be asked to speak in Chinese on a specific topic. Imagine you are making an oral presentation to your Chinese class. First, you will read and hear the topic for your presentation. You will have 4 minutes to prepare your presentation. Then you will have 2 minutes to record your presentation. Your presentation should be as complete as possible.

Choose ONE form of Chinese arts or crafts (e.g. brush painting, musical instruments, pottery, embroidery, etc). In your presentation, describe this art or craft form in detail and explain its significance.

[This marks the end of the audio track **Customs - Speaking**.]

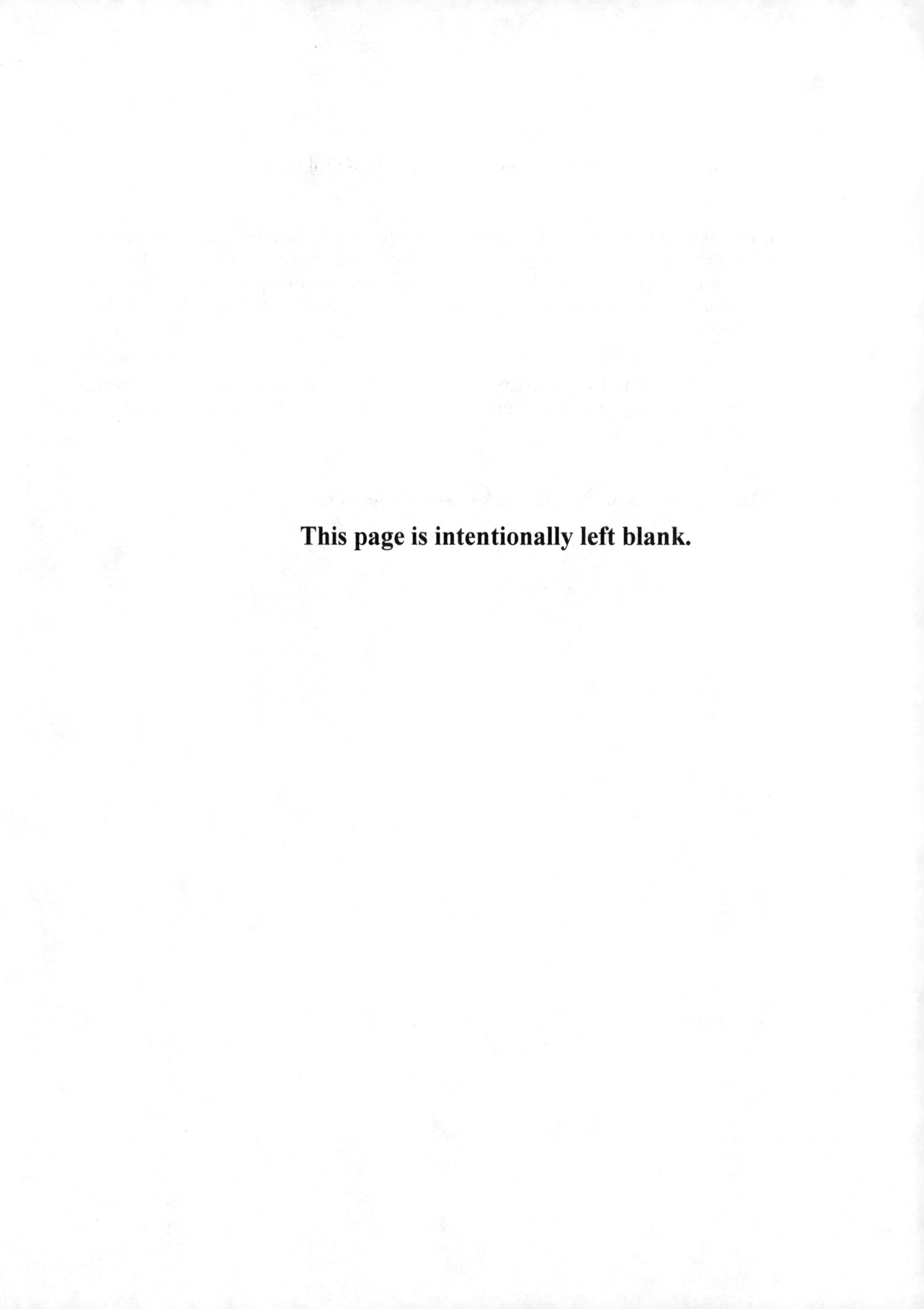

This page is intentionally left blank.

UNIT 2 DAILY LIFE

SECTION I: MULTIPLE CHOICE

PART A: LISTENING [20 minutes, 25% of final score]

[Listen to the audio track **Daily Life - Listening**.]

Note: In this part of the exam, you may NOT move back and forth among questions.

I. REJOINDERS [10 minutes, 10% of final score]

Directions: You will hear several short conversations or parts of conversations followed by 4 choices, designated (A), (B), (C), and (D). Choose the one that continues or completes the conversation in a logical and culturally appropriate manner. You will have 5 seconds to answer each question.

QUESTION NUMBER	STUDENT CHOICE			
1	(A)	(B)	(C)	(D)
2	(A)	(B)	(C)	(D)
3	(A)	(B)	(C)	(D)
4	(A)	(B)	(C)	(D)
5	(A)	(B)	(C)	(D)
6	(A)	(B)	(C)	(D)
7	(A)	(B)	(C)	(D)
8	(A)	(B)	(C)	(D)
9	(A)	(B)	(C)	(D)
10	(A)	(B)	(C)	(D)
11	(A)	(B)	(C)	(D)
12	(A)	(B)	(C)	(D)
13	(A)	(B)	(C)	(D)
14	(A)	(B)	(C)	(D)
15	(A)	(B)	(C)	(D)

II. LISTENING SELECTIONS [10 minutes, 15% of final score]

Directions: You will listen to several selections in Chinese. For each selection, you will be told whether it will be played once or twice. You may take notes as you listen. Your notes will not be graded. After listening to each selection, you will see questions in English. For each question, choose the response that is best according to the selection. You will have 12 seconds to answer each question.

SELECTION 1

16. What is the purpose of this announcement?
    (A) To announce a budget cut
    (B) To announce the library is open on Sunday
    (C) To announce the new library schedule
    (D) To extend the library hours

17. When do the announced changes take effect?
    (A) Immediately
    (B) Monday
    (C) March 1
    (D) January 3

18. Who makes the decision on this matter?
    (A) The library committee
    (B) The librarians
    (C) The budget controller
    (D) The library manager

19. How many hours was the library open on Mondays before the change?
    (A) Six hours
    (B) Eight hours
    (C) Ten hours
    (D) Twelve hours

SELECTION 2

20. The instructions are for
    (A) making an omelet
    (B) making fried noodles
    (C) making egg fried rice
    (D) making rice cake

21. What ingredient is mentioned in the instructions?
    (A) Soy sauce
    (B) Sugar
    (C) Salt
    (D) Oil

22. According to the instructions, what cooking utensils are used?
    (A) Frying pan and spoon
    (B) Frying pan and spatula
    (C) Frying pan and chopsticks
    (D) Frying pan and tongs

SELECTION 3

23. What is the main point of the message?
    (A) The speaker's car is broken.
    (B) The speaker will bring food to the meeting.
    (C) The speaker will be late for the meeting.
    (D) The speaker will take the bus to his friend's house.

24. What does the speaker want his friends to do before he arrives?
    (A) Discuss the Chinese New Year activities
    (B) Decide on the Chinese New Year activities
    (C) Have some light snacks while waiting for him
    (D) Brew a pot of tea and prepare snacks

25. Where is the speaker calling from?
    (A) His home
    (B) A bus stop
    (C) A teahouse
    (D) A train station

26. What does the speaker plan to do after he arrives?
    (A) Brew a pot of coffee
    (B) Have lunch with his friends
    (C) Rehearse for the upcoming event
    (D) Join the meeting while having tea

SELECTION 4

27. Why does the woman call the man?
    (A) To ask him for advice
    (B) To ask him to go out for coffee
    (C) To ask him to practice English conversation with her
    (D) To ask him to help with her English writing homework

28. The man would like the woman to
    (A) pay for the meal
    (B) treat him to a cup of coffee
    (C) buy a coffee mug for him
    (D) practice English first

29. What does the woman propose to do?
    (A) Have coffee on Friday
    (B) Order coffee in English
    (C) Meet during the coffee break
    (D) Have coffee and practice English

SELECTION 5

30. If today is Saturday, then what is Monday's weather forecast?
    (A) Cloudy
    (B) Sunny
    (C) Rainy
    (D) Windy

31. According to the report, what is tomorrow's temperature?
    (A) High of seventy-five and low of fifty degrees Fahrenheit
    (B) High of eighty and low of sixty-five degrees Fahrenheit
    (C) High of twenty and low of ten degrees Celsius
    (D) High of twenty-five and low of fifteen degrees Celsius

32. According to the forecast, which day will have thunderstorms?
    (A) Today
    (B) Tomorrow
    (C) Every day
    (D) The day after tomorrow

[This marks the end of the audio track **Daily Life - Listening**.]

PART B: READING [60 minutes, 25% of final score]

Note: In this part of the test, you may move back and forth among all the questions.

Directions: You will read several selections in Chinese. Each selection is accompanied by a number of questions in English. For each question, choose the response that is best according to the selection.

Read this advertisement

(Simplified Characters)	(Traditional Characters)
小提琴教学 张老师二十年经验专精儿童小提琴教学 25 美元/30 分钟或 45 美元/1 小时请电 925-123-4567	**小提琴教學** 張老師二十年經驗專精兒童小提琴教學 25 美元/30 分鐘或 45 美元/1 小時請電 925-123-4567

1. What type of advertisement is this?

   (A) Violin lessons for children

   (B) Musical instrument repair

   (C) Violin for rent

   (D) Teacher needed

2. How much does it cost for sixty minutes of the service advertised?

   (A) Sixty dollars

   (B) Fifty dollars

   (C) Forty-five dollars

   (D) Twenty-five dollars

Read this poster

(Simplified Characters)	(Traditional Characters)
禁止停泊车辆通告 ***国庆日花车游行路线*** 此处从七月三日下午五时起到七月四日下午八时禁止停泊车辆。违规车辆将被拖走。 屋仑市政府启	**禁止停泊車輛通告** ***國慶日花車遊行路線*** 此處從七月三日下午五時起到七月四日下午八時禁止停泊車輛。違規車輛將被拖走。 屋崙市政府啓

3. When are cars allowed to park?
   (A) After 5 p.m. on July 3
   (B) Before 5 p.m. on July 3
   (C) After 5 p.m. on July 4
   (D) Before 5 p.m. on July 4

4. Why are cars not allowed to park at the designated time?
   (A) Because of street cleaning
   (B) Because of road repair
   (C) Because of a protest demonstration
   (D) Because of a holiday parade

5. The notice is issued by
   (A) the City Hall
   (B) the Police Department
   (C) the Parking Enforcement Department
   (D) the Sheriff's Office

Read this passage

(Simplified Characters)	(Traditional Characters)
公历：二月十日 农历：元月初二 天气：多云 昨天一早妈妈给我打电话，说“今天是年初一”。我连忙向爸爸妈妈拜年，祝他们身体健康，然后向他们讨压岁钱。他们说已经准备好红包了，不过要等我回家时才能给我。妈妈说虽然学校不放假，但不要忘记下课后去中国餐馆吃一顿年饭来庆祝新年。要不是妈妈的提醒，我一定会忘记昨天是农历新年。 到了晚上，我便约了几位中国留学生一起去学校附近的中餐馆吃了年饭。正当大家兴高采烈地谈论着各自家乡过年的习俗时，陈小娟的眼睛突然红了，真是每逢佳节倍思亲啊！我们都劝她，再过几个月放暑假就可以回家了，而且在大年初一哭也不吉利，她才不好意思地点点头，擦干了眼泪。	公曆：二月十日 農曆：元月初二 天氣：多雲 昨天一早媽媽給我打電話，說“今天是年初一”。我連忙向爸爸媽媽拜年，祝他們身體健康，然後向他們討壓歲錢。他們說已經準備好紅包了，不過要等我回家時才能給我。媽媽說雖然學校不放假，但不要忘記下課後去中國餐館吃一頓年飯來慶祝新年。要不是媽媽的提醒，我一定會忘記昨天是農曆新年。 到了晚上，我便約了幾位中國留學生一起去學校附近的中餐館吃了年飯。正當大家興高采烈地談論著各自家鄉過年的習俗時，陳小娟的眼睛突然紅了，真是每逢佳節倍思親啊！我們都勸她，再過幾個月放暑假就可以回家了，而且在大年初一哭也不吉利，她才不好意思地點點頭，擦乾了眼淚。

6. This passage is most likely from
   (A) a letter
   (B) a diary
   (C) a postcard
   (D) a book

7. When did the writer's mother call?
   (A) February 9
   (B) February 10
   (C) February 11
   (D) February 12

8. The writer's mother called her
   (A) to ask her to go home for Chinese New Year
   (B) to return her inquiry about a Chinese recipe
   (C) to tell her that they will have dinner with her
   (D) to remind her to celebrate Chinese New Year

9. Why did one of the student's eyes turn red?
   (A) She had allergies.
   (B) She had an eye infection.
   (C) She missed her family.
   (D) She could not handle spicy food.

Read this chart

(Simplified Characters)

美国主要城市气象预报

城市	天气预报	最高气温（华氏）	最低气温（华氏）
纽约	小雪，一至二英寸	25	15
华盛顿	阳光普照，东北风，风势强劲	40	30
芝加哥	冰雹， 非常寒冷	-5	-15
三藩市	多云转阴，零星小雨，湿度百分之五十	65	50
洛杉矶	多云转晴，微风	70	60

(Traditional Characters)

美國主要城市氣象預報

城市	天氣預報	最高氣溫（華氏）	最低氣溫（華氏）
紐約	小雪，一至二英吋	25	15
華盛頓	陽光普照，東北風，風勢強勁	40	30
芝加哥	冰雹，非常寒冷	-5	-15
三藩市	多雲轉陰，零星小雨，濕度百分之五十	65	50
洛杉磯	多雲轉晴，微風	70	60

10. What is the weather forecast for San Francisco?
    (A) Strong wind
    (B) Scattered showers
    (C) Heavy rain
    (D) Freezing cold

11. Which city will be sunny?
    (A) San Jose
    (B) New Jersey
    (C) Los Angeles
    (D) Los Altos

12. Which city will have snow?
    (A) New York
    (B) Washington, D.C.
    (C) Boston
    (D) Chicago

13. Which city has a colder temperature forecast than New York?
    (A) Newark
    (B) Washington, D.C.
    (C) Chicago
    (D) Boston

Read this brochure

(Simplified Characters)

2009 牛年迎春联欢会

主持人：张英雄，陈安娜

致辞

蔡晶莹	校长	新春贺词

节目单

次序	表演者	节目
1	一年级	儿歌朗诵
2	学前班	合唱
3	三年级	舞蹈
4	全体老师	民乐合奏
5	五年级	短剧

(Traditional Characters)

2009 牛年迎春聯歡會

主持人：張英雄，陳安娜

致辭

蔡晶瑩	校長	新春賀詞

節目單

次序	表演者	節目
1	一年級	兒歌朗誦
2	學前班	合唱
3	三年級	舞蹈
4	全體老師	民樂合奏
5	五年級	短劇

14. What kind of brochure is this?
    (A) It is a program for a year-end music concert.
    (B) It is a program for a Chinese New Year celebration.
    (C) It is a program for a fundraising performance.
    (D) It is a program for a school talent show.

15. According to the brochure, who will give the opening speech?
    (A) Principal
    (B) Teacher
    (C) Parent
    (D) Student

16. How many classes are listed in the brochure?
    (A) Five
    (B) Four
    (C) Three
    (D) Two

17. Which class's performance is likely to involve more physical action?
    (A) First grade
    (B) Second grade
    (C) Third grade
    (D) Fourth grade

Read this letter

(Simplified Characters)

亲爱的外公外婆：

您们好吗？非常想念您们。

一转眼，我从香港回美国已经快一个月了。因为忙着做入学准备，所以一直都没能写信感谢您们对我在香港时的照顾，请原谅。

上星期六是大学开学第一天，爸爸妈妈送我到宿舍。整理好行李后，我们先去宿舍附近的餐馆吃午饭，然后在校园里参观游览了一番。天快黑时，爸爸妈妈才依依不舍地回家了。

我现在是大学生了，除了要用心学习外还要适应新的生活环境。在家里我和小弟都有自己的房间，可现在我要跟两个室友共用一间卧室。虽然他们都很友善，但我还是觉得有一点儿不习惯，但愿我很快就能适应。

我要去上课了。过几天再给您们写信。

祝身体健康！

外孙女　美仪 敬上
二〇〇九年九月十五日

(Traditional Characters)

親愛的外公外婆：

您們好嗎？非常想念您們。

一轉眼，我從香港回美國已經快一個月了。因為忙着做入學準備，所以一直都沒能寫信感謝您們對我在香港時的照顧，請原諒。

上星期六是大學開學第一天，爸爸媽媽送我到宿舍。整理好行李後，我們先去宿舍附近的餐館吃午飯，然後在校園裡參觀游覽了一番。天快黑時，爸爸媽媽才依依不捨地回家了。

我現在是大學生了，除了要用心學習外還要適應新的生活環境。在家裡我和小弟都有自己的房間，可現在我要跟兩個室友共用一間臥室。雖然他們都很友善，但我還是覺得有一點兒不習慣，但願我很快就能適應。

我要去上課了。過幾天再給您們寫信。

祝身體健康！

外孫女　美儀 敬上
二〇〇九年九月十五日

18. To whom is Mei Yi writing?
    (A) Her parents
    (B) Her college roommates
    (C) Her maternal grandparents
    (D) Her paternal grandparents

19. What do Mei Yi and her parents do together on the first day of school?
    (A) Walk around campus
    (B) Eat dinner at school cafeteria
    (C) Meet her academic advisor
    (D) Have lunch with her roommates

20. Which of the following statement is mentioned in the passage?
    (A) Mei Yi's brother attends the same school.
    (B) Mei Yi's grandparents live in America.
    (C) Mei Yi visited Hong Kong during the summer.
    (D) Mei Yi has been in college for a month.

21. According to the passage, what does Mei Yi have to do to adjust to college life?
    (A) Eat cafeteria food
    (B) Do her own laundry
    (C) Share a dorm room
    (D) Manage her money

22. What does Mei Yi promise to do in her letter?
    (A) Call her parents
    (B) Help her roommates
    (C) Take her parents to lunch
    (D) Write to her grandparents

Read this poster

(Simplified Characters)	(Traditional Characters)
糖尿病饮食讲座	**糖尿病飲食講座**
糖尿病患者 **如何在节日期间控制饮食**	**糖尿病患者** **如何在節日期間控制飲食**
主讲者: 李世晶医生 (洛杉矶医院营养辅导主任)	主講者: 李世晶醫生 (洛杉磯醫院營養輔導主任)
日期: 十一月五日(星期六) 或 十一月六日(星期日)	日期: 十一月五日(星期六) 或 十一月六日(星期日)
时间: 上、下午各一场 上午九点到十一点 下午一点到三点	時間: 上、下午各一場 上午九點到十一點 下午一點到三點
地点: 洛杉矶医院中心会议室	地點: 洛杉磯醫院中心會議室
电话: 1-800-321-4321 请打电话报名注册	電話: 1-800-321-4321 請打電話報名註冊

23. What is the poster about?
    (A) A seminar on healthy cooking
    (B) A seminar on weight control
    (C) A seminar on nutrition for athletes
    (D) A seminar on diet for people with diabetes

24. What is the main focus of this seminar?
    (A) How to control food intake during the holidays
    (B) How to manage the medical condition at home
    (C) How to measure blood sugar level
    (D) How to maintain a healthy weight

25. How many seminars will Dr. Li give at the hospital's conference room?
    (A) One
    (B) Two
    (C) Three
    (D) Four

Read this passage

(Simplified Characters)	(Traditional Characters)
每一天都有成千上万的消费者成为"身份盗用"受害者。身份盗用日趋严重。盗用者用偷取的个人资料，例如驾驶執照、信用卡或银行提款卡等，来购物、提款。当盗用者的诈骗罪行被发现时，往往他们已经给受害者留下了一笔沉重的债务负担。 为了避免身份被盗用，消费者必须采取行动来积极地保护自己。这本手册向大家介绍（一）什么是"安全冻结"（二）"安全冻结"的优点及缺点（三）如何正确使用"安全冻结"。	每一天都有成千上萬的消費者成為"身份盜用"受害者。身份盜用日趨嚴重。盜用者用偷取的個人資料，例如駕駛執照、信用卡或銀行提款卡等，來購物、提款。當盜用者的詐騙罪行被發現時，往往他們已經給受害者留下了一筆沉重的債務負擔。 為了避免身份被盜用，消費者必須採取行動來積極地保護自己。這本手冊向大家介紹（一）什麼是"安全凍結"（二）"安全凍結"的優點及缺點（三）如何正確使用"安全凍結"。

26. What kind of service is this brochure advertising?
    (A) Credit protection
    (B) Refrigerator repair
    (C) Credit check
    (D) Criminal background check

27. Which of the following is mentioned in this article?
    (A) Social Security card
    (B) Debit card
    (C) Insurance card
    (D) Credit card

28. According to the passage, what could be the cause of heavy debts?
    (A) Overspending on credit cards
    (B) High interest rate on loans
    (C) Identity theft
    (D) High cost of living

Read this public sign

(Simplified Characters)	(Traditional Characters)
申请驾照者请在柜台前红线处 排队等候服务	申請駕照者請在櫃檯前紅線處 排隊等候服務

29. Where would the sign most likely appear?
    (A) At a restaurant
    (B) At a theater
    (C) At a sports stadium
    (D) At the Department of Motor Vehicles

30. What does the sign ask people to do?
    (A) Line up at the service counter
    (B) Form a straight line
    (C) Wait in line for service
    (D) Wait to be seated

31. This sign is intended for
    (A) applicants
    (B) diners
    (C) ticket buyers
    (D) event goers

Read this story

(Simplified Characters)

钟先生的爱好

看书和看电视是钟先生的两大爱好。 你看他的家里堆满了书，每个房间都有，连洗手间也不例外。电视呢，也是每个房间都有，当然也包括洗手间。不过，他的爱中之爱还是体育。

钟先生一有空就看有关球赛的书籍和电视节目。他对每样球赛的规则和球赛的结果都能倒背如流，对球员的个人资料更是了如指掌。

那钟先生一定是个运动健将啰？其实不然。春天，钟先生看棒球赛，可是他不打棒球，他说打棒球很危险。夏天，钟先生看网球赛，可是他也不打网球，因为他怕晒。秋天，钟先生看橄榄球赛，但他从不参加橄榄球队，他说太容易受伤。冬天，钟先生看篮球赛，他又说他的个子太小会被人撞倒，所以还是坐在电视前看球赛最好，又安全又方便。

(Traditional Characters)

鍾先生的愛好

看書和看電視是鍾先生的兩大愛好。你看他的家裡堆滿了書，每個房間都有，連洗手間也不例外。電視呢，也是每個房間都有，當然也包括洗手間。不過，他的愛中之愛還是體育。

鍾先生一有空就看有關球賽的書籍和電視節目。他對每樣球賽的規則和球賽的結果都能倒背如流，對球員的個人資料更是瞭如指掌。

那鍾先生一定是個運動健將囉？其實不然。春天，鍾先生看棒球賽，可是他不打棒球，他說打棒球很危險。夏天，鍾先生看網球賽，可是他也不打網球，因為他怕曬。秋天，鍾先生看橄欖球賽，但他從不參加橄欖球隊，他說太容易受傷。冬天，鍾先生看籃球賽，他又說他的個子太小會被人撞倒，所以還是坐在電視前看球賽最好，又安全又方便。

32. What does Mr. Zhong most enjoy doing in his spare time?
    (A) Participating in individual sports
    (B) Participating in team sports
    (C) Watching sports on television
    (D) Discussing sports with friends

33. According to the story, which of the following statements is true about Mr. Zhong?
    (A) He enjoys watching TV more than sports.
    (B) He enjoys basketball more than football.
    (C) He has sports memorabilia in every room.
    (D) He memorizes all kinds of sports-related facts.

34. What sport does Mr. Zhong watch in the summer?
    (A) Baseball
    (B) Tennis
    (C) Swimming
    (D) Soccer

35. Mr. Zhong doesn't play basketball because
    (A) he is not tall enough
    (B) he is not coordinated
    (C) he doesn't run fast
    (D) he doesn't like to be in the sun

36. According to the story, what sport does Mr. Zhong enjoy playing?
    (A) Tennis
    (B) Golf
    (C) Baseball
    (D) Not mentioned

SECTION II: FREE RESPONSE

PART A: WRITING

[30 minutes, 25% of final score]

Note: In this part of the exam, you may NOT move back and forth among questions.

Directions: You will be asked to perform two writing tasks in Chinese. In each case, you will be asked to write for a specific purpose and to a specific person. You should write in as complete and as culturally appropriate a manner as possible, taking into account the purpose and the person described.

I. Story Narration [15 minutes, 15% of final score]

The four pictures present a story. Imagine you are writing the story to a friend. Narrate a complete story as suggested by the pictures. Give your story a beginning, middle, and an end.

II. E-MAIL RESPONSE [15 minutes, 10% of total score]

Read this e-mail from a friend and then type your response.

(Simplified Characters)

发件人：大卫
邮件主题：如何节约用水？

连续几年的干旱使我们地区的水库水位大幅下降，我们已经收到自来水公司的通知，要求城镇居民今年夏天控制用水量。你有什么节约用水的好主意吗？如果超过用水限额就得多付很多钱，但不浇足够的水，花草又会枯死，你说我该怎么办呢？

(Traditional Characters)

發件人：大衛
郵件主題：如何節約用水？

連續幾年的乾旱使我們地區的水庫水位大幅下降，我們已經收到自來水公司的通知，要求城鎮居民今年夏天控制用水量。你有什麼節約用水的好主意嗎？如果超過用水限額就得多付很多錢，但不澆足夠的水，花草又會枯死，你說我該怎麼辦呢？

PART B: SPEAKING [15 minutes, 25% of final score]

[Listen to the audio track **Daily Life - Speaking**.]

Note: In this part of the exam, you may NOT move back and forth among questions.

I. CONVERSATION [4 minutes, 10% of final score]

Directions: You will participate in a simulated conversation. Each time it is your turn to speak, you will have 20 seconds to record. You should respond as fully and as appropriately as possible.

You are having a conversation with your mother about your father's upcoming birthday celebration.

Mother: [Audio]
[TONE]
[Student records the response] (20 seconds)

Mother: [Audio]
[TONE]
[Student records the response] (20 seconds)

Mother: [Audio]
[TONE]
[Student records the response] (20 seconds)

Mother: [Audio]
[TONE]
[Student records the response] (20 seconds)

Mother: [Audio]
[TONE]
[Student records the response] (20 seconds)

Mother: [Audio]
[TONE]
[Student records the response] (20 seconds)

II. CULTURAL PRESENTATION [7 minutes, 15% of final score]

Directions: You will be asked to speak in Chinese on a specific topic. Imagine you are making an oral presentation to your Chinese class. First, you will read and hear the topic for your presentation. You will have 4 minutes to prepare your presentation. Then you will have 2 minutes to record your presentation. Your presentation should be as complete as possible.

Choose one of your favorite Chinese foods. In your presentation, describe it in detail, and then compare and contrast Chinese cuisine (Cantonese, Sichuan, Shandong cuisine, etc.) with that of another culture.

[This marks the end of the audio track **Daily Life - Speaking**.]

This page is intentionally left blank.

UNIT 3 ECONOMICS

SECTION I: MULTIPLE CHOICE

PART A: LISTENING [20 minutes, 25% of final score]

[Listen to the audio track **Economics - Listening.**]

Note: In this part of the exam, you may NOT move back and forth among questions.

I. REJOINDERS [10 minutes, 10% of final score]

Directions: You will hear several short conversations or parts of conversations followed by 4 choices, designated (A), (B), (C), and (D). Choose the one that continues or completes the conversation in a logical and culturally appropriate manner. You will have 5 seconds to answer each question.

QUESTION NUMBER	STUDENT CHOICE			
1	(A)	(B)	(C)	(D)
2	(A)	(B)	(C)	(D)
3	(A)	(B)	(C)	(D)
4	(A)	(B)	(C)	(D)
5	(A)	(B)	(C)	(D)
6	(A)	(B)	(C)	(D)
7	(A)	(B)	(C)	(D)
8	(A)	(B)	(C)	(D)
9	(A)	(B)	(C)	(D)
10	(A)	(B)	(C)	(D)
11	(A)	(B)	(C)	(D)
12	(A)	(B)	(C)	(D)
13	(A)	(B)	(C)	(D)
14	(A)	(B)	(C)	(D)
15	(A)	(B)	(C)	(D)

II. Listening Selections [10 minutes, 15% of final score]

Directions: You will listen to several selections in Chinese. For each selection, you will be told whether it will be played once or twice. You may take notes as you listen. Your notes will not be graded. After listening to each selection, you will see questions in English. For each question, choose the response that is best according to the selection. You will have 12 seconds to answer each question.

SELECTION 1

16. The business is announcing a change of
    (A) its official name
    (B) its office location
    (C) its office hours
    (D) its contact number

17. When does the change take effect?
    (A) On Monday
    (B) In the near future
    (C) April 7, 2009
    (D) July 4, 2009

18. Which of the following statements is true?
    (A) The business will be closed on weekends.
    (B) The business purchased a new office in 2009.
    (C) The business is located on the third floor.
    (D) The business will be moving to a new location.

19. How many hours per day is the business open?
    (A) Eight hours
    (B) Nine hours
    (C) Seven hours
    (D) Six hours

SELECTION 2

20. The instructions are for
    (A) checking the status of a shipment
    (B) activating a new credit card
    (C) closing a bank account
    (D) making a medical appointment

21. Which of the following information is asked for in the instructions?
    (A) A bank account number
    (B) A credit card number
    (C) A shipping number
    (D) An insurance policy number

22. How many digits does the user have to enter altogether for this procedure?
    (A) Sixteen
    (B) Twenty
    (C) Thirty
    (D) Thirty-two

SELECTION 3

23. What is the main purpose of the message?
    (A) The speaker needs Anna's help with his translation work.
    (B) The speaker wants to know if Anna could accompany him to a bank.
    (C) The speaker wants to know if Anna could be a tour guide in place of him.
    (D) The speaker is looking for a high-paying job.

24. Why does the speaker ask Anna for help?
    (A) He has lots of translation work to finish.
    (B) He has to go to the Bank of China tomorrow.
    (C) He does not know anything about the Bank of China.
    (D) He needs help with documents about the insurance business.

25. Why does the speaker think Anna is a good candidate for this task?
    (A) Anna is good at translation.
    (B) Anna loves high-paying jobs.
    (C) Anna is a good friend of the speaker.
    (D) Anna is very knowledgeable about the Bank of China.

26. What type of delegation is the speaker talking about?
    (A) A delegation of insurance agents
    (B) A delegation of business executives
    (C) A delegation of government officials
    (D) A delegation of diplomats

SELECTION 4

27. Why is the man giving the woman his phone number?
    (A) She is a potential customer.
    (B) She needs his referral to a doctor.
    (C) He is interested in dating her.
    (D) He is interested in hiring her.

28. What is the woman complaining about?
    (A) The living costs are escalating.
    (B) She had a hard time finding a job.
    (C) The health insurance premium has increased.
    (D) She received poor service at her doctor's office.

29. The man is most likely a
    (A) car salesman
    (B) insurance agent
    (C) department manager
    (D) healthcare professional

SELECTION 5

30. What is the main claim of this report?
    (A) Hong Kong's population has decreased dramatically.
    (B) Hong Kong's population has increased dramatically.
    (C) Hong Kong has become an aged society.
    (D) Hong Kong has comprehensive support systems for seniors.

31. According to this report, which of the following statements about Hong Kong is true?
    (A) General population has increased 12% in ten years.
    (B) Seniors count for about 12% of general population.
    (C) The general population has surpassed 8,500,000.
    (D) The population of senior citizens has reached 85,000.

32. According to the report, where did the statistics come from?
    (A) They were provided by the Hong Kong government.
    (B) They were provided by a Hong Kong news agency.
    (C) They were provided by a United Nations publication.
    (D) They were provided by an independent research group.

[This marks the end of the audio track **Economics - Listening**.]

PART B: READING [60 minutes, 25% of final score]

Note: In this part of the exam, you may move back and forth among all the questions.

Directions: You will read several selections in Chinese. Each selection is accompanied by a number of questions in English. For each question, choose the response that is best according to the selection.

Read this advertisement

(Simplified Characters)	(Traditional Characters)
二室二厅，全新装修，楼层景观俱佳，月租三千元。	二室二廳，全新裝修，樓層景觀俱佳，月租三千元。

1. The advertised property
   (A) is newly remodeled
   (B) is fully furnished
   (C) has two units
   (D) has two bathrooms

2. The property owner is looking for
   (A) a buyer
   (B) a roommate
   (C) a manager
   (D) a tenant

3. According to the advertisement, the property
   (A) is located on a desirable floor
   (B) has double-pane windows
   (C) is in an upscale neighborhood
   (D) offers the best value for the money

Read this advertisement

(Simplified Characters)	(Traditional Characters)
叮当书店，限时赠送 叮当书店，新年大酬宾。本周所有前来买书的顾客，每次购书满一百元，即可以得到免费图书一本，多买多送。 免费赠送仅限于价格二十元以下的图书。	**叮噹書店，限時贈送** 叮噹書店，新年大酬賓。本週所有前來買書的顧客，每次購書滿一百元，即可以得到免費圖書一本，多買多送。 免費贈送僅限於價格二十元以下的圖書。

4. What type of business is this advertisement for?
   (A) A department store
   (B) A grocery store
   (C) A bookstore
   (D) A flower shop

5. What kind of promotion does the advertisement offer?
   (A) A free book with every 100 *yuan* purchase
   (B) Up to twenty percent off for every 100 *yuan* purchase
   (C) A New Year's calendar with every 100 *yuan* purchase
   (D) A twenty *yuan* gift card with every 100 *yuan* purchase

6. When is the promotion period?
   (A) New Year's Day only
   (B) A week after New Year
   (C) This week only
   (D) Not specified in the advertisement

Read this article

(Simplified Characters)	(Traditional Characters)
上世纪的七八十年代，中国的经济建设刚刚重新起步，百废待兴。记得那时在报纸上读到一篇新闻报道，讲某国六个工人六天建成了一幢楼。这在当时的中国听起来就像天方夜谭。而我们的住房和校舍都是砖瓦结构，百分之百由人工砌成，大多数的建房工人恐怕连重型机械都没见过。 时光如梭，三十年后的今天，我再次来到上海，下榻的旅馆旁边正在建造一座足有一里长的大桥。住进旅馆的那天，我眼看着工人们搭起脚手架，把空荡荡的大桥骨架围了起来，短短的两、三个星期后，这座金碧辉煌的汉白玉大桥就完工了。这样的施工速度可真是今非昔比了。	上世紀的七八十年代，中國的經濟建設剛剛重新起步，百廢待興。記得那時在報紙上讀到一篇新聞報導，講某國六個工人六天建成了一幢樓。這在當時的中國聽起來就像天方夜譚。而我們的住房和校舍都是磚瓦結構，百分之百由人工砌成，大多數的建房工人恐怕連重型機械都沒見過。 時光如梭，三十年後的今天，我再次來到上海，下榻的旅館旁邊正在建造一座足有一里長的大橋。住進旅館的那天，我眼看著工人們搭起腳手架，把空蕩蕩的大橋骨架圍了起來，短短的兩、三個星期後，這座金碧輝煌的漢白玉大橋就完工了。這樣的施工速度可真是今非昔比了。

7. Where did the author learn that six workers constructed a building in six days?
   (A) From a TV news broadcast
   (B) From a newspaper
   (C) From a radio report
   (D) From a construction journal

8. According to the article, what was the most commonly used building material in China in the 1970s?
   (A) Wood
   (B) Brick
   (C) Concrete
   (D) Mud and clay

9. What project did the author witness in Shanghai?
   (A) The amazing renovation of an old bridge
   (B) The creation of contemporary sculptures along a historical bridge
   (C) The transformation of a stone bridge to a steel bridge
   (D) The construction of a new bridge from a bare frame to a lavish finish

10. According to the article, which of the following is true?
   (A) A bridge connecting two hotel buildings was under construction.
   (B) Most school dormitories were single story buildings in the 1970s.
   (C) Chinese workers completed a building in six days.
   (D) The author was in Shanghai thirty years ago.

Read this passage

(Simplified Characters)

网络的推广和物尽其用

近来常听朋友们提起淘宝网。看他们神采飞扬地讲述各桩买卖的经历，不禁让我感叹网络的巨大经济潜能。

一位朋友在家门前种了一棵参天棕榈，可是市容监管部门说这棵大树种的地方不符合城市规划要求，要砍掉。因为他不忍心看到心爱的大树遭此厄运，于是上淘宝网登了广告。没想到，当天就有个公司来把树挖走了，要知道这可是一棵很值钱的大树噢。

昨天，邻居家门前来了一对年轻人，开着一辆除了喇叭不响其他都响的老爷车。因为邻居是一对无儿无女的老夫妇，这立刻引起了我的好奇。谁知，他们还没敲门，隔壁的老先生已经笑嘻嘻地走出来，把一台旧照相机交到年轻人手里。看着我百思不解的样子，他告诉我，那老相机还能正常使用，只是旧了。既然没人用，不如让喜欢的人拥有它，当然，这又是一笔淘宝网上做的买卖。

若不是网络的推广，能物尽其用到这种程度，真是不可想象呢。

(Traditional Characters)

網絡的推廣和物盡其用

近來常聽朋友們提起淘寶網。看他們神彩飛揚地講述各樁買賣的經歷，不禁讓我感嘆網絡的巨大經濟潛能。

一位朋友在家門前種了一棵參天棕櫚，可是市容監管部門說這棵大樹種的地方不符合城市規劃要求，要砍掉。因為他不忍心看到心愛的大樹遭此厄運，於是上淘寶網登了廣告。沒想到，當天就有個公司來把樹挖走了，要知道這可是一棵很值錢的大樹噢。

昨天，鄰居家門前來了一對年輕人，開著一輛除了喇叭不響其他都響的老爺車。因為鄰居是一對無兒無女的老夫婦，這立刻引起了我的好奇。誰知，他們還沒敲門，隔壁的老先生已經笑嘻嘻地走出來，把一台舊照相機交到年輕人手裡。看著我百思不解的樣子，他告訴我，那老相機還能正常使用，只是舊了。既然沒人用，不如讓喜歡的人擁有它，當然，這又是一筆淘寶網上做的買賣。

若不是網絡的推廣，能物盡其用到這種程度，真是不可想像呢。

11. According to the article, what type of media does the market rely on?
    (A) Internet
    (B) Television
    (C) Newspaper
    (D) Radio

12. Why does the owner want the tree to be removed?
    (A) The tree is growing too tall.
    (B) The tree is blocking the view.
    (C) The location of the tree violates the city code.
    (D) The owner wants to sell the tree for profit.

13. According to the article, what drew the author's attention to the young couple?
    (A) They dug up the palm tree.
    (B) They drove an old clunker.
    (C) They played loud music on their car stereo.
    (D) They knocked on every door.

14. What is the relationship between the old gentleman and the author?
    (A) They are neighbors.
    (B) They are friends.
    (C) They are relatives.
    (D) They are colleagues.

15. What did the old gentleman give to the young couple?
    (A) An old battered car
    (B) An antique horn
    (C) An antique alarm clock
    (D) An old camera

Read this e-mail

(Simplified Characters)	(Traditional Characters)
发件人：孙先生 收件人：宁女士 主题：请查收附件	發件人：孫先生 收件人：寧女士 主題：請查收附件
宁女士，你好！ 随信附上设计图纸，请查收。图纸要用达芬奇绘图软件（2004以后的版本）才可以打开，如果你没有这个软件，我下次改成图片格式发给你。 以后有事情就给我发邮件好了，我每天都会上网查看邮件的。请放心，我们公司会认真地装修你的房子，就像对待自己的房子一样尽心尽力。 孙先生	寧女士，你好！ 隨信附上設計圖紙，請查收。圖紙要用達芬奇繪圖軟件（2004以後的版本）才可以打開，如果你沒有這個軟件，我下次改成圖片格式發給你。 以後有事情就給我發郵件好了，我每天都會上網查看郵件的。請放心，我們公司會認真地裝修你的房子，就像對待自己的房子一樣盡心盡力。 孫先生

16. Why does Mr. Sun send this e-mail to Ms. Ning?
    (A) To express his personal feelings toward her
    (B) To provide her with information on a remodeling project
    (C) To ask her opinions about a remodeling service
    (D) To give her instructions on how to use a software program

17. What is the relationship between the two?
    (A) He is her contractor.
    (B) He is her supervisor.
    (C) She is his older relative.
    (D) He is her husband.

18. What is the attachment that he sends with his e-mail?
    (A) An appraisal report
    (B) A copy of his resume
    (C) A design chart
    (D) A new version of the software

19. What does Mr. Sun promise to Ms. Ning?
    (A) To check his e-mail every day and keep in touch
    (B) To help her figure out how to use the software
    (C) To provide the best housekeeping services for her
    (D) To do his best with her project

Read this chart

(Simplified Characters)

美国主要经济指标一览

经济指标名称	近期数据	前期数据
国内生产总值（亿元）	1200	1100
国际贸易（亿元）	-40	-58
失业率（%）	7.2	6.7
消费物价升降指数（%）	-1.9	-2.2
个人收入增长率（%）	-0.2	0.3
消费信心指数	38.0	44.7
新屋开工（千）	407	407

(Traditional Characters)

美國主要經濟指標一覽

經濟指標名稱	近期數據	前期數據
國內生產總值（億元）	1200	1100
國際貿易（億元）	-40	-58
失業率（%）	7.2	6.7
消費物價升降指數（%）	-1.9	-2.2
個人收入增長率（%）	-0.2	0.3
消費信心指數	38.0	44.7
新屋開工（千）	407	407

20. According to the chart, what is the latest unemployment rate?
    (A) 6.7 percent
    (B) 7.2 percent
    (C) 0.2 percent decreased
    (D) 0.3 percent increased

21. What does the Consumer Confidence Index indicate?
    (A) Consumer confidence is unchanged.
    (B) Consumer confidence has gone up.
    (C) Consumer confidence has dropped.
    (D) The Consumer Confidence Index is not in this chart.

22. Based on this chart, what best describes the state of international trade?
    (A) There is a trade deficit, but it is getting smaller.
    (B) International trading is producing a surplus.
    (C) The trade deficit is increasing.
    (D) There is no significant change from the previous report.

23. Which of the follow indexes is not listed in the chart?
    (A) Gross Domestic Product
    (B) New Construction
    (C) Prime Interest Rate
    (D) Consumer Price Index

Read this story

(Simplified Characters)	(Traditional Characters)
钟先生的经济头脑	**鍾先生的經濟頭腦**
钟先生的聪明在朋友中是尽人皆知的。其中之一是他敏锐的经济头脑。	鍾先生的聰明在朋友中是盡人皆知的。其中之一是他敏銳的經濟頭腦。
钟先生对经商的兴趣在读小学时就已初露头角，他会推销给同学们一些不知从哪儿弄来的流行小玩意儿。	鍾先生對經商的興趣在讀小學時就已初露頭角，他會推銷給同學們一些不知從哪兒弄來的流行小玩意兒。
上高中期间，钟先生成立了自己的糖果销售公司，居然用两年里挣来的钱为自己添置了手提式电脑和手机。	上高中期間，鍾先生成立了自己的糖果銷售公司，居然用兩年裡掙來的錢為自己添置了手提式電腦和手機。
钟先生不仅会赚钱，书也是读得一流，现在是一所名牌大学的教授。	鍾先生不僅會賺錢，書也是讀得一流，現在是一所名牌大學的教授。
虽然钟先生现在的专业与经济不沾边，但他从来没有停止使用他的经济头脑。朋友中谁要买车了、买房了、要订旅馆了、订机票了，钟先生都会利用业余时间，详细地告诉他们当前最好的价格是什么，如何在最佳时机，用最短时间，拿到最好价钱。	雖然鍾先生現在的專業與經濟不沾邊，但他從來沒有停止使用他的經濟頭腦。朋友中誰要買車了、買房了、要訂旅館了、訂機票了，鍾先生都會利用業餘時間，詳細地告訴他們當前最好的價格是什麼，如何在最佳時機，用最短時間，拿到最好價錢。
时间长了，名声在外，来咨询的人越来越多。钟先生还是不厌其烦地回答每个人的问题。朋友们都纳闷，他为什么不开一家咨询公司呢？钟先生的经济头脑哪里去了？	時間長了，名聲在外，來諮詢的人越來越多。鍾先生還是不厭其煩地回答每個人的問題。朋友們都納悶，他為什麼不開一家諮詢公司呢？ 鍾先生的經濟頭腦哪裡去了？

24. According to the story, when was Mr. Zhong's first business experience?
    (A) When he was a salesman for a candy company
    (B) When he was in elementary school
    (C) When he was a teenager
    (D) When he was an employee of a consulting firm

25. What is Mr. Zhong's occupation?
    (A) Salesman
    (B) Consultant
    (C) Professor
    (D) Businessman

26. During his high school years, what did he earn from selling candy?
    (A) A laptop and a cell phone
    (B) A top sales award
    (C) A used car
    (D) College tuition

27. According to the article, which of the following is true about Mr. Zhong?
    (A) He is a chief consultant at a consulting company.
    (B) He is a professional advisor for a top university.
    (C) He is respected as a community leader.
    (D) He is known for his vast knowledge.

Read this poster

(Simplified Characters)	(Traditional Characters)
"邻里座谈"活动通知 海湾城的居民们： "邻里座谈"活动将于十月十九日上午九点在本社区服务中心多功能厅举行。 主要话题：目前的世界金融危机对本地经济和日常生活的影响；社区商业设施规划；周边环境及维护；物业管理费的使用情况通报。 欢迎社区广大居民群众踊跃参加。 海湾城社区中心 二OO九年十月五日	**"鄰里座談"活動通知** 海灣城的居民們： "鄰里座談"活動將於十月十九日上午九點在本社區服務中心多功能廳舉行。 主要話題：目前的世界金融危機對本地經濟和日常生活的影響；社區商業設施規劃；周邊環境及維護；物業管理費的使用情況通報。 歡迎社區廣大居民群眾踴躍參加。 海灣城社區中心 二OO九年十月五日

28. What event does the poster announce?
    (A) A community forum
    (B) A financial planning seminar
    (C) A public hearing
    (D) A board meeting

29. Which of the following topics is mentioned in the poster?
    (A) Community service
    (B) Investment strategy
    (C) World financial crisis
    (D) Neighborhood safety

30. Where will the event be held?
    (A) Local library
    (B) Service center
    (C) Business center
    (D) Community center

Read this article

(Simplified Characters)	(Traditional Characters)
吓人的结婚预算	**嚇人的結婚預算**
邓先生要结婚了。他和未婚妻的家境和收入都不错，那就买房、结婚同时办，来个双喜临门吧。	鄧先生要結婚了。他和未婚妻的家境和收入都不錯，那就買房、結婚同時辦，來個雙喜臨門吧。
考虑到将来要生孩子，买房子起码要两室两厅，那就至少要两百万元，二手房也得要一百六十万元。小两口所有的积蓄都拿去作首期付款了。	考慮到將來要生孩子，買房子起碼要兩室兩廳，那就至少要兩百萬元，二手房也得要一百六十萬元。小兩口所有的積蓄都拿去作首期付款了。
装修至少 10 万元，即使不请所有的亲朋好友，只请至亲密友，婚礼也得花 8 万元，这些都只好请父母赞助了。那可是他们大半辈子的积蓄啊！	裝修至少 10 萬元，即使不請所有的親朋好友，只請至親密友，婚禮也得花 8 萬元，這些都只好請父母贊助了。那可是他們大半輩子的積蓄啊！
如今的婚还真是不容易结啊！	如今的婚還真是不容易結啊！

31. What is the main issue addressed in the article?
    (A) The high cost of buying an apartment
    (B) The shocking cost of getting married
    (C) The extravagant wedding ceremony
    (D) The sky-rocketing cost of living

32. Which of the following expenses is mentioned in the budget?
    (A) Cost of raising a family
    (B) Honeymoon expenses
    (C) Cost of remodeling
    (D) Mortgage payments

33. According to the article, what is the financial condition of Mr. Deng and his fiancée?
    (A) They come from rich families but do not have enough money to support themselves.
    (B) They get by on their own without any help from their families.
    (C) They have a good income but no savings.
    (D) They have a good income and the financial support of both families.

Read the following table

(Simplified Characters)

厨房装修报价单

项目	单价	数量	合计
橱柜	6000 元/米	10	60000 元
台面	3000 元/米	5	15000 元
地砖	500 元/平米	50	25000 元
墙砖	700 元/平米	10	7000 元
抽油烟机	4000 元/台	1	4000 元
炉灶	3500 元/台	1	3500 元
微波炉	1000 元/台	1	1000 元
冰箱	13900 元/台	1	13900 元
人工	1100 元/天	5	5500 元
总计			134900 元

以上报价按已定材料和品牌型号为基准。任何选材变动完工后另行结算，多退少补。

(Traditional Characters)

廚房裝修報價單

項目	單價	數量	合計
櫃櫥	6000 圓/米	10	60000 圓
檯面	3000 圓/米	5	15000 圓
地磚	500 圓/平米	50	25000 圓
牆磚	700 圓/平米	10	7000 圓
抽油煙機	4000 圓/臺	1	4000 圓
爐灶	3500 圓/臺	1	3500 圓
微波爐	1000 圓/臺	1	1000 圓
冰箱	13900 圓/臺	1	13900 圓
人工	1100 圓/天	5	5500 圓
總計			134900 圓

以上報價按已定材料和品牌型號為基準。任何選材變動完工後另行結算，多退少補。

34. What kind of list is this?
    (A) A budget proposal
    (B) A remodeling estimate
    (C) An inventory report
    (D) An expense summary

35. According to the list, which item costs the most per unit?
    (A) Cabinets
    (B) Refrigerator
    (C) Floor tiles
    (D) Labor

36. How many working days will it take to complete the project?
    (A) Five
    (B) Four
    (C) Three
    (D) Information is not given

SECTION II: FREE RESPONSE

PART A: WRITING

[30 minutes, 25% of final score]

Note: In this part of the exam, the student may NOT move back and forth among questions.

Directions: You will be asked to perform two writing tasks in Chinese. In each case, you will be asked to write for a specific purpose and to a specific person. You should write in as complete and as culturally appropriate a manner as possible, taking into account the purpose and the person described.

I. Story Narration [15 minutes, 15% of final score]

The four pictures present a story. Imagine you are writing the story to a friend. Narrate a complete story as suggested by the pictures. Give your story a beginning, middle, and an end.

II. E-MAIL RESPONSE [15 minutes, 10% of total score]

Read this e-mail from a friend and then type your response.

(Simplified Characters)

发件人：安琪
邮件主题：球场铁丝围墙的安全问题

我们学校球场周围的铁丝围墙修建于多年以前，不符合现在的安全标准。家长们都很担心运动员的安全，多次要求校方维修。可是，由于教育经费缩减，学校在这件事上确实是心有余而力不足。大家想通过集资来解决这个问题，你能告诉我一些集资的好办法吗？如果你还有其他的主意，也请一并告知。谢谢你！

(Traditional Characters)

發件人：安琪
郵件主題：球場鐵絲圍牆的安全問題

我們學校球場周圍的鐵絲圍牆修建於多年以前，不符合目前的安全標準。家長們都很擔心運動員的安全，多次要求校方維修。可是，由於教育經費縮減，學校在這件事上確實是心有餘而力不足。大家想通過集資來解決這個問題，你能告訴我一些集資的好辦法嗎？如果你還有其他的主意，也請一並告知。謝謝你！

PART B: SPEAKING [15 minutes, 25% of final score]

 [Listen to the audio track **Economics - Speaking**.]

Note: In this part of the exam, you may NOT move back and forth among questions.

I. CONVERSATION [4 minutes, 10% of final score]

Directions: You will participate in a simulated conversation. Each time it is your turn to speak, you will have 20 seconds to record. You should respond as fully and as appropriately as possible.

You have a conversation with Mary, a reporter for your school's student-run newspaper.

Mary: [Audio]
[TONE]
[Student records the response] (20 seconds)

Mary: [Audio]
[TONE]
[Student records the response] (20 seconds)

Mary: [Audio]
[TONE]
[Student records the response] (20 seconds)

Mary: [Audio]
[TONE]
[Student records the response] (20 seconds)

Mary: [Audio]
[TONE]
[Student records the response] (20 seconds)

Mary: [Audio]
[TONE]
[Student records the response] (20 seconds)

II. CULTURAL PRESENTATION [7 minutes, 15% of final score]

Directions: You will be asked to speak in Chinese on a specific topic. Imagine you are making an oral presentation to your Chinese class. First, you will read and hear the topic for your presentation. You will have 4 minutes to prepare your presentation. Then you will have 2 minutes to record your presentation. Your presentation should be as complete as possible.

Auspicious Chinese symbols (e.g., peony flower, dragon, *pixiu*, etc.) are often found in Chinese business establishments such as restaurants, markets, and shops. Choose and describe one or two of such symbols and state where they would be seen. In your presentation, explain the cultural significance of those symbols.

[This marks the end of the audio track **Economics - Speaking**.]

UNIT 4 EDUCATION

SECTION I: MULTIPLE CHOICE

PART A: LISTENING [20 minutes, 25% of final score]

[Listen to the audio track **Education - Listening**.]

Note: In this part of the exam, you may NOT move back and forth among questions.

I. REJOINDERS [10 minutes, 10% of final score]

Directions: You will hear several short conversations or parts of conversations followed by 4 choices, designated (A), (B), (C), and (D). Choose the one that continues or completes the conversation in a logical and culturally appropriate manner. You will have 5 seconds to answer each question.

QUESTION NUMBER	STUDENT CHOICE			
1	(A)	(B)	(C)	(D)
2	(A)	(B)	(C)	(D)
3	(A)	(B)	(C)	(D)
4	(A)	(B)	(C)	(D)
5	(A)	(B)	(C)	(D)
6	(A)	(B)	(C)	(D)
7	(A)	(B)	(C)	(D)
8	(A)	(B)	(C)	(D)
9	(A)	(B)	(C)	(D)
10	(A)	(B)	(C)	(D)
11	(A)	(B)	(C)	(D)
12	(A)	(B)	(C)	(D)
13	(A)	(B)	(C)	(D)
14	(A)	(B)	(C)	(D)
15	(A)	(B)	(C)	(D)

II. Listening Selections [10 minutes, 15% of final score]

Directions: You will listen to several selections in Chinese. For each selection, you will be told whether it will be played once or twice. You may take notes as you listen. Your notes will not be graded. After listening to each selection, you will see questions in English. For each question, choose the response that is best according to the selection. You will have 12 seconds to answer each question.

SELECTION 1

16. What are these two students discussing?

    (A) Student registration

    (B) Course selection

    (C) An online project

    (D) A tennis class registration

17. Has the male student completed what he had originally planned to do?

    (A) No. He does not want to be caught in traffic for two hours.

    (B) No. His online project partner did not complete her work.

    (C) No. He does not want to stand in line for two hours.

    (D) No. He didn't get the class that he wanted.

18. According to the conversation, what will happen if students do not act soon?

    (A) They may not be able to get into the classes that they want.

    (B) They may not be able to get the most popular professors.

    (C) They have to spend more time waiting in line next week.

    (D) They will not have Internet access to class websites.

19. What does the woman suggest to the man?

    (A) To be put on the waiting list

    (B) To sign up for another class

    (C) To call his online project partner

    (D) To sign up for classes on the Internet

SELECTION 2

20. Who is making this announcement?
    (A) A PhD candidate
    (B) An undergraduate student
    (C) A graduate student
    (D) A college professor

21. What is the announcer's academic discipline?
    (A) Sociology
    (B) Music
    (C) Engineering
    (D) Biology

22. When does the tour begin?
    (A) In the morning
    (B) At noon
    (C) In the afternoon
    (D) In the evening

23. Which part of campus is included in the tour?
    (A) Gymnasium
    (B) Student union
    (C) Admission office
    (D) Biology laboratory

SELECTION 3

24. What type of competition are the instructions for?
    (A) A sports competition
    (B) A science competition
    (C) A math competition
    (D) A music competition

25. What is the rule for the individual contest?
    (A) There is a 30-minute time limit; discussion is allowed.
    (B) There is a 30-minute time limit; no discussion is allowed.
    (C) There is a 40-minute time limit; discussion is allowed.
    (D) There is a 40-minute time limit; no discussion is allowed.

26. What is the rule for the group contest?
    (A) There are three problems; discussion within the group is allowed.
    (B) There are three problems; discussion is not allowed.
    (C) There are six problems; discussion within the group is allowed.
    (D) There are six problems; discussion is not allowed.

SELECTION 4

27. This commercial is about
    (A) a SAT preparation book
    (B) a SAT tutoring class
    (C) a college admissions service
    (D) an academic counseling service

28. The woman plans to visit Xin Shi Dai tomorrow because
    (A) she needs to get college admissions information for her son
    (B) she is impressed by the academic achievement of the man's daughter
    (C) she wants to take her son to the academic consultation seminar
    (D) she wants to evaluate the tutoring class with her son

29. According to the man, which of the following statements is true?
    (A) His son's SAT score improved by 300 points.
    (B) His son attends a top-ranked university.
    (C) His daughter's SAT score improved by 300 points.
    (D) His daughter is a top-ranked student in her school.

SELECTION 5

30. What did Wang Yuan do before calling Lily?
    (A) Studying for an exam at the library
    (B) Finishing his lab report at school
    (C) Trying to solve a homework problem
    (D) Looking for his class assignment

31. Wang Yuan was having trouble with
    (A) Math assignment
    (B) English essay
    (C) Biology homework
    (D) Chemistry lab report

32. What did Wang Yuan ask Lily to do?
    (A) Meet him at the library
    (B) Call the teacher for help
    (C) Turn in the assignment for him
    (D) Help him with a homework problem

[This marks the end of the audio track **Education - Listening**.]

PART B: READING [60 minutes, 25% of final score]

Note: In this part of the exam, you may move back and forth among all the questions.

Directions: You will read several selections in Chinese. Each selection is accompanied by a number of questions in English. For each question, choose the response that is best according to the selection.

Read this poster

(Simplified Characters)	(Traditional Characters)
我校图书馆已完成内部装修，定于11月1日正式恢复对外开放。 装修调整后的图书分类如下：一楼为文学、艺术类；二楼为工程、医学类；三楼经济、英语、饮食类。	我校圖書館已完成內部裝修，定於11月1日正式恢復對外開放。 裝修調整後的圖書分類如下：一樓為文學、藝術類；二樓為工程、醫學類；三樓經濟、英語、飲食類。

1. According to the poster, what will happen on November 1?
   (A) The library hours will be shortened.
   (B) The library moved to a new location.
   (C) The library will be closed for remodeling.
   (D) The library will reopen.

2. Which category of books is mentioned in the poster?
   (A) Food
   (B) Law
   (C) Travel
   (D) Biography

3. The library
   (A) is newly remodeled
   (B) moved to a new building
   (C) opened a new location
   (D) has had its area reduced

Read this advertisement

(Simplified Characters)	(Traditional Characters)
最佳英文写作软件 帮助您检查语法和拼写，含字典功能，快速提高您的英文写作水平，欢迎下载试用！	**最佳英文寫作軟件** 幫助您檢查語法和拼寫，含字典功能，快速提高您的英文寫作水平，歡迎下載試用！

4. What product or service is this advertisement for?
   (A) Electronic dictionary
   (B) English writing software
   (C) English tutoring service
   (D) Language translation software

5. Who is the target audience of this advertisement?
   (A) People who are looking for online spell-check software
   (B) People who want to learn how to speak English fluently
   (C) People who want to improve their English writing
   (D) People who are looking for a dictionary

6. Which of the following statements is included in the advertisement?
   (A) This service is offered online only.
   (B) The grammar check function has to be downloaded separately.
   (C) A dictionary function is included in the package.
   (D) English is the provider's native language.

Read this schedule:

(Simplified Characters)

夏令营第一周课程表

时间	星 期 一	星 期 二	星 期 三	星 期 四	星 期 五
8:00–9:30	自我介绍 水平测试	拼音	中文	中文	中文
9:30–10:00	自由活动				
10:00–11:30	武术	国画	书法	武术	书法
11:30–1:00	午饭和午休				
1:00–2:00	民族乐器	会话	国画	民族乐器	会话
2:00–2:30	自由活动				
2:30–3:30	中国象棋	乒乓球	学做中国菜	民族舞	手工才艺

(Traditional Characters)

夏令營第一周課程表

時間	星 期 一	星 期 二	星 期 三	星 期 四	星 期 五
8:00–9:30	自我介紹 水平測試	拼音	中文	中文	中文
9:30–10:00	自由活動				
10:00–11:30	武術	國畫	書法	武術	書法
11:30–1:00	午飯和午休				
1:00–2:00	民族樂器	會話	國畫	民族樂器	會話
2:00–2:30	自由活動				
2:30–3:30	中國象棋	乒乓球	學做中國菜	民族舞	手工才藝

7. What kind of schedule is this?
   (A) It is a class schedule for a Chinese program in the United States.
   (B) It is a class schedule for a high school in China.
   (C) It is a schedule for the first week at a summer camp.
   (D) It is a class schedule for the first semester at a Chinese school.

8. On which day(s) and at what time(s) will martial arts be taught?
   (A) Monday and Thursday at 10:00 a.m.
   (B) Wednesday and Friday at 10:00 a.m.
   (C) Monday at 2:30 p.m.
   (D) Friday at 1:00 p.m.

9. Which of the following statements is most likely to be true?
   (A) The class schedule will be slightly different for the rest of the program.
   (B) The students will learn Chinese painting on the first day of the program.
   (C) There will be a class presentation in the first week of the program.
   (D) The students will not learn calligraphy since this is a program for beginners.

Read this report

(Simplified Characters)	(Traditional Characters)
中国人口占世界之首。仅十八岁以下的人口就有 3.67 亿。要保持长期稳定的经济增长，就需要不断提高全国人口的整体素质，特别是青少年的教育水平，这对于中国这样的人口大国尤其困难。	中國人口占世界之首。僅十八歲以下的人口就有 3.67 億。要保持長期穩定的經濟增長，就需要不斷提高全國人口的整體素質，特別是青少年的教育水平，這對於中國這樣的人口大國尤其困難。
当前中国教育改革的课题之一就是如何让年轻一代在继承中国优秀文化传统的同时，面向世界，吸收现代化的科学技术和知识理念。	當前中國教育改革的課題之一就是如何讓年輕一代在繼承中國優秀文化傳統的同時，面向世界，吸收現代化的科學技術和知識理念。
比较和分析世界上各个国家的教育传统、理念、方式和方法，可以为中国的教育改革开阔思路。比如说，美国式教育比较注重培养学生创新意识和思辨能力，而中国式教育则更强调扎实的理论知识和熟练的基础技能。	比較和分析世界上各個國家的教育傳統、理念、方式和方法，可以為中國的教育改革開闊思路。比如說，美國式教育比較注重培養學生創新意識和思辨能力，而中國式教育則更強調紮實的理論知識和熟練的基礎技能。
如果中国的教育体系既能够充分发扬光大中国传统教学的长处，同时加强培养学生的创新精神和实践能力，就有希望把中国所承受的巨大的人口压力转化为丰富的人力资源。	如果中國的教育體系既能夠充分發揚光大中國傳統教學的長處，同時加強培養學生的創新精神和實踐能力，就有希望把中國所承受的巨大的人口壓力轉化為豐富的人力資源。

10. According to the passage, what is one of the strong points of American education?
    (A) It encourages innovative ideas.
    (B) It emphasizes learning a wide range of knowledge.
    (C) It places importance on mastering the basic skills.
    (D) It values proficiency in all core subjects.

11. Which piece of information was given in the passage?
    (A) China is making an effort to improve school facilities.
    (B) China needs to advance the level of education for its population.
    (C) China has the largest population of college students in the world.
    (D) China has been undergoing economic transformation in recent years.

12. According to the passage, what is China's education reform attempting to accomplish?
    (A) Restoration of the traditional Chinese education system
    (B) Transforming China's large population into rich human resources
    (C) Establishing a brand-new system modeled after American education
    (D) Launching China's economy into the world market

Read this article

(Simplified Characters)	(Traditional Characters)
中国有两亿多学生，随着竞争的日益激烈，为了孩子能够脱颖而出或者不落人后，家长们往往会毫不犹豫地投资孩子的教育。 就是在这种环境下，课外辅导服务的需求快速增加，网校应运而生。 网校的优势在于它能提供便利的服务，孩子们不但可以不出家门就上补习课，而且还可以任意选择上课的时间，因此倍受家长和学生们的欢迎，特别是在缺乏课外辅导服务的地区，网校的建立就更是及时雨了。	中國有兩億多學生，隨著競爭的日益激烈，為了孩子能夠脫穎而出或者不落人後，家長們往往會毫不猶豫地投資孩子的教育。 就是在這種環境下，課外輔導服務的需求快速增加，網校應運而生。 網校的優勢在於它能提供便利的服務，孩子們不但可以不出家門就上補習課，而且還可以任意選擇上課的時間，因此倍受家長和學生們的歡迎，特別是在缺乏課外輔導服務的地區，網校的建立就更是及時雨了。

13. What is the main idea of this article?
    (A) Online tutoring school provides a much needed service to the market.
    (B) Parents are willing to invest in high-quality education.
    (C) Online schools have become more popular than traditional schools.
    (D) Competition among more than 200 million students has intensified.

14. What is one of the benefits of the service discussed in the article?
    (A) It awards high school diploma to its students.
    (B) It offers educational advice and support to parents.
    (C) It provides convenient tutoring to students.
    (D) It meets the increasing demand for population growth.

15. According to the article, which of the following statements is true?
    (A) Online school is especially helpful to students in bad weather conditions.
    (B) In some areas, after-school tutoring services are not available.
    (C) Due to limited Internet access, online school is not practical for most families.
    (D) Although it is favored by students, online school is not welcomed by parents.

Read this public notice

(Simplified Characters)	(Traditional Characters)
今天上午的历史课因老师生病停上，请互相转告！ 五月二十一日	今天上午的歷史課因老師生病停上，請互相轉告！ 五月二十一日

16. Where would you most likely see this notice?
    (A) At a bus stop
    (B) At a school cafeteria
    (C) On a classroom door
    (D) In a computer lab

17. What is the purpose of this notice?
    (A) To announce a location change for a gathering
    (B) To cancel a scheduled event
    (C) To postpone a scheduled meeting
    (D) To inform students about their teacher's health

18. What does the notice suggest viewers do?
    (A) To check back for the latest updates
    (B) To go to the office for more information
    (C) To visit the business at a new location
    (D) To pass on the message to others

Read this passage

(Simplified Characters)	(Traditional Characters)
钟先生和他的儿子	**鍾先生和他的兒子**
钟先生长得瘦瘦小小，斯斯文文，带着一副眼镜，见到球就躲得远远的。如果不说，估计谁也猜不到他对体育那份近于痴迷的热爱。	鍾先生長得瘦瘦小小，斯斯文文，帶著一副眼鏡，見到球就躲得遠遠的。如果不說，估計誰也猜不到他對體育那份近於痴迷的熱愛。
从儿子冬冬出生的那一刻起，钟先生对体育的热情似乎终于找到了释放渠道。钟先生为冬冬请的保姆是会气功的，冬冬还不会走路，那摩拳擦掌的架势就和保姆有几分神似。刚刚学步的冬冬去公园，爬沙堆、荡秋千、玩滑梯，钟先生全都一一奉陪。后来，冬冬开始打球了，游泳了，溜冰了，滑雪了，钟先生也从不错过，俨然一幅资深教练模样，手里拿着与冬冬的运动项目相关的理论书籍、还有一块不知用了多少年的旧秒表，可他就是动脑、动口、不动手。	從兒子冬冬出生的那一刻起，鍾先生對體育的熱情似乎終於找到了釋放渠道。鍾先生為冬冬請的保姆是會氣功的，冬冬還不會走路，那摩拳擦掌的架勢就和保姆有幾分神似。剛剛學步的冬冬去公園，爬沙堆、盪鞦韆、玩滑梯，鍾先生全都一一奉陪。後來，冬冬開始打球了，游泳了，溜冰了，滑雪了，鍾先生也從不錯過，儼然一幅資深教練模樣，手裡拿著與冬冬的運動項目相關的理論書籍、還有一塊不知用了多少年的舊秒錶，可他就是動腦、動口、不動手。
虽然俗话说，“龙生龙，凤生凤，老鼠的儿子会打洞”，但是如今的冬冬成了体育健将，跟毫无体育细胞的钟先生截然不同，看来还是后天的努力和培养更重要。	雖然俗話說，“龍生龍，鳳生鳳，老鼠的兒子會打洞”，但是如今的冬冬成了體育健將，跟毫無體育細胞的鍾先生截然不同，看來還是後天的努力和培養更重要。

19. According to the passage, Mr. Zhong's son has tried
    (A) skiing
    (B) surfing
    (C) snorkeling
    (D) bowling

20. According to the passage, who practices *qigong*?
    (A) Mr. Zhong
    (B) Mr. Zhong's son
    (C) Mr. Zhong's son's nanny
    (D) Mr. Zhong's son's coach

21. Which of the following statements is true?
    (A) Mr. Zhong is an experienced sports coach.
    (B) Mr. Zhong enjoys playing many sports.
    (C) Mr. Zhong's son has his father's talent in sports.
    (D) Mr. Zhong's son is a very good athlete.

22. What does Mr. Zhong do to support his son's sports activities?
    (A) Buys all the relevant instructional books for his son to read
    (B) Keeps a record of every sport his son has ever played
    (C) Accompanies his son to all his sports activities
    (D) Designs practice routines for his son

23. What does Mr. Zhong bring to his son's sports practice?
    (A) A training log and a cap
    (B) A training log and a stopwatch
    (C) A sports theory book and a cap
    (D) A sports theory book and a stopwatch

Read this letter

(Simplified Characters)

亲爱的公公婆婆:

您们好! 我非常想念您们。

我已经是大学二年级的学生了，正在申请一份暑期工作，这份工作是"在中国学中文"暑期班中做助教。

"在中国学中文"是美国华美文化基金会组织的暑期学中文强化班，已经成功地举办了多年。参加暑期班的美国学生利用暑假在北京和上海进行中文学习，效果相当不错。

我的一位美国同学，家里没有一个人懂中文。他去年参加了这个活动，初到北京时只能结结巴巴地讲一两句中文。经过两个月的学习，他的中文进步很大，现在他已经能与中国人进行日常对话交流了。

我对这份工作特别有兴趣，除了能练习中文、积累工作经验、挣点生活费以外，还能到上海去看望您们，实在是个一举多得的好机会。因为我中文讲得很流利，所以我对能争取到这份工作还是很有把握的。一旦有消息，我会马上写信告诉您们。

祝身体健康!

外孙女 小羽 敬上
二OO九年一月十五日

(Traditional Characters)

親愛的公公和婆婆:

您們好！我非常想念您們。

我已經是大學二年級的學生了，正在申請一份暑期工作，這份工作是"在中國學中文"暑期班中做助教。

"在中國學中文"是美國華美文化基金會組織的暑期學中文強化班，已經成功地舉辦了多年。參加暑期班的美國學生利用暑假在北京和上海進行中文學習，效果相當不錯。

我的一位美國同學，家裡沒有一個人懂中文。他去年參加了這個活動，初到北京時只能結結巴巴地講一兩句中文。經過兩個月的學習，他的中文進步很大，現在他已經能與中國人進行日常對話交流了。

我對這份工作特別有興趣，除了能練習中文、積累工作經驗、掙點生活費以外，還能到上海去看望您們，實在是個一舉多得的好機會。因為我中文講得很流利，所以我對能爭取到這份工作還是很有把握的。一旦有消息，我會馬上寫信告訴您們。

祝身體健康!

外孫女 小羽 敬上
二OO九年一月十五日

24. To whom does the author write this letter?
    (A) The author's maternal grandparents
    (B) The author's paternal grandparents
    (C) The author's parents
    (D) The author's friends

25. What does the author plan to do in the summer?
    (A) Learn Chinese in a language summer camp
    (B) Visit her parents in China
    (C) Work as a teaching assistant
    (D) Work for an organization in the United States

26. The "Study Chinese in China" program is organized by
    (A) the Chinese American Cultural Foundation
    (B) the Chinese government
    (C) a well-known university
    (D) a culture exchange group

27. Based on the information given in the letter, which of the following statements is true?
    (A) Last year, the author was not able to speak Chinese very well.
    (B) One of the author's classmates went to China last summer.
    (C) The author worked at the summer camp as an assistant last year.
    (D) The author plans to enroll in the "Study Chinese in China" program.

28. The author is interested in this program because
    (A) her friend is enrolled in the program
    (B) she can take the opportunity to tour China
    (C) it is part of her school requirement
    (D) she will be able to gain work experience

Read this form

(Simplified Characters)

中国中学生赴美夏令营报名表

姓名：		性别：	年龄：
出生日期：		出生地：	
家庭住址：		邮编：	
家庭电话：		手机号码：	
就读学校：			年级：
父母姓名：			
报名条件： （1）12岁以上，17岁以下（包括17岁在内），品学兼优的学生。 （2）报名时请提供十万存款证明。 （3）团体活动期间必须守时和遵守纪律。未经批准，不得私自离团。 （4）团员因病送医治疗，费用自理。			
学生签字：	日期：	家长签字：	日期：
学生所在学校意见/盖章	日期：	主办单位意见/盖章	日期：

(Traditional Characters)

中國中學生赴美夏令營報名表

姓名：		性別：	年齡：
出生日期：		出生地：	
家庭住址：		郵編：	
家庭電話：		手機號碼：	
就讀學校：			年級：
父母姓名：			
報名條件： （1）12歲以上，17歲以下（包括17歲在內），品學兼優的學生。 （2）報名時請提供十萬存款証明。 （3）團體活動期間必須守時和遵守紀律。未經批准，不得私自離團。 （4）團員因病送醫治療，費用自理。			
學生簽字：	日期：	家長簽字：	日期：
學生所在學校意見/蓋章	日期：	主辦單位意見/蓋章	日期：

29. What is this application form for?
    (A) Getting a student visa to visit China
    (B) Getting a student visa to visit the United States
    (C) Enrolling in a summer camp in China
    (D) Enrolling in a summer camp in the United States

30. The applicant must fill in
    (A) passport number
    (B) place of birth
    (C) emergency contact
    (D) e-mail address

31. Which of the following is one of the required qualifications?
    (A) Having an excellent academic record
    (B) Having 10,000 *yuan* bank deposit
    (C) Having direct relatives in the United States
    (D) Having a pre-travel physical examination

Read this report

(Simplified Characters)	(Traditional Characters)
上学读书，对在中国城市里的孩子们来说，似乎是理所当然的，可是，对于不少偏远贫困地区的孩子们来说，老师、书本、教室都是奢侈品。 生活在这些偏远贫困地区的人们，一旦有机会到条件好的地方去就不再愿意返回家乡工作，而生活在条件优越地方的人，就更不愿意往这种苦地方跑了。这样就形成了这些地区缺乏师资的状况。 为了解决这个问题，国家政府制定了一系列政策，鼓励大学毕业生到偏远地区从事教育工作。现在，不少有社会责任感的大学毕业生放弃了大城市舒适的环境，自愿奔赴偏远贫困地区短期当老师。支援偏远贫困地区教育之举，被称为“支教”。 支教的年轻人不仅给偏远贫困地区的孩子们带去了爱心，而且把他们带进了五彩缤纷的知识世界。而支教本身也给了这些年轻人一个磨练的机会。这些地区的物质贫乏，设备简陋，志愿者们面临重重困难，但是最大的挑战是孤独和寂寞。他们远离亲人，既不能上网，又没有电视，有些地方甚至连报纸都没有，对于这些在电子时代长大的年轻人来说，这简直就是与世隔绝了。但从孩子们盈盈的笑脸上，他们得到了丰厚的回报。	上學讀書，對在中國城市裡的孩子們來說，似乎是理所當然的，可是，對於不少偏遠貧困地區的孩子們來說，老師、書本、教室都是奢侈品。 生活在這些偏遠貧困地區的人們，一旦有機會到條件好的地方去就不再願意返回家鄉工作，而生活在條件優越地方的人，就更不願意往這種苦地方跑了。這樣就形成了這些地區缺乏師資的狀況。 為了解決這個問題，國家政府制定了一系列政策，鼓勵大學畢業生到偏遠地區從事教育工作。現在，不少有社會責任感的大學畢業生放棄了大城市舒適的環境，自願奔赴偏遠貧困地區短期當老師。支援偏遠貧困地區教育之舉，被稱為“支教”。 支教的年輕人不僅給偏遠貧困地區的孩子們帶去了愛心，而且把他們帶進了五彩繽紛的知識世界。而支教本身也給了這些年輕人一個磨練的機會。這些地區的物質貧乏，設備簡陋，志願者們面臨重重困難，但是最大的挑戰是孤獨和寂寞。他們遠離親人，既不能上網，又沒有電視，有些地方甚至連報紙都沒有，對於這些在電子時代長大的年輕人來說，這簡直就是與世隔絕了。但從孩子們盈盈的笑臉上，他們得到了豐厚的回報。

32. Why is it difficult for children to get an education in some remote areas?

    (A) It is not possible to transport children to the nearest schools.
    (B) There are not enough teachers in these areas.
    (C) Parents do not see the importance of education.
    (D) Parents prefer for their children to be educated in urban cities.

33. What is the main objective of the government sponsored program?

    (A) To provide financial sponsorship to children in poor areas
    (B) To promote economic development in remote areas
    (C) To provide education for children in remote areas
    (D) To offer financial assistance to people in poor areas

34. What do the college graduates bring to the children in the remote areas?

    (A) Knowledge
    (B) Television
    (C) Telephones
    (D) Necessities

35. What is the reward mentioned in this article for those college graduates who go to the remote areas?

    (A) Good salary
    (B) Time away from the city
    (C) Minimum distraction
    (D) The children's smiles

36. According to the article, what is the biggest challenge faced by those college graduates?

    (A) Lack of teaching resources
    (B) Lack of convenient transportation
    (C) Lack of communication means
    (D) Lack of community support

SECTION II: FREE RESPONSE

PART A: WRITING [30 minutes, 25% of final score]

Note: In this part of the exam, you may NOT move back and forth among questions.

Directions: You will be asked to perform two writing tasks in Chinese. In each case, you will be asked to write for a specific purpose and to a specific person. You should write in as complete and as culturally appropriate a manner as possible, taking into account the purpose and the person described.

I. STORY NARRATION [15 minutes, 15% of final score]

The four pictures present a story. Imagine you are writing the story to a friend. Narrate a complete story as suggested by the pictures. Give your story a beginning, middle, and an end.

II. E-mail Response [15 minutes, 10% of total score]

Read this e-mail from a friend and then type your response.

(Simplified Characters)

发件人：大卫

邮件主题：听听你的建议

刚刚收到成绩单，这学期我的成绩有所下降。我知道，父母虽然嘴上不说，但心里在替我着急，怕我考不上好大学。我不知道怎么做才能不让他们担心，你有什么好建议吗？另外，你在学习上有什么好方法可以给我介绍一下吗？

(Traditional Characters)

發件人：大衛

郵件主題：聽聽你的建議

剛剛收到成績單，這學期我的成績有所下降。我知道，父母雖然嘴上不說，但心裡在替我着急，怕我考不上好大學。我不知道怎麼做才能不讓他們擔心，你有什麼好建議嗎？另外，你在學習上有什麼好方法可以给我介绍一下吗？

PART B: SPEAKING [15 minutes, 25% of final score]

[Listen to the audio track **Education - Speaking**.]

Note: In this part of the exam, you may NOT move back and forth among questions.

I. CONVERSATION [4 minutes, 10% of final score]

Directions: You will participate in a simulated conversation. Each time it is your turn to speak, you will have 20 seconds to record. You should respond as fully and as appropriately as possible.

Anna has just moved to the United States from China with her family and enrolled in your high school. She wants to ask you some questions about high school life in the United States.

Anna: [Audio]
[TONE]
[Student records the response] (20 seconds)

Anna: [Audio]
[TONE]
[Student records the response] (20 seconds)

Anna: [Audio]
[TONE]
[Student records the response] (20 seconds)

Anna: [Audio]
[TONE]
[Student records the response] (20 seconds)

Anna: [Audio]
[TONE]
[Student records the response] (20 seconds)

Anna: [Audio]
[TONE]
[Student records the response] (20 seconds)

II. CULTURAL PRESENTATION [7 minutes, 15% of final score]

Directions: You will be asked to speak in Chinese on a specific topic. Imagine you are making an oral presentation to your Chinese class. First, you will read and hear the topic for your presentation. You will have 4 minutes to prepare your presentation. Then you will have 2 minutes to record your presentation. Your presentation should be as complete as possible.

Choose ONE ancient Chinese invention (e.g., paper making, movable type printing, the compass, etc.). In your presentation, describe this invention in detail and explain its significance.

[This marks the end of the audio track **Education - Speaking**.]

This page is intentionally left blank.

UNIT 5 ENTERTAINMENT

SECTION I: MULTIPLE CHOICE

PART A: LISTENING [20 minutes, 25% of final score]

[Listen to the audio track **Entertainment - Listening**.]

Note: In this part of the exam, you may NOT move back and forth among questions.

I. REJOINDERS [10 minutes, 10% of final score]

Directions: You will hear several short conversations or parts of conversations followed by 4 choices, designated (A), (B), (C), and (D). Choose the one that continues or completes the conversation in a logical and culturally appropriate manner. You will have 5 seconds to answer each question.

QUESTION NUMBER	STUDENT CHOICE			
1	(A)	(B)	(C)	(D)
2	(A)	(B)	(C)	(D)
3	(A)	(B)	(C)	(D)
4	(A)	(B)	(C)	(D)
5	(A)	(B)	(C)	(D)
6	(A)	(B)	(C)	(D)
7	(A)	(B)	(C)	(D)
8	(A)	(B)	(C)	(D)
9	(A)	(B)	(C)	(D)
10	(A)	(B)	(C)	(D)
11	(A)	(B)	(C)	(D)
12	(A)	(B)	(C)	(D)
13	(A)	(B)	(C)	(D)
14	(A)	(B)	(C)	(D)
15	(A)	(B)	(C)	(D)

II. Listening Selections [10 minutes, 15% of final score]

Directions: You will listen to several selections in Chinese. For each selection, you will be told whether it will be played once or twice. You may take notes as you listen. Your notes will not be graded. After listening to each selection, you will see questions in English. For each question, choose the response that is best according to the selection. You will have 12 seconds to answer each question.

SELECTION 1

16. Why did Liu Yun leave the message?
    (A) To tell Xiao Li that a new movie is on.
    (B) To tell Xiao Li that she is going to a concert
    (C) To ask Xiao Li to go to a movie with her
    (D) To ask Xiao Li to wait for her at home

17. When is the event?
    (A) In two hours
    (B) Tonight
    (C) Tomorrow
    (D) In two days

18. Who cannot make it to the event?
    (A) Liu Yun's roommate
    (B) Liu Yun's boyfriend
    (C) Xiao Li
    (D) Liu Yun

19. What does Liu Yun want Xiao Li to do?
    (A) Meet Liu Yun at the concert hall
    (B) Tell Liu Yun if she is available
    (C) Meet Liu Yun at the movie theater
    (D) Call other friends

SELECTION 2

20. What is the purpose of the announcement?
    (A) To cancel the tennis matches
    (B) To cancel all the doubles matches
    (C) To change the time and location for the tennis matches
    (D) To move singles matches to Washington High School

21. What is the situation that led to the announcement?
    (A) There is a thunderstorm in the area.
    (B) There are not enough players.
    (C) The tennis courts are overbooked.
    (D) The courts are still too wet.

22. According to the announcement, what will happen to the women's doubles matches?
    (A) The matches will be canceled.
    (B) The matches will be delayed for three hours.
    (C) The matches will be moved to Washington High School.
    (D) The matches will be held at the nearby recreational center.

23. What does the announcement suggest people do?
    (A) Get directions at the registration desk
    (B) Get directions at the school entrance
    (C) Get directions from the Internet
    (D) Get directions from the coaches

SELECTION 3

24. What event is the announcement about?
    (A) A concert
    (B) A movie
    (C) A sports game
    (D) A musical show

25. According to the announcement, each person is allowed to purchase
    (A) one ticket
    (B) two tickets
    (C) three tickets
    (D) four tickets

26. How much does a child's ticket cost?
    (A) Twenty *yuan*
    (B) Fifteen *yuan*
    (C) Twelve *yuan*
    (D) Ten *yuan*

SELECTION 4

27. What is Li Mei's occupation?
    (A) Movie director
    (B) Screenwriter
    (C) Actress
    (D) Photographer

28. Where is Li Mei when this conversation is taking place?
    (A) On a train
    (B) On a farm
    (C) In a coffee shop
    (D) In a movie studio

SELECTION 5

29. What is this TV report about?
    (A) The NBA Rockets will be playing their last game in China.
    (B) Fans are disappointed to learn that the game has been postponed.
    (C) It is about how to get a ticket to the NBA game in China.
    (D) The NBA Rockets are playing against Team China in the United States.

30. According to the report, which of the following statements is true?
    (A) Tickets for the game are still available for sale.
    (B) The stadium is completely packed.
    (C) Tickets were completely sold out a week before the game.
    (D) Fans have camped out to buy tickets.

31. When does the speaker make this report?
    (A) After the game
    (B) The day before the game
    (C) A few minutes before the game
    (D) During the game

32. According to the report, the fans are
    (A) disappointed
    (B) excited
    (C) cheering
    (D) screaming

[This marks the end of the audio track **Entertainment - Listening**.]

PART B: READING

[60 minutes, 25% of final score]

Note: In this part of the exam, you may move back and forth among all the questions.

Directions: You will read several selections in Chinese. Each selection is accompanied by a number of questions in English. For each question, choose the response that is best according to the selection.

Read this advertisement

(Simplified Characters)	(Traditional Characters)
浪漫京城 2009	**浪漫京城 2009**
中外爱情经典名片音乐 大型交响音乐会	**中外愛情經典名片音樂 大型交響音樂會**
• 情人节专场：“浪漫京城 2009”音乐会，将为观众献上一组最浪漫的中、外爱情电影音乐，祝愿天下有情人幸福快乐。	• 情人節專場：“浪漫京城 2009”音樂會，將為觀眾獻上一組最浪漫的中、外愛情電影音樂，祝願天下有情人幸福快樂。
• 规模盛大：大型交响乐团由近百人组成，现场演奏。	• 規模盛大：大型交響樂團由近百人組成，現場演奏。
• 曲目经典：音乐选自《乱世佳人》、《罗马假日》、《马路天使》、《泰塔尼克号》、《音乐之声》、《梁祝》等。	• 曲目經典：音樂選自《亂世佳人》、《羅馬假日》、《馬路天使》、《泰塔尼克號》、《音樂之聲》、《梁祝》等。
演出时间：2009.2.14 晚 8:30 演出地点：国家音乐厅 票价：贵宾票 299 元 普通票 199 元 订票热线：8324-9834	演出時間：2009.2.14 晚 8:30 演出地點：國家音樂廳 票價：貴賓票 299 元 普通票 199 元 訂票熱線：8324-9834

1. What is this advertisement promoting?
   (A) A new movie
   (B) An orchestra concert
   (C) A movie award
   (D) A pop music concert

2. What special occasion is this event for?
   (A) An international movie festival
   (B) A music festival
   (C) Valentine's Day
   (D) New Year's Day

3. According to this advertisement, what does this event offer?
   (A) A live concert by a world-renowned orchestra
   (B) Love songs from well-known Chinese movies
   (C) Clips from award-winning romantic movies
   (D) A live performance of romantic music from classic movies

4. Where will this event most likely take place?
   (A) Nanjing, China
   (B) Tianjin, China
   (C) Beijing, China
   (D) Shanghai, China

Read this e-mail

(Simplified Characters)	(Traditional characters)
大卫， 你好！ 到中国旅行有好几天了，直到今天才有时间给你写信。 昨天晚上朋友请我去看了一场京剧。她说，京剧已经有 200 多年的历史了，被誉为中国的国粹，到中国来的外国人都应该去体验一下。我们看的这出京剧叫《白蛇传》，讲的是中国的一个古老的传说。 京剧真是很独特的艺术，我尤其喜欢里面热闹的武打场面，但给我印象最深的是脸谱。脸谱用鲜艳的色彩、夸张的面部造型来区别剧中各种角色，不同的人物性格用不同的脸谱，即使听不懂京剧的人也能看出谁是好人、谁是坏人。 这是我第一次看京剧，虽然有许多听不明白的地方，不过借助脸谱和中英双语字幕，我还是能把剧情猜出个大概。 朋友告诉我，为了推广这门传统艺术， 艺术家们在剧中融入了其他艺术手法，例如，多媒体影像、民间舞、交响乐等等， 让古老的京剧呈现了新风貌。 这真是一次很有意思的经历。 祝好！ 珍妮	大衛， 你好！ 到中國旅行有好幾天了，直到今天才有時間給你寫信。 昨天晚上朋友請我去看了一場京劇。她說，京劇已經有 200 多年的歷史了，被譽為中國的國粹，到中國來的外國人都應該去體驗一下。我們看的這齣京劇叫《白蛇傳》，講的是中國的一個古老的傳說。 京劇真是很獨特的藝術，我尤其喜歡裡面熱鬧的武打場面，但給我印象最深的是臉譜。臉譜用鮮豔的色彩、誇張的面部造型來區別劇中各種角色，不同的人物性格用不同的臉譜，即使聽不懂京劇的人也能看出誰是好人、誰是壞人。 這是我第一次看京劇，雖然有許多聽不明白的地方，不過借助臉譜和中英雙語字幕，我還是能把劇情猜出個大概。 朋友告訴我，為了推廣這門傳統藝術，藝術家們在劇中融入了其他藝術手法，例如，多媒體影像、民間舞、交響樂等等，讓古老的京劇呈現了新風貌。 這真是一次很有意思的經歷。 祝好！ 珍妮

5. Why did the author's friend take her to see Beijing Opera?
   (A) Because the author asked to see it
   (B) Because she thought the author should experience it
   (C) Because the author had nothing else to do in the evening
   (D) Because she is an opera enthusiast

6. According to the author, what aspect of the opera left her with the deepest impression?
   (A) The story line
   (B) Martial art fighting scenes
   (C) Beijing opera masks
   (D) The modern aspects of the show

7. According to the passage, can one tell the good characters from the evil characters in Beijing Opera?
   (A) No, because all the characters wear heavy makeup.
   (B) Yes, because the good characters and the evil characters wear different costumes.
   (C) No, because the good characters and the evil characters both wear masks.
   (D) Yes, because the good characters and the evil characters wear distinctive masks.

8. What helped the author to understand Beijing Opera more?
   (A) Her friend's translation
   (B) The multimedia effects
   (C) The fighting scenes
   (D) The English/Chinese subtitles

9. According to the passage, what new element has been incorporated into today's Beijing Opera?
   (A) Acrobats
   (B) Folk dance
   (C) Modern costume
   (D) Facial makeup

Read this article

(Simplified Characters)	(Traditional Characters)
家长如何引导孩子健康上网？	**家長如何引導孩子健康上網？**
目前中国的中小学生学习紧张，压力很大，而且这些独生子女们因为没有兄弟姐妹所以会感到孤独。他们渴望结交年龄相仿的伙伴，互联网给孩子们提供了一个互相交流和舒解压力的平台。如何引导孩子健康上网成了家长们的新课题。	目前中國的中小學生學習緊張，壓力很大，而且這些獨生子女們因為沒有兄弟姐妹所以會感到孤獨。他們渴望結交年齡相仿的伙伴，互聯網給孩子們提供了一個互相交流和舒解壓力的平台。如何引導孩子健康上網成了家長們的新課題。
首先家长们要对网络这个新鲜事物多加了解，认识网路的好处和弊端，理解网络在我们现代生活中的重要性。	首先家長們要對網絡這個新鮮事物多加瞭解，認識網路的好處和弊端，理解網絡在我們現代生活中的重要性。
其次，家长也要学会上网，善用网络，引导孩子选择有利于成才的健康网站。	其次，家長也要學會上網，善用網絡，引導孩子選擇有利於成材的健康網站。
最后，家长要注意监督和控制孩子的上网时间和上网内容，培养孩子上网自制力，并郑重告诫孩子不要涉足色情网站。	最後，家長要注意監督和控制孩子的上網時間和上網內容，培養孩子上網自制力，並鄭重告誡孩子不要涉足色情網站。

10. According to the article, some Chinese children feel lonely because
    (A) they do not have any siblings
    (B) they have limited internet access
    (C) they have no time to socialize with peers
    (D) their parents are too busy to spend time with them

11. According to the article, the children want to go online
    (A) to do homework
    (B) to play games
    (C) to chat with classmates
    (D) to make friends

12. According to the article, what is the new parenting issue for Chinese parents?
    (A) To spend quality time with their children
    (B) To encourage their children's curiosity
    (C) To guide their children to use the Internet responsibly
    (D) To communicate with their children

13. What does the article suggest parents do?
    (A) Do outdoor activities together
    (B) Get involved in their children's school functions
    (C) Prohibit their children's Internet access
    (D) Monitor their children's online activities

14. According to the article, what aspect of their children's Internet usage should parents monitor?
    (A) Friends made online
    (B) Time spent online
    (C) Instant messages
    (D) E-mail correspondence

Read this article

(Simplified Characters)

2003 年，姚明还是 NBA 的新秀，当明星队的名单公布时，姚明高票当选，让很多人感到意外，他的选票竟然超过了超级球星奥尼尔，成为西部明星队首发阵容的一员。从此，姚明年年榜上有名，就连 2007 年他膝盖受了伤也不例外。

2009 年姚明又一次入选 NBA 明星队。七年来，姚明入选西部明星队已经是没有悬念的事了。可是，在全明星赛场上，他却一直是个配角。

然而，与常规赛季的比赛不同，全明星赛不仅是东西两队一决胜负的时刻，更是明星们展现个人高超球技的大好机会。而姚明在这样的场合中就显得比较拘谨，与其他球星们截然不同，他不大善于表现自己。

意识到自己的弱点，姚明大胆地做过不少尝试。例如，三年前他在球场上为球迷们献上一段霹雳舞，虽然观众認为很“僵硬”，但他却自嘲地说: “(舞)虽然跳得很烂，那可是我跳得最好的一次。”

姚明就是这样一位不断努力，不断超越自己的球星。

(Traditional Characters)

2003 年，姚明還是 NBA 的新秀，當明星隊的名單公佈時，姚明高票當選，讓很多人感到意外，他的選票竟然超過了超級球星奧尼爾，成為西部明星隊首發陣容的一員。從此，姚明年年榜上有名，就連 2007 年他膝蓋受了傷也不例外。

2009 年姚明又一次入選 NBA 明星隊，七年來，姚明入選西部明星隊已經是沒有懸念的事了。可是，在全明星賽場上，他卻一直是個配角。

然而，與常規賽季的比賽不同，全明星賽不僅是東西兩隊一決勝負的時刻，更是明星們展現個人高超球技的大好機會。而姚明在這樣的場合中就顯得比較拘謹，與其他球星們截然不同，他不大善於表現自己。

意識到自己的弱點，姚明大膽地做過不少嘗試。例如，三年前他在球場上為球迷們獻上一段霹靂舞，雖然觀眾認為很“僵硬”，但他卻自嘲地說: “(舞)雖然跳得很爛，那可是我跳得最好的一次。”

姚明就是這樣一位不斷努力，不斷超越自己的球星。

15. What is this article about?
    (A) Yao Ming's career on an NBA team
    (B) Yao Ming's NBA All-Star experience
    (C) Yao Ming's experience in show business
    (D) Yao Ming's career on a Chinese basketball team

16. From 2003 to 2009, how many times has Yao Ming been an All-Star?
    (A) Four
    (B) Five
    (C) Six
    (D) Seven

17. After Yao Ming suffered a knee injury in 2007,
    (A) he missed the All-Star game
    (B) he had complicated knee surgery
    (C) he was still selected for the All-Star team
    (D) he canceled an appearance for his fans

18. What is the main contrast between Yao Ming and other All-Star basketball players?
    (A) Yao Ming loves to be a star more than others.
    (B) Yao Ming cannot dance as well as others.
    (C) Yao Ming does not show off on the court like others.
    (D) Yao Ming is more outgoing than others.

Read this passage

(Simplified Characters)	(Traditional Characters)
在大众的热切期盼中，香港电影金像奖公布了第 28 届入围名单。年度大片《赤壁》人气最旺，赢得了十九个奖项中的十五项提名，同时，来自大陆的女演员们表现不凡，在最佳女主角、最佳女配角和最佳新人等热门奖项中，获得六项提名。 功夫演员出身的甄子丹近年来成绩突出，以《叶问》中的上乘表演备受赞许，首次获得最佳男主角提名。面对竞争，甄子丹坦率地表示，"动作片向来都得不到同等对待，但我花费心力去演，能够获得提名已经很难得了！" 相对甄子丹的成功，周星驰和徐克却显得有些失落。力争最佳导演的周星驰竟然没能得到提名，而他极力扶持的年轻演员徐娇也只得到最佳新人的提名。最不得志的恐怕要数徐克，他去年的两部作品中只有《深海寻人》得到最佳视觉效果和最佳原创歌曲两项提名。	在大眾的熱切期盼中，香港電影金像獎公佈了第 28 屆入圍名單。年度大片《赤壁》人氣最旺，贏得了十九個獎項中的十五項提名。同時，來自大陸的女演員們表現不凡，在最佳女主角、最佳女配角和最佳新人等熱門獎項中，獲得六項提名。 功夫演員出身的甄子丹近年來成績突出，以《葉問》中的上乘表演備受讚許，首次獲得最佳男主角提名。面對競爭，甄子丹坦率地表示，"動作片向來都得不到同等對待，但我花費心力去演，能夠獲得提名已經很難得了！" 相對甄子丹的成功，周星馳和徐克卻顯得有些失落。力爭最佳導演的周星馳竟然沒能得到提名，而他極力扶持的年輕演員徐嬌也只得到最佳新人的提名。最不得志的恐怕要數徐克，他去年的兩部作品中只有《深海尋人》得到最佳視覺效果和最佳原創歌曲兩項提名。

19. What kind of award is mentioned in this news article?
    (A) A Chinese movie award
    (B) A Chinese drama award
    (C) A Chinese television program award
    (D) A Chinese music award

20. This special award ceremony is held in which city?
    (A) Taipei
    (B) Los Angeles
    (C) Beijing
    (D) Hong Kong

21. The "Red Cliff" is considered the most successful entry in the event because
    (A) it did best at the box office
    (B) it got the most award nominations
    (C) it features many superstars
    (D) it is directed by the most popular director

22. Zeng Zidan is nominated for
    (A) the best dramatic tenor
    (B) the best supporting actor
    (C) the best leading singer
    (D) the best leading actor

23. Xu Jiao is nominated for
    (A) the best songwriter
    (B) the best director
    (C) the best visual effects
    (D) the best new actress

Read this article

(Simplified Characters)	(Traditional Characters)
琴、棋、书、画是中国古代的四大艺术，其中的棋，指的就是围棋。	琴、棋、書、畫是中國古代的四大藝術，其中的棋，指的就是圍棋。
根据中国国家体育总局的《围棋规则》，对局双方各执一色棋子；黑先白后，交替下子，棋子下在棋盘的交叉点上，每次只能下一子；棋子下定后，不允许再挪动位置；轮流下子是双方的权利。虽然围棋的玩法简单易懂，但是要想真正下得好，并不容易。	根據中國國家體育總局的《圍棋規則》，對局雙方各執一色棋子；黑先白後，交替下子，棋子下在棋盤的交叉點上，每次只能下一子；棋子下定後，不允許再挪動位置；輪流下子是雙方的權利。雖然圍棋的玩法簡單易懂，但是要想真正下得好，並不容易。
围棋不仅是一门艺术，也是一项训练战略战术的智力游戏。下围棋能够训练应变能力，激发空间想像力，培养敏锐的观察力。常下围棋，还有益于孩子们的大脑发育，有助于老年人保持记忆力。	圍棋不僅是一門藝術，也是一項訓練戰略戰術的智力遊戲。下圍棋能夠訓練應變能力，激發空間想像力，培養敏銳的觀察力。常下圍棋，還有益於孩子們的大腦發育、有助於老年人保持記憶力。
围棋艺术流传数千年，如今已经遍及全世界。	圍棋藝術流傳數千年，如今已經遍及全世界。

24. As one of the four ancient art forms, Qi refers to
    (A) Go
    (B) Wuzi chess
    (C) Chinese chess
    (D) Chinese checkers

25. How long is the history of this art form?
    (A) One thousand years
    (B) A few thousand years
    (C) One hundred years
    (D) A few centuries

26. Which of the following rules is mentioned in this article?
    (A) A player has a time limit for each move.
    (B) There is a standard for the size of the board.
    (C) A player may give up a turn.
    (D) Black makes the first move.

27. According to the article, what is true about this art form?
    (A) It is easy to learn and easy to be good at it.
    (B) It is easy to learn but hard to be good at it.
    (C) It is hard to learn but easy to be good at it.
    (D) It is hard to learn and hard to be good at it.

28. In the article, which is mentioned as a benefit of practicing this art form?
    (A) Improving math skills
    (B) Practicing patience
    (C) Retaining memory
    (D) Developing sagacity

Read this e-mail

(Simplified Characters)	(Traditional Characters)
大卫，	大衛，
上封邮件我给你讲了我去看京剧的体验，这次我告诉你我去卡拉 OK 的感想吧。	上封郵件我給你講了我去看京劇的體驗，這次我告訴你我去卡拉 OK 的感想吧。
没有去卡拉 OK 歌厅之前，我一点也不知道中国人如此热衷于这种娱乐 。在美国，我几乎没见过这种自唱自娱的地方，而卡拉 OK 在中国的大小城市里，却是遍地开花，真可以说是最受中国人喜爱的休闲场所之一。	沒有去卡拉 OK 歌廳之前，我一點也不知道中國人如此熱衷於這種娛樂。在美國，我幾乎看不到這種自唱自娛的地方，而卡拉 OK 在中國的大小城市裡，卻是遍地開花，真可以說是最受中國人喜愛的休閒場所之一。
最让我惊讶的是，在歌厅里，平时很腼腆的中国人好像都变得很大方，人人都是歌星， 个个都有拿手的歌曲。他们从中国歌唱到外国歌，让我对这些中国朋友们不得不刮目相看了！	最讓我驚訝的是，在歌廳裡，平時很靦腆的中國人好像都變得很大方，人人都是歌星，個個都有拿手的歌曲。他們從中國歌唱到外國歌，讓我對這些中國朋友們不得不刮目相看了！
在朋友们的鼓励声中，我也拿起了麦克风。平时大大方方的我，这时却紧张得不得了，好不容易唱完了一首英文歌，就再也不愿意当众献丑了。其实， 在旁边听他们唱也很开心。我想，和朋友一块儿唱歌也是调剂生活、舒解压力的一种方式吧。	在朋友們的鼓勵聲中，我也拿起了麥克風。平時大大方方的我，這時卻緊張得不得了，好不容易唱完了一首英文歌，就再也不願意當眾獻醜了。其實，在旁邊聽他們唱也很開心。我想，和朋友一塊兒唱歌也是調劑生活、舒解壓力的一種方式吧。
下次你有机会来中国，一定要到卡拉 OK 歌厅亲身体验一下哦。	下次你有機會來中國，一定要到卡拉 OK 歌廳親身體驗一下哦。
祝好！	祝好！
珍妮	珍妮

29. According to this e-mail, what is true about Karaoke in China?
    (A) It is only popular in big cities.
    (B) It is an expensive form of entertainment.
    (C) You can find Karaoke lounges everywhere.
    (D) All Karaoke lounges are decorated with flowers.

30. What is the best word to describe the author's impression of her Chinese friends before this experience?
    (A) Bashful
    (B) Outgoing
    (C) Talkative
    (D) Cautious

31. What did the author learn about her Chinese friends from this experience?
    (A) They are average singers.
    (B) They are still shy when singing.
    (C) They can only sing their specialty songs.
    (D) They can sing songs in other languages.

32. Which of the following statements is true about the author?
    (A) She felt intensely nervous when singing.
    (B) She did not enjoy Karaoke.
    (C) She enjoyed singing in front of people very much.
    (D) She felt pressured and uncomfortable.

33. According to this e-mail, Jenny thinks
    (A) her friend David should try Karaoke
    (B) Karaoke is popular among college students
    (C) her Chinese friends want to become pop stars
    (D) her Chinese friends are under a lot of pressure

Read this short notice

(Simplified Characters)	(Traditional Characters)
告示 今晚的《哈里波特》电影票全部售完。本售票处将提前出售明天的票。您也可以上网预定明天或其他日期的票。谢谢合作！	告示 今晚的《哈里波特》電影票全部售完。本售票處將提前出售明天的票。您也可以上網預定明天或其他日期的票。謝謝合作！

34. Where would you most likely see this notice?
    (A) At a movie theater box office
    (B) At a music hall box office
    (C) On a theater's website
    (D) On a movie screen before the show starts

35. Which statement about purchasing tickets for tomorrow is true?
    (A) All tomorrow's tickets are sold out.
    (B) Tickets can only be purchased at the theater today.
    (C) Tickets can be pre-ordered online.
    (D) Tomorrow's tickets are available for sale tomorrow only.

Read this sign

(Simplified Characters)	(Traditional Characters)
本周流行音乐排行榜	本週流行音樂排行榜

36. This sign is a
    (A) weekly classical music ranking
    (B) weekly popular music ranking
    (C) annual classical music ranking
    (D) annual popular music ranking

SECTION II: FREE RESPONSE

PART A: WRITING [30 minutes, 25% of final score]

Note: In this part of the exam, you may NOT move back and forth among questions.

Directions: You will be asked to perform two writing tasks in Chinese. In each case, you will be asked to write for a specific purpose and to a specific person. You should write in as complete and as culturally appropriate a manner as possible, taking into account the purpose and the person described.

I. STORY NARRATION [15 minutes, 15% of final score]

The four pictures present a story. Imagine you are writing the story to a friend. Narrate a complete story as suggested by the pictures. Give your story a beginning, middle, and an end.

II. E-MAIL RESPONSE [15 minutes, 10% of total score]

Read this e-mail from a friend and then type your response.

(Simplified Characters)

发件人：苏珊

邮件主题： 在中国期间的活动安排

真高兴你今年八月份要来中国。我去打听了一下，在你逗留期间，杂技表演、羽毛球比赛和音乐会还都有票， 请尽快告诉我你哪几天晚上有空，我好替你订票。另外，我还帮你找了一位导游，请你回信时告诉我你想去游览的地方，这样我可以让导游提前为你做安排。

(Traditional Characters)

發件人：蘇珊

郵件主題：在中國期間的活動安排

真高興你今年八月份要來中國。我去打聽了一下，在你逗留期間，雜技表演、羽毛球比賽和音樂會還都有票，請盡快告訴我你哪幾天晚上有空，我好替你訂票。另外，我還幫你找了一位導遊，請你回信時告訴我你想去遊覽的地方，这樣我可以讓導遊提前為你做安排。

PART B: SPEAKING [15 minutes, 25% of final score]

 [Listen to the audio track **Entertainment - Speaking**.]

Note: In this part of the exam, you may NOT move back and forth among questions.

I. CONVERSATION [4 minutes, 10% of final score]

Directions: You will participate in a simulated conversation. Each time it is your turn to speak, you will have 20 seconds to record. You should respond as fully and as appropriately as possible.

You are having a conversation with David, a college student who is conducting a survey about people's opinions regarding the Internet and its use.

David: [Audio]
[TONE]
[Student records the response] (20 seconds)

David: [Audio]
[TONE]
[Student records the response] (20 seconds)

David: [Audio]
[TONE]
[Student records the response] (20 seconds)

David: [Audio]
[TONE]
[Student records the response] (20 seconds)

David: [Audio]
[TONE]
[Student records the response] (20 seconds)

David: [Audio]
[TONE]
[Student records the response] (20 seconds)

II. CULTURAL PRESENTATION [7 minutes, 15% of final score]

Directions: You will be asked to speak in Chinese on a specific topic. Imagine you are making an oral presentation to your Chinese class. First, you will read and hear the topic for your presentation. You will have 4 minutes to prepare your presentation. Then you will have 2 minutes to record your presentation. Your presentation should be as complete as possible.

Choose ONE form of Chinese performing arts (Beijing Opera, acrobatics, martial arts, etc). In your presentation, describe this art form in detail and explain its significance.

[This marks the end of the audio track **Entertainment - Speaking**.]

UNIT 6 FAMILY

SECTION I: MULTIPLE CHOICE

PART A: LISTENING [20 minutes, 25% of final score]

[Listen to the audio track **Family - Listening**.]

Note: In this part of the exam, you may NOT move back and forth among questions.

I. REJOINDERS [10 minutes, 10% of final score]

Directions: You will hear several short conversations or parts of conversations followed by 4 choices, designated (A), (B), (C), and (D). Choose the one that continues or completes the conversation in a logical and culturally appropriate manner. You will have 5 seconds to answer each question.

QUESTION NUMBER	STUDENT CHOICE			
1	(A)	(B)	(C)	(D)
2	(A)	(B)	(C)	(D)
3	(A)	(B)	(C)	(D)
4	(A)	(B)	(C)	(D)
5	(A)	(B)	(C)	(D)
6	(A)	(B)	(C)	(D)
7	(A)	(B)	(C)	(D)
8	(A)	(B)	(C)	(D)
9	(A)	(B)	(C)	(D)
10	(A)	(B)	(C)	(D)
11	(A)	(B)	(C)	(D)
12	(A)	(B)	(C)	(D)
13	(A)	(B)	(C)	(D)
14	(A)	(B)	(C)	(D)
15	(A)	(B)	(C)	(D)

II. Listening Selections [10 minutes, 15% of final score]

Directions: You will listen to several selections in Chinese. For each selection, you will be told whether it will be played once or twice. You may take notes as you listen. Your notes will not be graded. After listening to each selection, you will see questions in English. For each question, choose the response that is best according to the selection. You will have 12 seconds to answer each question.

SELECTION 1

16. What is the purpose of the message?
    (A) To make wedding arrangements
    (B) To plan for a honeymoon
    (C) To find a ride for the speaker's daughter
    (D) To arrange an airport pickup

17. Who just got married?
    (A) Jasmine's daughter
    (B) Jasmine's cousin
    (C) Jasmine's sister
    (D) Jasmine's niece

18. What should Lily do first when she gets the message?
    (A) Call Jasmine's cell phone
    (B) Call Jasmine's home phone
    (C) Pick up Jasmine from the airport
    (D) Pick up Jasmine's daughter

19. Why did Jasmine's relative come to America?
    (A) To get married
    (B) To attend a wedding
    (C) To visit Lily
    (D) To go on her honeymoon

SELECTION 2

20. What did the man and his friends do during the weekend?
    (A) Went skiing
    (B) Went bowling
    (C) Went to a movie
    (D) Went to a concert

21. According to the recording,
    (A) some bowling lanes are closed
    (B) all bowling lanes are occupied
    (C) the bowling alley is dark
    (D) the bowling alley is noisy

22. According to the recording, which of the following statements is true?
    (A) The heavy snowstorm is perfect for snowboarding.
    (B) It is fun to have a large group of people bowling together.
    (C) The movie they watched was not very exciting.
    (D) The ski trip was canceled because of the weather.

SELECTION 3

23. What does the lady ask Baobao and Beibei to do?
    (A) Come over for dinner
    (B) Keep track of the time
    (C) Clean up the house
    (D) Take care of the garden

24. What is the relationship between Baobao and Beibei?
    (A) Sisters
    (B) Father and son
    (C) Brothers
    (D) Brother and sister

25. According to the recording, which of the following statements is true?
   (A) They will go out for dinner together.
   (B) The woman asks both Baobao and Beibei to paint the fence.
   (C) It will be too late to eat out after they finish the yard work.
   (D) Baobao and Beibei have other activities to attend.

26. Which of the following do Baobao or Beibei have to do?
   (A) Mow the lawn
   (B) Water the plants
   (C) Plant flowers
   (D) Rake leaves

SELECTION 4

27. What are they talking about?
   (A) A holiday vacation
   (B) College life
   (C) The sandy beaches
   (D) The Thanksgiving parade

28. Which place does the man think his brother would prefer to visit?
   (A) New York
   (B) Hawaii
   (C) Florida
   (D) California

29. Who wants to go to New York?
   (A) The man's brother
   (B) The woman's brother
   (C) The man
   (D) The woman

SELECTION 5

30. Where is this announcement made?
    (A) In a restaurant
    (B) In a theater
    (C) In a museum
    (D) In a shopping mall

31. What is the announcement about?
    (A) A visitor's guide
    (B) An annual sales promotion
    (C) A lost and found
    (D) A Family Week special

32. Who is eligible for the promotion?
    (A) Children who come with their parents
    (B) Teenagers who come with their grandparents
    (C) All parents
    (D) All seniors

[This marks the end of the audio track **Family - Listening**.]

PART B: READING

[60 minutes, 25% of final score]

Note: In this part of the exam, you may move back and forth among all the questions.

Directions: You will read several selections in Chinese. Each selection is accompanied by a number of questions in English. For each question, choose the response that is best according to the selection.

Read this advertisement

(Simplified Characters)	(Traditional Characters)
聘请保姆 家有九十岁母亲，不能独立生活，诚请保姆一名。包吃包住，工资优厚。有意者请电：650-123-3456	**聘請保姆** 家有九十歲母親，不能獨立生活，誠請保姆一名。包吃包住，工資優厚。有意者請電：650-123-3456

1. What is the purpose of this advertisement?
   (A) To look for a babysitter
   (B) To hire a licensed nurse
   (C) To look for a caregiver
   (D) To offer a caregiver service

2. Whom is the advertisement intended for?
   (A) Parent
   (B) Nurses
   (C) Seniors
   (D) Caregivers

3. In addition to salary, what are the other benefits offered in the advertisement?
   (A) Free room and board
   (B) Health insurance
   (C) Overtime payment
   (D) Paid vacation days

Read this advertisement

(Simplified Characters)	(Traditional Characters)
征婚启事 家在苏州，30 岁，健康帅气，高等学历，有自己的公司，寻有缘人共度一生。要求：25 岁以下女性，160cm 以上，心地善良，孝顺父母，性情温和。非诚勿扰。 有意者请电：1234-5678	**徵婚啟事** 家在蘇州，30 歲，健康帥氣，高等學歷，有自己的公司，尋有緣人共度一生。要求：25 歲以下女性，160cm 以上，心地善良，孝順父母，性情溫和。非誠勿擾。 有意者請電：1234-5678

4. What is this man looking for?
   (A) He is looking for a roommate.
   (B) He is looking for a nanny.
   (C) He is looking for a secretary.
   (D) He is looking for a wife.

5. How does the advertiser describe himself?
   (A) Wealthy, middle-aged
   (B) Government employee, handsome
   (C) Well educated, business owner
   (D) Tall, healthy

6. What kind of person is he looking for?
   (A) Even-tempered and has good references
   (B) Good personality and respectful to the elderly
   (C) Hardworking and has previous experience
   (D) Under twenty-five years old and highly educated

Read this e-mail

(Simplified Characters)	(Traditional Characters)
小佳： 你好！ 最近没有收到你的邮件，是不是正忙着期中考试呢？ 你上次来信说，这次放春假你要去旧金山舅舅家，虽然我和爸爸都很想念你，希望你能回家来住几天，但去看望舅舅和舅妈也是个不错的主意。你的表弟和表妹知道你要去一定非常高兴。 去舅舅家时，要记得带些小礼品，不用太贵重。给你的表弟和表妹也带些小玩具或糖果零食什么的。在舅舅家，要主动帮舅妈做些家务活儿，自己能做的事就不要麻烦他们，因为他们俩工作都挺忙的。 旧金山气候好，风景美，你一定会过得很愉快的。到了舅舅家记着给我和爸爸打电话报平安，免得我们惦记。代我和爸爸问候舅舅舅妈好！ 祝你一路顺风！ 妈妈	小佳： 你好！ 最近沒有收到你的郵件，是不是正忙著期中考試呢？ 你上次來信說，這次放春假你要去舊金山舅舅家，雖然我和爸爸都很想念你，希望你能回家來住幾天，但去看望舅舅和舅媽也是個不錯的主意。你的表弟和表妹知道你要去一定非常高興。 去舅舅家時，要記得帶些小禮品，不用太貴重。給你的表弟和表妹也帶些小玩具或糖果零食什麼的。在舅舅家，要主動幫舅媽做些家務活兒，自己能做的事就不要麻煩他們，因為他們倆工作都挺忙的。 舊金山氣候好，風景美，你一定會過得很愉快的。到了舅舅家記著給我和爸爸打電話報平安，免得我們惦記。代我和爸爸問候舅舅舅媽好！ 祝你一路順風！ 媽媽

7. Whom is Xiaojia going to visit?
   (A) Her uncle on her mother's side
   (B) Her aunt on her mother's side
   (C) Her uncle on her father's side
   (D) Her aunt on her father's side

8. The mother wants her daughter to
   (A) bring a birthday gift for her uncle
   (B) help with her cousins' homework
   (C) do sightseeing in San Francisco
   (D) call home when she arrives

9. Which of the following statements is true?
   (A) Both of her cousins are boys.
   (B) Both of her cousins are girls.
   (C) Xiaojia is older than her cousins.
   (D) Xiaojia is younger than her cousins.

Read this letter

(Simplified Characters)	(Traditional Characters)
亲爱的老公，	親愛的老公，
岁月如梭，我们已携手共度了二十多个春秋。从相识到相知，从相知到相爱，渐渐地融入了彼此的天地。我深信，如今，已经没有什么能把我们分开了。	歲月如梭，我們已攜手共渡了二十多個春秋。從相識到相知，從相知到相愛，漸漸地融入了彼此的天地。我深信，如今，已經沒有什麼能把我們分開了。
人生漫漫，未来难料，但是，只要我们能够一起面对生活中遇到的困难，互相包容和信任，美好的幸福就会永恒常驻。	人生漫漫，未來難料，但是，只要我們能夠一起面對生活中遇到的困難，互相包容和信任，美好的幸福就會永恆常駐。
为了你的健康和我们的将来，今天，我对你有一个请求：多锻炼少熬夜。我知道做到这些不容易，但我相信，为了我，为了你，你能努力做到！	為了你的健康和我們的將來，今天，我對你有一個請求：多鍛煉少熬夜。我知道做到這些不容易，但我相信，為了我，為了你，你能努力做到！
“执子之手，与子偕老”不是梦想，而是我们对彼此的承诺。	“執子之手，與子偕老”不是夢想，而是我們對彼此的承諾。
永远爱你的妻子	永遠愛你的妻子

10. What type of letter is this?
    (A) A letter from a man to his girlfriend
    (B) A letter from a wife to her husband
    (C) A letter from a grandson to his grandfather
    (D) A letter from a mother to her son

11. According to the letter, how long have they been in their current relationship?
    (A) Over twenty years
    (B) About two years
    (C) Over forty years
    (D) About ten years

12. What does the letter writer want the recipient to do?
    (A) Help with household chores
    (B) Exercise more
    (C) Drink and smoke less
    (D) Eat healthier food

Read this essay

(Simplified Characters)	(Traditional Characters)
我快乐的家	**我快樂的家**
我和父母及一个妹妹生活在美国东部的一个小城市，宁静而快乐。	我和父母及一個妹妹生活在美國東部的一個小城市，寧靜而快樂。
五岁那年，我随父母从上海移民到美国后，就一直住在这个小城市。起先，我不大喜欢这里，在上海看惯了高楼大厦和车水马龙，觉得这个小城市太安静和太荒凉了。我很想念我上海的家和那里小朋友们。	五歲那年，我隨父母從上海移民到美國後，就一直住在這個小城市。起先，我不大喜歡這裡，在上海看慣了高樓大廈和車水馬龍，覺得這個小城市太安靜和太荒涼了。我很想念我上海的家和那裡小朋友們。
过了两年，爸爸妈妈给我添了一个小妹妹，这一下我们家就热闹多了。我每天放学回来就和妹妹玩，周末全家人一起去公园。我慢慢喜欢上我住的地方了。新鲜的空气，美丽的风光，热情的邻里，使我越来越热爱这个小城的生活了。	過了兩年，爸爸媽媽給我添了一個小妹妹，這一下我們家就熱鬧多了。我每天放學回來就和妹妹玩，週末全家人一起去公園。我慢慢喜歡上我住的地方了。新鮮的空氣，美麗的風光，熱情的鄰里，使我越來越熱愛這個小城的生活了。
现在，爸爸在一家电脑公司做工程师，妈妈上午在一家商店里上班，下午在家照顾我和妹妹，送我们参加各种有趣的课外活动。我喜欢游泳，妹妹喜欢踢足球。今年我是高中二年级的学生了，功课很多，但游泳能帮助我增强体质，减轻压力，所以我一直在坚持游泳训练。	現在，爸爸在一家電腦公司做工程師，媽媽上午在一家商店裡上班，下午在家照顧我和妹妹，送我們參加各種有趣的課外活動。我喜歡游泳，妹妹喜歡踢足球。今年我是高中二年級的學生了，功课很多，但游泳能幫助我增强體質，減輕壓力，所以我一直在堅持游泳訓練。
我的一家生活得很快乐，我爱我的家人，也爱我的小城。	我的一家生活得很快樂，我愛我的家人，也愛我的小城。

13. Where was the author originally from?
    (A) A small town in China
    (B) A big city in China
    (C) A small town in the United States
    (D) A big city in the United States

14. Why did the author initially dislike the new town?
    (A) It was too noisy and busy.
    (B) There were too many tall buildings.
    (C) It was too quiet and remote.
    (D) There was no friend to play with.

15. What is the favorite sports activity of the author's sister?
    (A) Soccer
    (B) Tennis
    (C) Baseball
    (D) Swimming

16. Does the author's mother work outside of the house?
    (A) No, she is a homemaker.
    (B) No, she works from home.
    (C) Yes, she works full time in a store.
    (D) Yes, she works part time in a store.

17. According to the passage, what activity does the author do to reduce his/her stress?
    (A) Playing soccer
    (B) Swimming
    (C) Playing with his/her sister
    (D) Walking in the park

Read this note

(Simplified Characters)	(Traditional Characters)
玛丽， 我送弟弟去棒球场训练，晚上八点钟才能回来。你放学回家后，先吃些点心，然后自己做功课，六点左右，请你帮忙煮一下米饭。我已经把菜做好放在冰箱里了。你饿了的话可以把菜在微波炉里热一下，自己先吃。不然可以等我和弟弟回来一起吃。 晚上见！ 妈妈	瑪麗， 我送弟弟去棒球場訓練，晚上八點鐘才能回來。你放學回家後，先吃些點心，然後自己做功課，六點左右，請你幫忙煮一下米飯。我已經把菜做好放在冰箱裡了。你餓了的話可以把菜在微波爐裡熱一下，自己先吃。不然可以等我和弟弟回來一起吃。 晚上見！ 媽媽

18. What kind of sport does Mary's brother play?
    (A) Basketball
    (B) Baseball
    (C) Soccer
    (D) Volleyball

19. According to the note, what does Mary need to do around 6 p.m.?
    (A) Wash vegetables
    (B) Do homework
    (C) Cook rice
    (D) Eat dinner

20. What time will Mary's mother be back?
    (A) 8 p.m.
    (B) 6 p.m.
    (C) 8 a.m.
    (D) 6 a.m.

21. According to the note, what should Mary do if she is hungry?
    (A) Order takeout
    (B) Eat dinner
    (C) Eat snacks
    (D) Cook rice

Read this short message

(Simplified Characters)	(Traditional Characters)
天增岁月人增寿，新春伊始，祝您身体健康，万事如意。	天增歲月人增壽，新春伊始，祝您身體健康，萬事如意。

22. What type of message is this?
    (A) A birthday greeting
    (B) A get well message
    (C) A Chinese New Year greeting
    (D) A Mid-Autumn Festival message

23. In this message, the writer wishes the receiver to
    (A) have a happy birthday
    (B) feel better soon
    (C) become richer
    (D) stay healthy

Read this passage

(Simplified Characters)

年夜饭

一年中，中国人家庭最重要的一顿家宴要数年夜饭了。

大年夜也叫除夕，是中国农历年的最后一天。人们辞旧迎新，工作再忙，离家再远，都要赶回家，和家人一起吃年夜饭。家人甚至会为实在赶不回来的亲人留个位子，放一副碗筷，以示团聚。可见，年夜饭是中国人最重视的团圆饭。

年夜饭当然少不了一桌美味丰盛的年菜了。一家人团坐在一起，享受满桌的佳肴和快乐的气氛，是中国人家最愉快的一刻。对于年菜，中国人非常重视和讲究， 每一道菜，不但要美味， 而且要吉祥。由于中国国土辽阔，从南到北，过年风俗也不尽相同。北方人过年要吃饺子，而南方人传统上要吃米糕元宵。而年菜中，鱼一定是一道必不可少的菜，因为“有鱼”和“有余”谐音，表示人们希望来年中生活上更丰盛而有所盈余。由于人员的流通， 很多天南海北的习俗都融合在一起了。现代人还不断地创造出一些新式的吉祥菜肴，比如 ，“五福临门”，“团团圆圆”，“笑口常开” 等等。

过年是中国文化中很重要的一部分，而年夜饭作为过年的主要传统一定会源远流长。

(Traditional Characters)

年夜飯

一年中，中國人家庭最重要的一頓家宴要數年夜飯了。

大年夜也叫除夕，是中國農曆年的最後一天，人們辭舊迎新，工作再忙，離家再遠，都要趕回家，和家人一起吃年夜飯，家人甚至會為實在趕不回家的親人留個位子，放一副碗筷，以示團聚。可見，年夜飯是中國人最重視的團圓飯。

年夜飯當然少不了一桌美味豐盛的年菜了。一家人團坐在一起，享受滿桌的佳餚和快樂的氣氛，是中國人家最愉快的一刻。對於年菜，中國人非常重視和講究，每一道菜，不但要美味，而且要吉祥。由於中國國土遼闊，從南到北，過年風俗也不盡相同。北方人過年要吃餃子，而南方人傳統上要吃米糕元宵。但年菜中，魚一定是一道必不可少的菜，因為“有魚”和“有餘”諧音，表示人們希望來年中生活上更豐盛而有所盈餘。由於人員的流通，很多天南海北的習俗都融合在一起了。現代人還不斷地創造出一些新式的吉祥菜餚，比如，“五福臨門”，“團團圓圓”，“笑口常開”等等。

過年是中國文化中很重要的一部分，而年夜飯作為過年的主要傳統一定會源遠流長。

24. According to the article, Chinese will have their most important meal on
    (A) Chinese New Year's Eve
    (B) Chinese New Year's Day
    (C) Mid-Autumn Festival
    (D) Lantern Festival

25. Where is the most desirable place to have this meal?
    (A) At a friend's house
    (B) At a relative's place
    (C) At a fancy restaurant
    (D) At home with family

26. According to the article, people usually favor dishes with
    (A) rare meat
    (B) exotic seafood
    (C) auspicious names
    (D) colorful presentation

27. If a family member is absent for the meal,
    (A) this person will host the next family event
    (B) a seat will be reserved for this person
    (C) the family will save some food for this person
    (D) a makeup dinner will be scheduled for this person

Read this invitation

(Simplified Characters)	(Traditional Characters)
** 请柬 **	** 請柬 **
敬请 金启朗夫妇 光临	敬請 金啟朗夫婦 光臨
刘小林	**劉小林**
张莹婷	**張瑩婷**
金婚庆典	金婚慶典
刘氏子女共同敬邀	劉氏子女共同敬邀
庆典时间: 2009 年 5 月 1 日(星期五)	慶典時間: 2009 年 5 月 1 日(星期五)
下午 5 时	下午 5 時
庆典地点: 上海喜福来大酒店	慶典地點: 上海喜福來大酒店
上海市南京路 888 号	上海市南京路 888 號
21-12349876	21-12349876
** 敬请光临 **	** 敬請光臨 **

28. This invitation is for a
    (A) birthday party
    (B) family reunion
    (C) wedding ceremony
    (D) golden anniversary

29. How many people does this invitation invite to the event?
    (A) One
    (B) Two
    (C) Three
    (D) Four

30. What is the most likely age range of Zhang Yingting and Liu Xiaolin?
    (A) In their teens
    (B) In their twenties
    (C) In their fifties
    (D) In their seventies

31. Who sent this invitation?
    (A) The parents of Zhang Yingting and Liu Xiaolin
    (B) The friends of Zhang Yingting and Liu Xiaolin
    (C) The children of Zhang Yingting and Liu Xiaolin
    (D) Zhang Yingting and Liu Xiaolin

Read this article

(Simplified Characters)

到中国人家做客

古老的中国被称为“礼仪之邦”，很多传统礼仪在今天的日常生活中也依然随处可见。中国人热情好客，常常邀请亲朋好友到家里吃饭。如果了解一些做客的基本礼仪，能帮助你在赴家宴时举止得当。

去中国人家做客要守时，衣着要整洁得体，带些小礼品，以表示对主人的尊重。

客人要等主人邀请后才能入席落座 。入座后，千万不能急于动筷子，要等主人举杯示意开始，客人才能用餐。

夹菜时一次不要夹得太多，也不能伸长胳膊去夹远处的菜，还要记得一定要用公筷。千万要避免玩弄筷子，或用筷子翻菜，或把筷子含在嘴里这些不礼貌的行为。

如果餐桌上有一壶茶水在你的旁边，你要记得常常为你周围的客人斟茶。如果别人给你斟茶，你应该用手指轻轻敲击桌面，以示感谢之意。

宴毕后不要滞留过久，告辞时要向主人道谢，也是应有的礼节。

(Traditional Characters)

到中國人家做客

古老的中國被稱為“禮儀之邦”，很多傳統禮儀在今天的日常生活中也依然隨處可見。中國人熱情好客，常常邀請親朋好友到家裡吃飯。如果瞭解一些做客的基本禮儀，能幫助你在赴家宴時舉止得當。

去中國人家做客要守時，衣著要整潔得體，帶些小禮品，以表示對主人的尊重。

客人要等主人邀請後才能入席落座。入座後，千萬不能急於動筷子，要等主人舉杯示意開始，客人才能用餐。

夾菜時一次不要夾得太多，也不能伸長胳膊去夾遠處的菜，還要記得一定要用公筷。千萬要避免玩弄筷子，或用筷子翻菜，或把筷子含在嘴裡這些不禮貌的行為。

如果餐桌上有一壺茶水在你的旁邊，你要記得常常為你周圍的客人斟茶。如果別人給你斟茶，你應該用手指輕輕敲擊桌面，以示感謝之意。

宴畢後不要滯留过久，告辭時要向主人道谢，也是應有的禮節。

32. According to the article, which of the following statements is true?
    (A) Chinese people love to receive gifts.
    (B) Guests should accept an invitation happily.
    (C) Traditional Chinese etiquette is no longer in practice.
    (D) Guests should arrive on time.

33. According to this article, when can a guest start to eat?
    (A) As soon as the guest arrives
    (B) After all the guests are seated
    (C) When the host signals to start
    (D) After the host sets the table

34. According to the article, which of the following is considered an appropriate use of chopsticks?
    (A) To get food for yourself
    (B) To stir food in the dishes
    (C) To play with after eating
    (D) To tap the table for attention

35. According to the article, how should tea be served?
    (A) Everyone helps himself or herself to tea.
    (B) The person who sits closest to the teapot will usually serve.
    (C) Underage people will not be served tea.
    (D) The host will serve tea to everyone.

36. According to the article, what should you do when someone serves you tea?
    (A) Say "Thank you!"
    (B) Nod your head politely
    (C) Tap the surface of the table lightly with your fingertips
    (D) Do not drink the tea until the person who served you sits down

SECTION II: FREE RESPONSE

PART A: WRITING

[30 minutes, 25% of final score]

Note: In this part of the exam, the student may NOT move back and forth among questions.

Directions: You will be asked to perform two writing tasks in Chinese. In each case, you will be asked to write for a specific purpose and to a specific person. You should write in as complete and as culturally appropriate a manner as possible, taking into account the purpose and the person described.

I. STORY NARRATION [15 minutes, 15% of final score]

The four pictures present a story. Imagine you are writing the story to a friend. Narrate a complete story as suggested by the pictures. Give your story a beginning, middle, and an end.

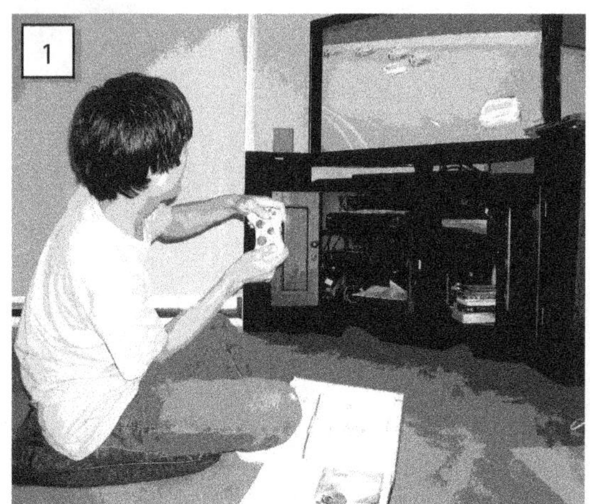

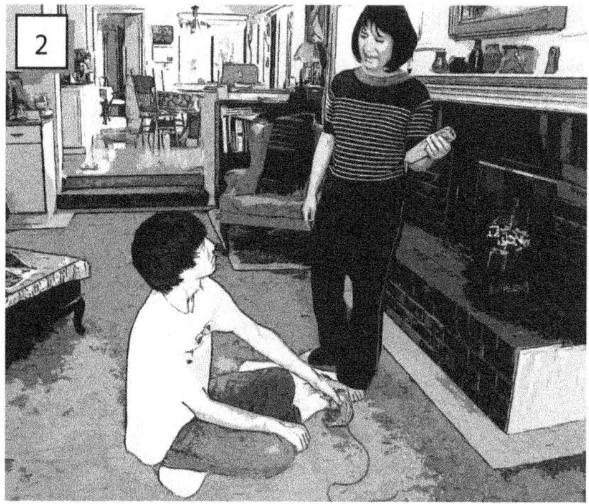

II. E-MAIL RESPONSE [15 minutes, 10% of total score]

Read this e-mail from a friend and then type your response.

(Simplified Characters)

发件人： 安妮 邮件主题：请帮我推荐一下旅游目的地
今年圣诞期间，我们全家打算出门旅游。可是每个人想去的地方都不一样，一家人为此争得面红耳赤的。我想，如果有一个地方大家都想去，事情就好办了。你常常到世界各地旅游，你能不能帮我推荐一两个适合在圣诞期间游玩的地方？再讲讲为什么这些地方值得去。我相信你的建议有助于说服大家。

(Traditional Characters)

發件人： 安妮 郵件主題： 幫我推薦一下旅遊目的地
今年聖誕期間，我們全家打算出門旅遊。可是每個人想去的地方都不一樣，一家人為此爭得面紅耳赤的。我想，如果有一個地方大家都想去，事情就好辦了。你常常到世界各地旅遊，你能不能幫我推薦一兩個適合在聖誕期間遊玩的地方？再講講為什麼這些地方值得去。我相信你的建議有助於說服大家。

PART B: SPEAKING [15 minutes, 25% of final score]

 [Listen to the audio track **Family - Speaking**.]

Note: In this part of the exam, the student may NOT move back and forth among questions.

I. CONVERSATION [4 minutes, 10% of final score]

Directions: You will participate in a simulated conversation. Each time it is your turn to speak, you will have 20 seconds to record. You should respond as fully and as appropriately as possible.

You are having a conversation with your mother about your summer plans.

Mom: [Audio]
[TONE]
[Student records the response] (20 seconds)

Mom: [Audio]
[TONE]
[Student records the response] (20 seconds)

Mom: [Audio]
[TONE]
[Student records the response] (20 seconds)

Mom: [Audio]
[TONE]
[Student records the response] (20 seconds)

Mom: [Audio]
[TONE]
[Student records the response] (20 seconds)

Mom: [Audio]
[TONE]
[Student records the response] (20 seconds)

II. Cultural Presentation [7 minutes, 15% of final score]

Directions: You will be asked to speak in Chinese on a specific topic. Imagine you are making an oral presentation to your Chinese class. First, you will read and hear the topic for your presentation. You will have 4 minutes to prepare your presentation. Then you will have 2 minutes to record your presentation. Your presentation should be as complete as possible.

Choose ONE aspect of Chinese family relationships (husband and wife, parents and children, etc.). In your presentation, describe the relationship and discuss traditional Chinese values embodied in this relationship.

[This marks the end of the audio track **Family - Speaking**.]

This page is intentionally left blank.

UNIT 7 GEOGRAPHY

SECTION I: MULTIPLE CHOICE

PART A: LISTENING [20 minutes, 25% of final score]

[Listen to the audio track **Geography - Listening**.]

Note: In this part of the exam, you may NOT move back and forth among questions.

I. REJOINDERS [10 minutes, 10% of final score]

Directions: You will hear several short conversations or parts of conversations followed by 4 choices, designated (A), (B), (C), and (D). Choose the one that continues or completes the conversation in a logical and culturally appropriate manner. You will have 5 seconds to answer each question.

QUESTION NUMBER	STUDENT CHOICE			
1	(A)	(B)	(C)	(D)
2	(A)	(B)	(C)	(D)
3	(A)	(B)	(C)	(D)
4	(A)	(B)	(C)	(D)
5	(A)	(B)	(C)	(D)
6	(A)	(B)	(C)	(D)
7	(A)	(B)	(C)	(D)
8	(A)	(B)	(C)	(D)
9	(A)	(B)	(C)	(D)
10	(A)	(B)	(C)	(D)
11	(A)	(B)	(C)	(D)
12	(A)	(B)	(C)	(D)
13	(A)	(B)	(C)	(D)
14	(A)	(B)	(C)	(D)
15	(A)	(B)	(C)	(D)

II. LISTENING SELECTIONS [10 minutes, 15% of final score]

Directions: You will listen to several selections in Chinese. For each selection, you will be told whether it will be played once or twice. You may take notes as you listen. Your notes will not be graded. After listening to each selection, you will see questions in English. For each question, choose the response that is best according to the selection. You will have 12 seconds to answer each question.

SELECTION 1

16. Where will most likely you hear this announcement?

    (A) On a plane

    (B) On a train

    (C) On a bus

    (D) On a ferry

17. What is the name of the next stop?

    (A) Shanghai

    (B) Beijing

    (C) Tianjin

    (D) Nanjing

18. What is mentioned in this announcement?

    (A) Table reservation is required.

    (B) Meals are included.

    (C) All seats are pre-assigned.

    (D) Free drinks are provided.

19. Which of following food items is offered?

    (A) Rice

    (B) Soup

    (C) Porridge

    (D) Noodles

SELECTION 2

20. Which type of business is most likely to air this commercial?
    (A) A resort booking service
    (B) An insurance company
    (C) A charter bus service
    (D) A travel agency

21. According to the woman, what is an attractive feature of the business?
    (A) Friendly tour guide
    (B) Door to door service
    (C) Free room upgrade
    (D) Competitive insurance rate

22. Which of the following is covered by the payment?
    (A) Show tickets
    (B) Meals
    (C) Gratuities
    (D) Room service

SELECTION 3

23. In this voice message, the speaker mentions
    (A) his flight destination
    (B) his dinner menu
    (C) his arrival time
    (D) his flight number

24. What does the speaker want his mother to do?
    (A) Wait for him for dinner
    (B) Make dinner for him
    (C) Have dinner without him
    (D) Wait for him at the airport

25. What does the speaker ask his father to do?
    (A) Wait for him at the airport
    (B) Pick him up as soon as possible
    (C) Check the flight arrival time before going to the airport
    (D) Wait for him for dinner

26. What does the speaker apologize for?
    (A) Having eaten dinner at the airport already
    (B) Missing the flight
    (C) Not being able to have dinner with his parents
    (D) Not remembering his flight number

SELECTION 4

27. The man asks the woman
    (A) when she will buy the plane ticket
    (B) which day she will come home
    (C) how she is getting to the airport
    (D) where she is going for vacation

28. The woman plans to
    (A) take a train to go home
    (B) go home on Friday
    (C) buy a plane ticket to go home
    (D) take the subway to the airport

29. What does the man offer to the woman?
    (A) To lend his car to her
    (B) To take the train with her to the airport
    (C) To drive her to the airport
    (D) To buy the airline ticket for her

SELECTION 5

30. In which city is the hotel located?
    (A) San Francisco
    (B) San Jose
    (C) Santa Monica
    (D) San Bruno

31. When and where does the Christmas tree lighting event take place?
    (A) December 5 in the hotel lobby
    (B) December 5 in the hotel parking lot
    (C) December 7 on the hotel front lawn
    (D) December 7 in the hotel grand ballroom

32. Which of the following is offered during the event?
    (A) Raffle tickets
    (B) A live concert
    (C) Flower bouquets
    (D) A free gift

[This marks the end of the audio track **Geography - Listening**.]

PART B: READING

[60 minutes, 25% of final score]

Note: In this part of the exam, you may move back and forth among all the questions.

Directions: You will read several selections in Chinese. Each selection is accompanied by a number of questions in English. For each question, choose the response that is best according to the selection.

Read this poster

(Simplified Characters)	(Traditional Characters)
北京、上海、杭州七日美食团	**北京、上海、杭州七日美食團**
$1,499 起， 两人成团	$1,499 起，兩人成團
各地美食	各地美食
北京—仿膳、北京烤鸭 上海—大闸蟹、八宝鸭 杭州—西湖醋魚、东坡肉	北京—仿膳、北京烤鴨 上海—大閘蟹、八寶鴨 杭州—西湖醋魚、東坡肉
各地景点	各地景點
北京—长城、故宫 上海—外滩、东方明珠 杭州—西湖、灵隐寺	北京—長城、故宮 上海—外灘、東方明珠 杭州—西湖、靈隱寺
平安旅行社：1-800-123-4567	平安旅行社：1-800-123-4567

1. What is the theme of this advertised tour?
   (A) Shopping
   (B) Asian cities
   (C) Gourmet food
   (D) Architecture

2. What is the minimum number of people required to form a tour group?
   (A) Two
   (B) Three
   (C) Seven
   (D) Eight

3. Which of the following places is included in the tour?
   (A) Ming Tombs
   (B) Temple of Heaven
   (C) Forbidden City
   (D) Summer Palace

Read this note

(Simplified Characters)	(Traditional Characters)
迈克， 刚刚接到你妈妈从中国打来的电话。今天下午两点多在四川发生了八级大地震，连北京和上海都感觉到了，灾情严重。 她要我转告你，因为成都离震中汶川比较远，尽管你家房子的外墙有些裂纹，但家里人并没有受伤，叫你不用担心。 我马上要去实验室工作，大概很晚才回来。你看了这便条后赶紧给家里打电话吧！ 大卫	邁克， 剛剛接到你媽媽從中國打來的電話。今天下午兩點多在四川發生了八級大地震，連北京和上海都感覺到了，災情嚴重。 她要我轉告你，因為成都離震中汶川比較遠，儘管你家房子的外牆有些裂紋，但家裡人並沒有受傷，叫你不用擔心。 我馬上要去實驗室工作，大概很晚才回來。你看了這便條後趕緊給家裡打電話吧！ 大衛

4. Why does David leave the note for Mike?
   (A) To relay a telephone message
   (B) To tell Mike that he is going to the library
   (C) To urge Mike to watch the news
   (D) To tell Mike that he is not coming home tonight

5. Where was the epicenter of the earthquake?
   (A) Chengdu
   (B) Wenchuan
   (C) Beijing
   (D) Shanghai

6. The earthquake measured
   (A) 2.0 on the Richter scale
   (B) 4.0 on the Richter scale
   (C) 6.0 on the Richter scale
   (D) 8.0 on the Richter scale

Read this public sign

(Simplified Characters)	(Traditional Characters)
请带走您的照片，别带走任何植物。 请留下您的足迹，别留下任何垃圾。	請帶走您的照片，別帶走任何植物。 請留下您的足跡，別留下任何垃圾。

7. Where would you most likely find this public sign?
   (A) At a photography studio
   (B) At a botanical garden
   (C) At a beach
   (D) At a garbage dump

8. Which of the following statements about the sign is true?
   (A) It says, “Off limits, this is a dump site.”
   (B) It says, “Don’t take pictures of exotic plants.”
   (C) It says, “Don’t step on the newly planted lawn.”
   (D) It says, “Don’t litter or take any plants.”

Read this e-mail

(Simplified Characters)	(Traditional Characters)
发件人：周云云 收件人：周志诚 邮件主题：云南照片	發件人：周雲雲 收件人：周志誠 郵件主題：雲南照片
亲爱的爷爷， 您好！ 今天是我到达云南的第三天。附上两张数码照片。一张是我戴着彝族的银头饰、穿着色彩缤纷的彝族服装照的。您看，我像不像一个彝族姑娘？另外一张照片是在昆明的石林拍摄的。置身在一座座拔地而起的奇峰怪石中，我好像进入了迷宫。 这次旅游，我是与四位大学同学一道来的。我们是自助游，没有参加旅游团。我们都会说汉语，而且这里的交通也很方便，请不用担心。我们后天晚上离开云南，乘飞机回美国。回家后再发电邮和照片给您。 云云	親愛的爺爺， 您好！ 今天是我到達雲南的第三天。附上兩張數碼照片。一張是我戴著彝族的銀頭飾、穿著色彩繽紛的彝族服裝照的。您看，我像不像一個彝族姑娘？另外一張照片是在昆明的石林拍攝的。置身在一座座拔地而起的奇峰怪石中，我好像進入了迷宮。 這次旅遊，我是與四位大學同學一道來的。我們是自助遊，沒有參加旅遊團。我們都會說漢語，而且這裡的交通也很方便，請不用擔心。我們後天晚上離開雲南，乘飛機回美國。回家後再發電郵和照片給您。 雲雲

9. What is the relationship between the e-mail sender and the recipient?
   (A) Friends
   (B) Classmates
   (C) Relatives
   (D) Coworkers

10. What is special about the costume?
    (A) The headpiece and the clothing are made of silk.
    (B) The headpiece and the clothing are very colorful.
    (C) The headpiece is made of silver and the clothing is made of silk.
    (D) The headpiece is made of silver and the clothing is colorful.

11. How many people are traveling together in this group?
    (A) Two
    (B) Three
    (C) Four
    (D) Five

12. How many days is the e-mail sender staying in Yunnan?
    (A) Three days
    (B) Four days
    (C) Five days
    (D) Six days

Read this story

(Simplified Characters)	(Traditional Characters)
钟先生曾经是一家贸易公司的经理，因工作需要，常常出差。按照公司的规定，飞行时间超过六小时就可以坐商务舱。有一次，他要去香港开会，因为从纽约直飞香港要十六个小时，所以钟先生准备在飞机上好好睡一觉，到达目的地后马上就去开会。 这一天，钟先生的秘书休病假，他只好请新来的办公室助理彼得帮他订票："请帮我订一张星期二下午去香港、星期五下午回纽约的来回机票和两晚旅馆。" 三个小时后，彼得很高兴地对钟先生说："我已经帮你在网上订了机票。今天运气真好，我找到一家航空公司，他们经济舱的票比别家便宜五十元，只要转两次航班。我还帮你订了三晚的青年旅社的床位。你知道星期二到星期五是三个晚上而不是两个晚上吗？" 钟先生听了哭笑不得地对彼得说："你难道不知道当我到达香港的时候已经是星期三了吗？"	鍾先生曾經是一家貿易公司的經理，因工作需要，常常出差。按照公司的規定，飛行時間超過六小時就可以坐商務艙。有一次，他要去香港開會，因為從紐約直飛香港要十六個小時，所以鍾先生準備在飛機上好好睡一覺，到達目的地後馬上就去開會。 這一天，鍾先生的秘書休病假，他只好請新來的辦公室助理彼得幫他訂票："請幫我訂一張星期二下午去香港、星期五下午回紐約的來回機票和兩晚旅館。" 三個小時後，彼得很高興地對鍾先生說："我已經幫你在網上訂了機票。今天運氣真好，我找到一家航空公司，他們經濟艙的票比別家便宜五十元，只要轉兩次航班。我還幫你訂了三晚的青年旅社的床位。 你知道星期二到星期五是三個晚上而不是兩個晚上嗎？" 鍾先生聽了哭笑不得地對彼得說："你難道不知道當我到達香港的時候已經是星期三了嗎？"

13. What type of company does Mr. Zhong work for?
    (A) A trading company
    (B) A travel agency
    (C) A hotel
    (D) An airline

14. What does Mr. Zhong plan to do immediately upon arrival at his destination?
    (A) Go to sleep
    (B) Attend a meeting
    (C) Join a city tour
    (D) Check-in to the hotel

15. On which day does Mr. Zhong plan to depart for Hong Kong?
    (A) Tuesday
    (B) Wednesday
    (C) Thursday
    (D) Friday

16. Who made the travel arrangements for Mr. Zhong?
    (A) Mr. Zhong himself
    (B) Mr. Zhong's secretary
    (C) The office manager
    (D) The office assistant

17. How did Mr. Zhong feel about the travel arrangements?
    (A) He was happy because he saved money on the airfare.
    (B) He was happy because he could spend an extra day in Hong Kong.
    (C) He was not pleased because he expected a direct flight.
    (D) He was not pleased because the assistant booked the ticket online.

Read this brochure

(Simplified Characters)	(Traditional Characters)
杭州湖畔国际大饭店 新开张大酬宾 杭州湖畔国际大饭店是由北京鸿湖集团投资兴建的国家四星级旅游饭店，它座落在中外闻名的西湖岸边。凭窗远望，西湖美景尽入眼帘，美不胜收。 杭州湖畔国际大饭店的设施齐全，设有标准房及豪华套房，每套房内均有互联网接头。有川粤餐厅，商务中心，礼品店，并提供旅游咨询和预订。服务周到，保证您百分之百的满意。 新开张期间，所有客房打五折酬宾，预订从速！ 地址：杭州西湖路 123 号 电话：0571-12345678	**杭州湖畔國際大飯店 新開張大酬賓** 杭州湖畔國際大飯店是由北京鴻湖集團投資興建的國家四星級旅遊飯店，它座落在中外聞名的西湖岸邊。憑窗遠望，西湖美景盡入眼簾，美不勝收。 杭州湖畔國際大飯店的設施齊全，設有標準房及豪華套房，每套房內均有互聯網接頭。有川粵餐廳，商務中心，禮品店，並提供旅遊諮詢和預訂。服務周到，保證您百分之百的滿意。 新開張期間，所有客房打五折酬賓，預訂從速！ 地址：杭州西湖路 123 號 電話：0571-12345678

18. The hotel is having a promotion for
    (A) a grand opening
    (B) an anniversary celebration
    (C) a re-opening after remodeling
    (D) the holiday season

19. Where is the hotel located?
    (A) Near the golf course
    (B) Near the airport
    (C) By the lake
    (D) By the beach

20. What amenity is mentioned in the brochure?
    (A) Complimentary breakfast
    (B) Business center
    (C) Fitness center
    (D) Day spa

21. What type of cuisine is served in the hotel?
    (A) Sichuan
    (B) Beijing
    (C) Shanghai
    (D) Hunan

Read these instructions

(Simplified Characters)	(Traditional Characters)
美国护照更新指南	**美國護照更新指南**
▪ **身份证明**	▪ **身份證明**
申请者必需呈递现有美国护照正本（原件）。如果申请者的姓名有别于现有美国护照正本，申请者必需提交结婚证明书或法庭颁发的更改姓名证明书。	申請者必需呈遞現有美國護照正本（原件）。如果申請者的姓名有別於現有美國護照正本，申請者必需提交結婚證明書或法庭頒發的更改姓名證明書。
▪ **照片**	▪ **照片**
两张半身无冠正面彩色近照（2x2英寸），照片必须于最近6个月内拍摄。	兩張半身無冠正面彩色近照（2x2英吋），照片必須於最近6個月內拍攝。
▪ **收费方式**	▪ **收費方式**
接受私人支票，银行支票或邮政局汇票。不接受现金或信用卡。	接受私人支票，銀行支票或郵政局匯票。不接受現金或信用卡。

22. What are the instructions about?
    (A) How to apply for a U.S. passport
    (B) How to replace a U.S. passport
    (C) How to extend a U.S. passport
    (D) How to renew a U.S. passport

23. Which of the following documents is mentioned?
    (A) Copy of the passport
    (B) Drivers license
    (C) Original birth certificate
    (D) Certificate of name change

24. The passport photographs must be taken within
    (A) four weeks
    (B) six weeks
    (C) twenty-six weeks
    (D) fifty-two weeks

25. According to the instructions, which method of payment is acceptable?
    (A) Personal check
    (B) Cash
    (C) Credit card
    (D) Debit card

Read this passage

(Simplified Characters)	(Traditional Characters)
“桂林山水甲天下” 是世人对这座风景名城的赞誉。桂林的山，拔地而起，千姿百态；桂林的水，清澈明丽，婀娜多姿。 据地质学家考证，3.7 亿年前，桂林是一片汪洋大海，后来由于地壳隆起，海水消退，自然风化，慢慢地形成了许多石峰。 桂林气候温热，水源丰富，河流众多。秀丽的漓江更是名闻遐迩，她围绕着奇峰异石，缓缓地流动，河流表面上看起来平静得没有一丝波纹。群峰倒映在镜子一般的水面上，令人过目难忘。 本书通过精美的照片和独特的介绍，让读者们仿佛身临其境地欣赏山清水秀的桂林，感受大自然的鬼斧神工。	“桂林山水甲天下” 是世人對這座風景名城的讚譽。桂林的山，拔地而起，千姿百態；桂林的水，清澈明麗，婀娜多姿。 據地質學家考證，3.7 億年前，桂林是一片汪洋大海， 後來由於地殼隆起，海水消退，自然風化，慢慢地形成了許多石峰。 桂林氣候溫熱，水源豐富，河流眾多。秀麗的漓江更是名聞遐邇，她圍繞著奇峰異石，緩緩地流動，河流表面上看起來平靜得沒有一絲波紋。群峰倒映在鏡子一般的水面上，令人過目難忘。 本書通過精美的照片和獨特的介紹，讓讀者們彷彿身臨其境地欣賞山清水秀的桂林，感受大自然的鬼斧神工。

26. According to the passage, Guilin is known for
    (A) its beautiful scenery
    (B) its long history
    (C) its tall mountains
    (D) its natural caverns

27. According to the passage, Li River is special because
    (A) it is featured on the twenty *yuan* banknote
    (B) it is one of the eight famous sights in Guilin
    (C) its bank are covered with lush bamboo
    (D) its surface appears as smooth as mirror

28. According to the geologist, what was Guilin like about 370 million years ago?
    (A) A vast ocean
    (B) A rocky mountain
    (C) A subtropical forest
    (D) An ancient city

29. The author is trying to promote
    (A) Guilin tourism
    (B) nature preservation
    (C) an illustrated book
    (D) Li River paintings

Read this article

(Simplified Characters)	(Traditional Characters)
郑和下西洋	**鄭和下西洋**
郑和是中国伟大的航海家。他七次下西洋，从 1405 年到 1433 年，前前后后历时 28 年。郑和带领的船队有两百多艘船及两万多人。他的船队从中国苏州出发，最远曾到达非洲，航行 10 万多里，共访问了 30 多个国家。郑和的远航时间之长，规模之大，航线之远是中国航海历史上的创举。	鄭和是中國偉大的航海家。他七次下西洋，從 1405 年到 1433 年，前前後後歷時 28 年。鄭和帶領的船隊有兩百多艘船及兩萬多人。他的船隊從中國蘇州出發，最遠曾到達非洲，航行 10 萬多里，共訪問了 30 多個國家。鄭和的遠航時間之長，規模之大，航線之遠是中國航海歷史上的創舉。
郑和也是明朝的外交和贸易代表， 他把丝绸、瓷器、茶叶等礼品赠送给沿途各国的元首，不但表达了中国人民的友好情谊、传播了中国的灿烂文化，而且籍此为中国开拓了新的贸易市场。同时，郑和还把各国的特产和珍奇动物带回中国，例如：胡椒、象牙、长颈鹿、狮子等等。郑和远航促进了中国与各国之间的贸易交往和文化交流。	鄭和也是明朝的外交和貿易代表，他把絲綢、瓷器、茶葉等禮品贈送給沿途各國的元首，不但表達了中國人民的友好情誼、傳播了中國的燦爛文化，而且籍此為中國開拓了新的貿易市場。同時，鄭和還把各國的特產和珍奇動物帶回中國，例如：胡椒、象牙、長頸鹿、獅子等等。鄭和遠航促進了中國與各國之間的貿易交往和文化交流。
在第七次航程中，郑和因劳累过度，不幸在船上去世，船队由副舵手率领返航。郑和的过世和当时明朝财政困难，给下西洋的远征画上了句号。	在第七次航程中，鄭和因勞累過度，不幸在船上去世，船隊由副舵手率領返航。鄭和的過世和當時明朝財政困難，給下西洋的遠征畫上了句號。

30. Zheng He was a great
    (A) navigator
    (B) politician
    (C) historian
    (D) geographer

31. According to the article, what was the furthest place Zheng He visited on his expeditions?
    (A) Asia
    (B) Europe
    (C) Africa
    (D) Australia

32. According to the article, why did Zheng He bring silk, porcelain, and tea to the countries he visited?
    (A) To sell for profit
    (B) To exchange for favors
    (C) To show off his wealth
    (D) To offer friendship

33. What did Zheng He bring back to China?
    (A) Eagles
    (B) Tigers
    (C) Elephants
    (D) Giraffes

34. What happened to Zheng He on his seventh voyage?
    (A) Zheng He stayed in an overseas country.
    (B) Zheng He passed away during the journey.
    (C) Zheng He experienced financial difficulties.
    (D) Zhang He cut the voyage short.

Read this advertisement

(Simplified Characters)	(Traditional Characters)
留学中国医疗保险 适合前往中国学习的学生，保费每月五十美元起。电话：800-123-4567	**留學中國醫療保險** 適合前往中國學習的學生，保費每月五十美元起。電話：800-123-4567

35. What is this advertisement for?
    (A) Travel insurance
    (B) A Chinese language class
    (C) Medical insurance
    (D) A tutoring class

36. Who are the potential customers?
    (A) Chinese students who will study in the United States
    (B) Chinese workers who will work in the United States
    (C) Foreign students who will study in China
    (D) Foreign workers who will work in China

37. Where would you most likely see this advertisement?
    (A) In a college newspaper
    (B) In a local newspaper
    (C) In a trade journal
    (D) In an entertainment magazine

SECTION II: FREE RESPONSE

PART A: WRITING [30 minutes, 25% of final score]

Note: In this part of the exam, you may NOT move back and forth among questions.

Directions: You will be asked to perform two writing tasks in Chinese. In each case, you will be asked to write for a specific purpose and to a specific person. You should write in as complete and as culturally appropriate a manner as possible, taking into account the purpose and the person described.

I. Story Narration [15 minutes, 15% of final score]

The four pictures present a story. Imagine you are writing the story to a friend. Narrate a complete story as suggested by the pictures. Give your story a beginning, middle, and an end.

II. E-MAIL RESPONSE [15 minutes, 10% of total score]

Read this e-mail from a friend and then type your response.

(Simplified Characters)

发件人：大卫

邮件主题：推荐中国城市

老师给我们布置了一个有关中国地理的小组作业。我们可以任选一个中国的城市，详细介绍它的地理位置、人口、历史背景等等。我们小组五个人意見不一，决定不了到底选哪个城市。我们知道你常常去中国旅游，请你给我们推荐两个风格不同的城市作为参考。同时，请告诉我你推荐这两个城市的理由。

(Traditional Characters)

發件人：大衛

郵件主題：推薦中國城市

老師給我們佈置了一個有關中國地理的小組作業。我們可以任選一個中國的城市，詳細介紹它的地理位置、人口、歷史背景等等。我們小組五個人意見不一，決定不了到底選哪個城市。我們知道你常常去中國旅遊，請你給我們推薦兩個風格不同的城市作為參考。同時，請告訴我你推薦這兩個城市的理由。

PART B: SPEAKING [15 minutes, 25% of final score]

 [Listen to the audio track **Geography - Speaking**.]

Note: In this part of the exam, you may NOT move back and forth among questions.

I. CONVERSATION [4 minutes, 10% of final score]

Directions: You will participate in a simulated conversation. Each time it is your turn to speak, you will have 20 seconds to record. You should respond as fully and as appropriately as possible.

Your friend David plans to visit China with a tour group this summer. He wants to get some information from you about China and its cities.

David: [Audio]
[TONE]
[Student records the response] (20 seconds)

David: [Audio]
[TONE]
[Student records the response] (20 seconds)

David: [Audio]
[TONE]
[Student records the response] (20 seconds)

David: [Audio]
[TONE]
[Student records the response] (20 seconds)

David: [Audio]
[TONE]
[Student records the response] (20 seconds)

David: [Audio]
[TONE]
[Student records the response] (20 seconds)

II. CULTURAL PRESENTATION [7 minutes, 15% of final score]

Directions: You will be asked to speak in Chinese on a specific topic. Imagine you are making an oral presentation to your Chinese class. First, you will read and hear the topic for your presentation. You will have 4 minutes to prepare your presentation. Then you will have 2 minutes to record your presentation. Your presentation should be as complete as possible.

Choose ONE of the Chinese dynasties (e.g., Qin Dynasty, Tang Dynasty, Qing Dynasty, etc). In your presentation, state the key facts about this dynasty and explain its significance in Chinese history.

[This marks the end of the audio track **Geography - Speaking**.]

UNIT 8 MIXED THEME

SECTION I: MULTIPLE CHOICE

PART A: LISTENING [20 minutes, 25% of final score]

[Listen to the audio track **Mixed Theme - Listening**.]

Note: In this part of the exam, you may NOT move back and forth among questions.

I. REJOINDERS [10 minutes, 10% of final score]

Directions: You will hear several short conversations or parts of conversations followed by 4 choices, designated (A), (B), (C), and (D). Choose the one that continues or completes the conversation in a logical and culturally appropriate manner. You will have 5 seconds to answer each question.

QUESTION NUMBER	STUDENT CHOICE			
1	(A)	(B)	(C)	(D)
2	(A)	(B)	(C)	(D)
3	(A)	(B)	(C)	(D)
4	(A)	(B)	(C)	(D)
5	(A)	(B)	(C)	(D)
6	(A)	(B)	(C)	(D)
7	(A)	(B)	(C)	(D)
8	(A)	(B)	(C)	(D)
9	(A)	(B)	(C)	(D)
10	(A)	(B)	(C)	(D)
11	(A)	(B)	(C)	(D)
12	(A)	(B)	(C)	(D)
13	(A)	(B)	(C)	(D)
14	(A)	(B)	(C)	(D)
15	(A)	(B)	(C)	(D)

II. Listening Selections [10 minutes, 15% of final score]

Directions: You will listen to several selections in Chinese. For each selection, you will be told whether it will be played once or twice. You may take notes as you listen. Your notes will not be graded. After listening to each selection, you will see questions in English. For each question, choose the response that is best according to the selection. You will have 12 seconds to answer each question.

SELECTION 1

16. Why is the woman looking for the man?
    (A) She is a foreign student who needs a physical examination.
    (B) She is ill and needs immediate medical attention.
    (C) She has just arrived in the United States and needs a physical examination.
    (D) She is a new student who needs to take an assessment test.

17. What does the man ask the woman to do?
    (A) Register as a new foreign student
    (B) Fill out a form and then take a blood test
    (C) Have a physical examination in the United States
    (D) Take an entrance examination for foreign students

18. Which of the following statements is true?
    (A) The woman has had a blood test.
    (B) The woman has never had a physical examination.
    (C) The woman is looking for a medical doctor.
    (D) The woman had a physical examination last month.

SELECTION 2

19. The man is in a big hurry
    (A) to see his grandmother
    (B) to visit a sick patient
    (C) to get back to work
    (D) to purchase a gift

20. According to the conversation, the man uses ginseng
    (A) as a diet supplement
    (B) as a birthday present
    (C) for his herbology research
    (D) for a special recipe

21. How old is the relative mentioned in the conversation?
    (A) In her seventies
    (B) In her eighties
    (C) In her nineties
    (D) Over one hundred

SELECTION 3

22. What type of business is the commercial for?
    (A) An accounting firm
    (B) A public relations agency
    (C) An international law firm
    (D) A translation services company

23. Which of the following services is provided by this company?
    (A) Public notary service
    (B) Medical insurance filing
    (C) Unemployment training
    (D) Over-the-phone interpretation

24. The company's clients include
    (A) medical doctors
    (B) insurance companies
    (C) foreign embassies
    (D) international banks

SELECTION 4

25. What are these two friends talking about?
    (A) Going to a concert
    (B) Going to a dance
    (C) Going to a movie
    (D) Going to a game

26. Why does not the man want to go with the woman?
    (A) He would rather study.
    (B) He cannot stand the loud music.
    (C) He has made other plans for the night.
    (D) He has asked Xiao Zhang to a movie.

27. According to the dialogue, what does the woman think of the event?
    (A) Dancing is enjoyable.
    (B) Watching movies helps her to relax.
    (C) The event brings friends together.
    (D) The music is the best part of the event.

SELECTION 5

28. What did the girl ask her father to do?
    (A) Give a presentation for her class
    (B) Help her with course selection
    (C) Volunteer at a school event
    (D) Help her with homework

29. Why did the girl ask her father for help?
    (A) Because the teacher specifically requested it
    (B) Because her mother was not at home
    (C) Because he is the one she usually asks
    (D) Because she values his opinion

30. What was her father's response?
    (A) He requested more detailed information.
    (B) He promised to be a better father in the future.
    (C) He asked her mother to take care of the matter.
    (D) He agreed to help as much as he could.

SELECTION 6

31. These are instructions for applying for
    (A) American citizenship
    (B) Chinese passport
    (C) a driver's license
    (D) a travel visa

32. According to the announcement, applicants must bring
    (A) a valid passport
    (B) a birth certificate
    (C) a driver's license
    (D) a personal check

33. This procedure is only applicable to
    (A) legal aliens
    (B) all nationalities
    (C) American citizens
    (D) Chinese nationals

34. What is the normal application processing time?
    (A) One working day
    (B) Four working days
    (C) One week
    (D) Four weeks

[This marks the end of the audio track **Mixed Theme - Listening**.]

PART B: READING

[60 minutes, 25% of final score]

Note: In this part of the exam, you may move back and forth among all the questions.

Directions: You will read several selections in Chinese. Each selection is accompanied by a number of questions in English. For each question, choose the response that is best according to the selection.

Read this sign

(Simplified Characters)	(Traditional Characters)
请把相关证件准备好，在此排队等候安全检查。	請把相關證件準備好，在此排隊等候安全檢查。

1. What is the purpose of this sign?
   (A) To direct passengers to the customs inspection
   (B) To direct passengers to find their connecting flights
   (C) To direct passengers to the security inspection
   (D) To direct passengers to pick up their luggage

2. The sign asks passengers to have their
   (A) check-in luggage ready
   (B) relevant documents ready
   (C) boarding pass ready
   (D) custom form ready

Read this sign

(Simplified Characters)	(Traditional Characters)
四川餐馆	**四川餐館**
冬季营业时间 （十月至二月） 周一至周五：上午十点至晚上九点 周六：上午十点至晚上十一点 周日：休息	冬季營業時間（十月至二月） 週一至週五：上午十點至晚上九點 週六：上午十點至晚上十一點 週日：休息
夏季营业时间（三月至九月） 周一至周五：上午九点至晚上十点 周六：上午九点至晚上十二点 周日：中午十二点至晚上十点	夏季營業時間（三月至九月） 週一至週五：上午九點至晚上十點 週六：上午九點至晚上十二點 週日：中午十二點至晚上十點
以下节假日休息： 感恩节，圣诞节	以下節假日休息： 感恩節，聖誕節

3. During the winter season, what time does the place open on Wednesdays?
   (A) 9 a.m.
   (B) 10 a.m.
   (C) 11 a.m.
   (D) 5 p.m.

4. On which days is this place open the longest?
   (A) Sundays during the summer season
   (B) Sundays during the winter season
   (C) Saturdays during the summer season
   (D) Saturdays during the winter season

5. On which of the following days is this place open?
   (A) Thanksgiving Day
   (B) Christmas Day
   (C) Sunday, January 7
   (D) Sunday, July 4

Read this journal

(Simplified Characters)	(Traditional Characters)
日期：五月十三日 星期五 天气：雨 明天是情人节，爸爸带我去商店给妈妈挑礼物。 我问爸爸："你想买什么样的礼物给妈妈?" 爸爸说："茜茜，这就是为什么我要你一起来的原因。说真的，买一件有意义又让你妈喜欢的礼物真不容易。" 我建议说："妈妈最喜欢花，就买束鲜花给妈妈嘛！" 爸爸说："就是知道她爱花，所以年年情人节，我都送给她一打红玫瑰。你妈嘴上说好喜欢，可我看得出，她看着美丽的玫瑰花没几天就凋谢了，特别心疼！所以，今年我想换个花样。你帮我出出主意。" 我想了想，拽着爸爸，走进了妈妈最喜欢去的花圃园艺商店，给妈妈买了一盆盛开的兰花。	日期：五月十三日 星期五 天氣：雨 明天是情人節，爸爸帶我去商店給媽媽挑禮物。 我問爸爸："你想買什麼樣的禮物給媽媽?" 爸爸說："茜茜，這就是為什麼我要你一起來的原因。說真的，買一件有意義又讓你媽喜歡的禮物真不容易。" 我建議說："媽媽最喜歡花，就買束鮮花給媽媽嘛！" 爸爸說："就是知道她愛花，所以年年情人節，我都送給她一打紅玫瑰。你媽嘴上說好喜歡，可我看得出，她看著美麗的玫瑰花沒幾天就凋謝了，特別心疼！所以，今年我想換個花樣。你幫我出出主意。" 我想了想，拽著爸爸，走進了媽媽最喜歡去的花圃園藝商店，給媽媽買了一盆盛開的蘭花。

6. The special occasion mentioned in the passage is
   (A) Mother's Day
   (B) an anniversary
   (C) Valentine's Day
   (D) a birthday

7. According to the passage, what did the author's father buy for her mother last year?
   (A) A bouquet of carnations
   (B) A dozen roses
   (C) A piece of jewelry
   (D) A gift card

8. What did the author's father buy for her mother this year?
   (A) A bouquet of flowers
   (B) A box of chocolates
   (C) A piece of jewelry
   (D) A pot of orchids

Read this flyer

(Simplified Characters)	(Traditional Characters)
"边摇边滚"元宵晚会	**"邊搖邊滾"元宵晚會**
二月十二日晚上六点，一年一度的元宵晚会将在星光学院学生餐厅举行。周边城市的市长们也将参加我们传统的元宵节活动。	二月十二日晚上六點，一年一度的元宵晚會將在星光學院學生餐廳舉行。周邊城市的市長們也將參加我們傳統的元宵節活動。
今年元宵节的庆祝活动将与往年有所不同。我们将在现场"边摇边滚"做元宵。餐厅将提供滚元宵的工具、糯米粉和馅。	今年元宵節的慶祝活動將與往年有所不同。我們將在現場"邊搖邊滾"做元宵。餐廳將提供滾元宵的工具、糯米粉和餡。
参加者将围着餐桌，一起动手滚元宵，自产自消，多摇多吃，少摇少吃。餐厅的师傅们负责煮元宵。欢迎大家踊跃参加。	參加者將圍著餐桌，一起動手滾元宵，自產自消，多搖多吃，少搖少吃。餐廳的師傅們負責煮元宵。歡迎大家踴躍參加。
门票：每人3元 售票处：星光学院学生餐厅	門票：每人3元 售票處：星光學院學生餐廳

9. The event is to celebrate
   (A) Lantern Festival
   (B) Duanwu Festival
   (C) Mid-Autumn Festival
   (D) Chong Yang Festival

10. According to the flyer, where will the event be held?
   (A) In a theater
   (B) In a dining hall
   (C) In a ballroom
   (D) In an assembly hall

11. According to the flyer, what is new about this year's event?
   (A) The event will present a group of famous chefs.
   (B) A rock band will perform at the event.
   (C) The participants will make the food for themselves.
   (D) Mayors of nearby cities will join the event for the first time.

12. According to the flyer, which of the following statements is true?
   (A) Mayors are invited to the parade every year.
   (B) Dancing with chefs after dinner is a tradition.
   (C) Lanterns are lit up like stars in the dining hall.
   (D) Cooking materials are provided at the event.

Read this passage

(Simplified Characters)	(Traditional Characters)
有志者，事竟成 大卫在大学计算机系毕业后，顺利地进入了美国的一家跨国公司工作。五年后，晋升为软件开发部经理。不过，他很快发现不少在这家公司工作几十年的老职员，跟不上新技术的发展速度，干起管理工作来很吃力。再看看每年新招进来的年轻人，学习和运用新知识的能力一个个又都比他强。于是，他开始考虑转行，当一名越老越值钱的会计师。 他重返学校，经过两年的苦读，获得了商学院硕士学位。毕业后，又到华尔街实习了两年，加上他在以前的工作中积累了不少经验，所以很快就被一家公司聘为会计师，不久，他又顺利地通过了注册会计师的考试。现在，他自己开办了一家规模不小的会计事务所。 真是有志者，事竟成！	**有志者，事竟成** 大衛在大學計算機系畢業後，順利地進入了美國的一家跨國公司工作。五年後，晉升為軟件開發部經理。不過，他很快發現不少在這家公司工作幾十年的老職員，跟不上新技術的發展速度，幹起管理工作來很吃力。再看看每年新招進來的年輕人，學習和運用新知識的能力一個個又都比他強。於是，他開始考慮轉行，當一名越老越值錢的會計師。 他重返學校，經過兩年的苦讀，獲得了商學院碩士學位。畢業後，又到華爾街實習了兩年，加上他在以前的工作中積累了不少經驗，所以很快就被一家公司聘為會計師，不久，他又順利地通過了註冊會計師的考試。現在，他自己開辦了一家規模不小的會計事務所。 真是有志者，事竟成！

13. According to the article, what is the moral of the story?
    (A) Where there is a will, there is a way.
    (B) Some people are able to do the impossible.
    (C) Nothing is impossible with the right timing.
    (D) Only those who have ambitions will succeed.

14. According to the article, why did David change his career?
    (A) Because he did not make enough money at his previous job
    (B) Because he did not want to be a manager in his previous company
    (C) Because he did not have a sense of job security in his previous profession
    (D) Because he did not have the computer skills to stay at his previous job

15. According to the article, David earned his master's degree in
    (A) computer science
    (B) public administration
    (C) international relations
    (D) business administration

16. According to the article, what is David's current occupation?
    (A) Business owner
    (B) Accountant
    (C) Manager
    (D) Student

Read this passage

(Simplified Characters)	(Traditional Characters)
喝乌龙，摆乌龙	**喝烏龍，擺烏龍**
乌，是黑色的意思，乌龙就是黑色的龙。乌龙还是一种茶的名字呢。	烏，是黑色的意思，烏龍就是黑色的龍。烏龍還是一種茶的名字呢。
据说很早以前，有个叫乌龙的人发明了一种制作茶叶的办法，这种茶叶看上去是“绿叶红镶边”，喝起来既有红茶的浓郁，又有绿茶的清香。为了纪念他，人们称这茶中极品为“乌龙茶”。	據說很早以前，有個叫烏龍的人發明了一種製作茶葉的辦法，這種茶葉看上去是“綠葉紅鑲邊”，喝起來既有紅茶的濃郁，又有綠茶的清香。為了紀念他，人們稱這茶中極品為“烏龍茶”。
另外还有个传说，很久以前，由于连年干旱，人们跪在地上祈求龙王降雨，可是雨没有求到，倒呼出了一条大黑龙，这条乌龙给百姓带来了更多的灾难。	另外還有個傳說，很久以前，由於連年乾旱，人們跪在地上祈求龍王降雨，可是雨沒有求到，倒呼出了一條大黑龍，這條烏龍給百姓帶來了更多的災難。
从此，人们就把好心做事，却得到了事与愿违的结果叫“摆乌龙”，后来又引申出做事颠三倒四的意思。	從此，人們就把好心做事，卻得到了事與願違的結果叫“擺烏龍”，後來又引伸出做事顛三倒四的意思。

17. According to the passage, which of the following statements is true about *wulong* tea?
    (A) It looks like green tea but tastes like black tea.
    (B) It looks like black tea but tastes like green tea.
    (C) It combines the flavors of black tea and green tea.
    (D) It has the fragrance of red flowers and green leaves.

18. According to the passage, *wulong* also refers to
    (A) a dragon king
    (B) a person's name
    (C) a severe drought
    (D) a devastating disaster

19. In the story, what did people do when there was a drought?
    (A) They drank *wulong* tea.
    (B) They wore black clothing.
    (C) They knelt down and prayed.
    (D) They begged the black dragon for rain.

20. The idiom "*bai wulong*" from the legend means
    (A) to practice three or four times until the work is perfect
    (B) to get the opposite result of what one wishes for
    (C) to serve *wulong* tea to honor guests
    (D) to display a black dragon to pray for rain

Read this journal

(Simplified Characters)	(Traditional Characters)
日期：六月一日 天气：晴 清晨，我和朋友们一起到五龙潭公园游玩。 五龙潭之美在于泉水。园内有二十六处形态各异的泉池。公园西北角有一处叫“清泉石上流”，泉水自池底涌出，漫过泉池，流淌在青石板上，缓缓地汇入附近的另一股清泉，在泉畔的石阶上形成约一米来宽、半米多高的小瀑布。 顺着弯弯的小路，我们来到了鱼塘。池水清澈，小鱼游来游去，真是惬意。我们围在鱼塘边，一边吃午饭，一边喂鱼。一只水鸟一头扎过来，想吃游到水面觅食的小鱼儿。几次三番，却一条鱼也没抓到，小鱼儿也真够机灵的！ 不知不觉，天暗下来了，明亮的月光透过松林洒在水面上，真是“明月松间照，清泉石上流”。我们这才依依不舍地回家了。 今天玩得好开心。五龙潭，梦中再会！	日期：六月一日 天氣：晴 清晨，我和朋友們一起到五龍潭公園遊玩。 五龍潭之美在於泉水。園內有二十六處形態各異的泉池。公園西北角有一處叫“清泉石上流”，泉水自池底湧出，漫過泉池，流淌在青石板上，緩緩地匯入附近的另一股清泉，在泉畔的石階上形成約一米來寬、半米多高的小瀑布。 順著彎彎的小路，我們來到了魚塘。池水清澈，小魚游來游去，真是愜意。我們圍在魚塘邊，一邊吃午飯，一邊餵魚。一隻水鳥一頭扎過來，想吃游到水面覓食的小魚兒。幾次三番，卻一條魚也沒抓到，小魚兒也真夠機靈的！ 不知不覺，天暗下來了，明亮的月光透過松林灑在水面上，真是“明月松間照，清泉石上流”。我們這才依依不捨地回家了。 今天玩得好開心。五龍潭，夢中再會！

21. According to the journal, the park that the writer visited is well known for its
    (A) night scenery
    (B) clear springs
    (C) goldfish in the pond
    (D) Five-Dragon Pond

22. How long did the writer and her friends stay in the park?
    (A) From dawn to dusk
    (B) From the late afternoon until dark
    (C) From the morning until it started to rain
    (D) Not enough information to determine

23. While the writer and her friends were feeding the fish, what was the bird doing?
    (A) Flying around in the woods playfully
    (B) Trying to catch the fish that surfaced for food
    (C) Snatching the food that people threw to the fish
    (D) Sitting still on a rock and watching from a distance

24. What did the writer do in the park?
    (A) Feed birds
    (B) Catch fish
    (C) Eat lunch
    (D) Wade in the water

Read this passage

(Simplified Characters)	(Traditional Characters)
重阳节 农历九月九日，是中国的一个古老的传统佳节 — 重阳节。古老的《易经》称九为“阳”数之最。九月九日，正好是两个最大的阳数重叠在一起，因此叫“重阳”。 过重阳节，历来有登高的风俗，金秋九月，天高气爽，登高望远不但可以锻炼身体，而且还有步步高升的吉祥之意。 重阳节的时候，正是粮食收获季节。吃重阳糕最早是为了庆祝丰收，后来因为糕和高同音，人们用吃“糕”代替登“高”，重阳糕就慢慢地成了这个节日的传统食品。 每逢重阳，菊花盛开，所以赏菊也是重阳节必不可少的一项活动。 九九重阳，因为“九九”与“久久”同音、有长寿的意思，所以重阳节又是中国传统的敬老节。在一九八九年以后，九月九日正式成为中国的老人节。如今，政府部门、社区团体都在重阳节这一天组织敬老活动。晚辈们也通常会回家探望家里的长辈，或者陪伴老人到郊外，出游赏景、登山健身。 中国人对重阳节一向有着特殊的感情。	**重陽節** 農曆九月九日，是中國的一個古老的傳統佳節 — 重陽節。古老的《易經》稱九為“陽”數之最。九月九日，正好是兩個最大的陽數重疊在一起，因此叫“重陽”。 過重陽節，歷來有登高的風俗，金秋九月，天高氣爽，登高望遠不但可以鍛煉身體，而且還有步步高升的吉祥之意。 重陽節的時候，正是糧食收穫季節。吃重陽糕最早是為了慶祝豐收，後來因為糕和高同音，人們用吃“糕”代替登“高”，重陽糕就慢慢地成了這個節日的傳統食品。 每逢重陽，菊花盛開，所以賞菊也是重陽節必不可少的一項活動。 九九重陽，因為“九九”與“久久”同音、有長壽的意思，所以重陽節又是中國傳統的敬老節。在一九八九年以後，九月九日正式成為中國的老人節。如今，政府部門、社區團體都在重陽節這一天組織敬老活動。晚輩們也通常會回家探望家裡的長輩，或者陪伴老人到郊外，出遊賞景、登山健身。 中國人對重陽節一向有著特殊的感情。

25. In what season is Chong Yang Festival most likely celebrated?
    (A) Spring
    (B) Summer
    (C) Autumn
    (D) Winter

26. Chong Yang Festival is also known as
    (A) Fitness Day
    (B) Senior Day
    (C) Harvest Festival
    (D) Chrysanthemum Festival

27. How do people celebrate Chong Yang Festival?
    (A) By climbing mountains
    (B) By having a special dinner
    (C) By wearing double-nine lucky charms
    (D) By planting chrysanthemums in the gardens

28. What is the significance of 1989 in this article?
    (A) The United Nations officially designated Senior Day in 1989.
    (B) The very first Chong Yang Festival was celebrated in 1989.
    (C) China has officially celebrated Senior Day since 1989.
    (D) China officially changed Senior Day to Chong Yang Festival in 1989.

29. Which of the following is true about Chong Yang Festival?
    (A) It is the day to plant chrysanthemums.
    (B) Outdoor excursions are common activities.
    (C) It is a special day for people reaching their 99th birthday.
    (D) The food for the celebration must be made from new crops.

Read this passage

(Simplified Characters)	(Traditional Characters)
适量的午睡有助于集中精力和提高工作效率。但是，有利于健康的午睡不宜过长，以十五分钟到三十分钟为宜。	適量的午睡有助於集中精力和提高工作效率。但是，有利於健康的午睡不宜過長，以十五分鐘到三十分鐘為宜。
一项科学研究发现，二十四分钟的午睡，能够最有效地帮助人们集中精力、提高效率。如果睡的时间长于三十分钟，会在刚刚睡醒的半小时内，有轻微的头痛、心跳过快和全身无力的感觉，不利于下午的学习和工作。因此，午睡不宜超过三十分钟。如果晚上睡眠时间少于八小时，那么适宜的午睡就更加重要了。	一項科學研究發現，二十四分鐘的午睡， 能夠最有效地幫助人們集中精力、提高效率。如果睡的時間長於三十分鐘，會在剛剛睡醒的半小時內，有輕微的頭痛、心跳過快和全身無力的感覺，不利於下午的學習和工作。因此，午睡不要超過三十分鐘。如果晚上睡眠時間少於八小時，那麼適宜的午睡就更加重要了。
专家建议，要养成每天定时、定量午睡的习惯。	專家建議，要養成每天定時、定量午睡的習慣。

30. What is the main idea of this article?
    (A) The counter-productivity of taking naps during the day
    (B) The benefit of getting eight hours of sleep each day
    (C) The myth about taking naps and longevity
    (D) The benefit of taking a short nap each day

31. According to the article, what would happen if a person naps for more than 30 minutes?
    (A) The person may have difficulty sleeping at night.
    (B) The person may get a mild headache.
    (C) The person may feel more energetic.
    (D) The person may sleep less each day.

32. According to the article, how long should a person nap?
    (A) About twenty-four minutes
    (B) Less than fifteen minutes
    (C) More than thirty minutes
    (D) At least sixty minutes

Read this advertisement

(Simplified Characters)	(Traditional Characters)
功夫学院招生 全美一流中国功夫学院隆重推出一套完整的武术教程。从踢、打、摔、拿到刀、枪、棍、棒，应有尽有。 所有课程都由顶级教练执教。总教练曾获得全美武术比赛冠军。 从初学者到功夫高手都欢迎前来免费试课一次。 地点：圣罗蒙市笛山大道八号 电话：800-123-4567	**功夫學院招生** 全美一流中國功夫學院隆重推出一套完整的武術教程。從踢、打、摔、拿到刀、槍、棍、棒，應有盡有。 所有課程都由頂級教練執教。總教練曾獲得全美武術比賽冠軍。 從初學者到功夫高手都歡迎前來免費試課一次。 地點：聖羅蒙市笛山大道八號 電話：800-123-4567

33. A kung fu academy is advertising for
    (A) a full-time instructor
    (B) its grand opening
    (C) a new class
    (D) an upcoming competition

34. Which of the following is mentioned in the advertisement?
    (A) Spears
    (B) Whips
    (C) Tumbling
    (D) Wrestling

35. According to the passage, who is the head coach?
    (A) A winner of a national martial arts competition
    (B) An all-around champion in taekwondo
    (C) A black belt kung fu master
    (D) A professional trainer

SECTION II: FREE RESPONSE

PART A: WRITING

[30 minutes, 25% of final score]

Note: In this part of the exam, you may NOT move back and forth among questions.

Directions: You will be asked to perform two writing tasks in Chinese. In each case, you will be asked to write for a specific purpose and to a specific person. You should write in as complete and as culturally appropriate a manner as possible, taking into account the purpose and the person described.

I. STORY NARRATION [15 minutes, 15% of final score]

The four pictures present a story. Imagine you are writing the story to a friend. Narrate a complete story as suggested by the pictures. Give your story a beginning, middle, and an end.

II. E-MAIL RESPONSE [15 minutes, 10% of total score]

Read this e-mail from a friend/relative and then type your response.

(Simplified Characters)

发件人：小丽
邮件主题：猪流感疫情状况

再有两个星期，我们就要启程到美国旅游了。这是我们盼望已久的行程，花了很大精力才安排好的。可是，国内每天都在报道猪流感在很多国家蔓延的消息，美国也已经发现不少猪流感病例。现在美国的疫情到底如何？如果我决定按原计划到美旅游，你说我应该采取些什么防范措施？

(Traditional Characters)

發件人： 小麗
郵件主題：豬流感疫情狀況

再有兩個星期，我們就要啟程到美國旅遊了。這是我們盼望已久的行程，花了很大精力才安排好的。可是，國內每天都在報道豬流感在很多國家蔓延的消息，美國也已經發現不少豬流感病例。現在美國的疫情到底如何？如果我決定按原計劃到美旅遊，你說我應該採取些什麼防範措施？

PART B: SPEAKING [15 minutes, 25% of final score]

 [Listen to the audio track **Mixed Theme - Speaking**.]

Note: In this part of the exam, you may NOT move back and forth among questions.

I. CONVERSATION [4 minutes, 10% of final score]

Directions: You will participate in a simulated conversation. Each time it is your turn to speak, you will have 20 seconds to record. You should respond as fully and as appropriately as possible.

Imagine you are having a conversation with David, a friend of yours who has been to China many times, about your very first trip to China this summer.

David: [Audio]
[TONE]
[Student records the response] (20 seconds)

David: [Audio]
[TONE]
[Student records the response] (20 seconds)

David: [Audio]
[TONE]
[Student records the response] (20 seconds)

David: [Audio]
[TONE]
[Student records the response] (20 seconds)

David: [Audio]
[TONE]
[Student records the response] (20 seconds)

David: [Audio]
[TONE]
[Student records the response] (20 seconds)

II. Cultural Presentation [7 minutes, 15% of final score]

Directions: You will be asked to speak in Chinese on a specific topic. Imagine you are making an oral presentation to your Chinese class. First, you will read and hear the topic for your presentation. You will have 4 minutes to prepare your presentation. Then you will have 2 minutes to record your presentation. Your presentation should be as complete as possible.

Choose ONE well-known Chinese historical or contemporary structure that you are familiar with (the Forbidden City, the Great Wall of China, the Bird's Nest, etc.). In your presentation, describe this structure and explain its significance.

[This marks the end of the audio track **Mixed Theme - Speaking**.]

STUDENT ANSWER SHEET

Section I: Multiple Choice

Part A: Listening

1.	Ⓐ	Ⓑ	Ⓒ	Ⓓ
2.	Ⓐ	Ⓑ	Ⓒ	Ⓓ
3.	Ⓐ	Ⓑ	Ⓒ	Ⓓ
4.	Ⓐ	Ⓑ	Ⓒ	Ⓓ
5.	Ⓐ	Ⓑ	Ⓒ	Ⓓ
6.	Ⓐ	Ⓑ	Ⓒ	Ⓓ
7.	Ⓐ	Ⓑ	Ⓒ	Ⓓ
8.	Ⓐ	Ⓑ	Ⓒ	Ⓓ
9.	Ⓐ	Ⓑ	Ⓒ	Ⓓ
10.	Ⓐ	Ⓑ	Ⓒ	Ⓓ
11.	Ⓐ	Ⓑ	Ⓒ	Ⓓ
12.	Ⓐ	Ⓑ	Ⓒ	Ⓓ
13.	Ⓐ	Ⓑ	Ⓒ	Ⓓ
14.	Ⓐ	Ⓑ	Ⓒ	Ⓓ
15.	Ⓐ	Ⓑ	Ⓒ	Ⓓ
16.	Ⓐ	Ⓑ	Ⓒ	Ⓓ
17.	Ⓐ	Ⓑ	Ⓒ	Ⓓ
18.	Ⓐ	Ⓑ	Ⓒ	Ⓓ
19.	Ⓐ	Ⓑ	Ⓒ	Ⓓ
20.	Ⓐ	Ⓑ	Ⓒ	Ⓓ
21.	Ⓐ	Ⓑ	Ⓒ	Ⓓ
22.	Ⓐ	Ⓑ	Ⓒ	Ⓓ
23.	Ⓐ	Ⓑ	Ⓒ	Ⓓ
24.	Ⓐ	Ⓑ	Ⓒ	Ⓓ
25.	Ⓐ	Ⓑ	Ⓒ	Ⓓ
26.	Ⓐ	Ⓑ	Ⓒ	Ⓓ
27.	Ⓐ	Ⓑ	Ⓒ	Ⓓ
28.	Ⓐ	Ⓑ	Ⓒ	Ⓓ
29.	Ⓐ	Ⓑ	Ⓒ	Ⓓ
30.	Ⓐ	Ⓑ	Ⓒ	Ⓓ
31.	Ⓐ	Ⓑ	Ⓒ	Ⓓ
32.	Ⓐ	Ⓑ	Ⓒ	Ⓓ
33.	Ⓐ	Ⓑ	Ⓒ	Ⓓ
34.	Ⓐ	Ⓑ	Ⓒ	Ⓓ
35.	Ⓐ	Ⓑ	Ⓒ	Ⓓ

Part B: Reading

1.	Ⓐ	Ⓑ	Ⓒ	Ⓓ
2.	Ⓐ	Ⓑ	Ⓒ	Ⓓ
3.	Ⓐ	Ⓑ	Ⓒ	Ⓓ
4.	Ⓐ	Ⓑ	Ⓒ	Ⓓ
5.	Ⓐ	Ⓑ	Ⓒ	Ⓓ
6.	Ⓐ	Ⓑ	Ⓒ	Ⓓ
7.	Ⓐ	Ⓑ	Ⓒ	Ⓓ
8.	Ⓐ	Ⓑ	Ⓒ	Ⓓ
9.	Ⓐ	Ⓑ	Ⓒ	Ⓓ
10.	Ⓐ	Ⓑ	Ⓒ	Ⓓ
11.	Ⓐ	Ⓑ	Ⓒ	Ⓓ
12.	Ⓐ	Ⓑ	Ⓒ	Ⓓ
13.	Ⓐ	Ⓑ	Ⓒ	Ⓓ
14.	Ⓐ	Ⓑ	Ⓒ	Ⓓ
15.	Ⓐ	Ⓑ	Ⓒ	Ⓓ
16.	Ⓐ	Ⓑ	Ⓒ	Ⓓ
17.	Ⓐ	Ⓑ	Ⓒ	Ⓓ
18.	Ⓐ	Ⓑ	Ⓒ	Ⓓ
19.	Ⓐ	Ⓑ	Ⓒ	Ⓓ
20.	Ⓐ	Ⓑ	Ⓒ	Ⓓ
21.	Ⓐ	Ⓑ	Ⓒ	Ⓓ
22.	Ⓐ	Ⓑ	Ⓒ	Ⓓ
23.	Ⓐ	Ⓑ	Ⓒ	Ⓓ
24.	Ⓐ	Ⓑ	Ⓒ	Ⓓ
25.	Ⓐ	Ⓑ	Ⓒ	Ⓓ
26.	Ⓐ	Ⓑ	Ⓒ	Ⓓ
27.	Ⓐ	Ⓑ	Ⓒ	Ⓓ
28.	Ⓐ	Ⓑ	Ⓒ	Ⓓ
29.	Ⓐ	Ⓑ	Ⓒ	Ⓓ
30.	Ⓐ	Ⓑ	Ⓒ	Ⓓ
31.	Ⓐ	Ⓑ	Ⓒ	Ⓓ
32.	Ⓐ	Ⓑ	Ⓒ	Ⓓ
33.	Ⓐ	Ⓑ	Ⓒ	Ⓓ
34.	Ⓐ	Ⓑ	Ⓒ	Ⓓ
35.	Ⓐ	Ⓑ	Ⓒ	Ⓓ
36.	Ⓐ	Ⓑ	Ⓒ	Ⓓ
37.	Ⓐ	Ⓑ	Ⓒ	Ⓓ
38.	Ⓐ	Ⓑ	Ⓒ	Ⓓ
39.	Ⓐ	Ⓑ	Ⓒ	Ⓓ
40.	Ⓐ	Ⓑ	Ⓒ	Ⓓ

Section II: Free Response

Part A: Writing - Story Narration

Part A: Writing - E-mail Response

ANSWER KEY

UNIT 1 CUSTOMS

PART A: LISTENING

1 B	6 D	11 D	16 A	21 D	26 D	31 C
2 C	7 B	12 B	17 A	22 C	27 C	32 D
3 D	8 B	13 A	18 D	23 C	28 B	
4 A	9 B	14 C	19 B	24 D	29 D	
5 B	10 B	15 D	20 B	25 A	30 A	

PART B: READING

1 D	6 B	11 B	16 A	21 B	26 C	31 D	36 D
2 B	7 C	12 D	17 D	22 A	27 A	32 A	
3 D	8 A	13 C	18 B	23 C	28 C	33 C	
4 C	9 B	14 D	19 B	24 D	29 B	34 A	
5 D	10 B	15 C	20 C	25 A	30 C	35 D	

UNIT 2 DAILY LIFE

PART A: LISTENING

1 B	6 D	11 D	16 C	21 D	26 D	31 B
2 D	7 B	12 D	17 C	22 B	27 C	32 A
3 A	8 B	13 C	18 A	23 C	28 B	
4 A	9 B	14 C	19 B	24 A	29 D	
5 D	10 B	15 D	20 C	25 B	30 A	

PART B: READING

1 A	6 B	11 C	16 B	21 C	26 A	31 A	36 D
2 C	7 A	12 A	17 C	22 D	27 D	32 C	
3 B	8 D	13 C	18 C	23 D	28 C	33 D	
4 D	9 C	14 B	19 A	24 A	29 D	34 B	
5 A	10 B	15 A	20 C	25 D	30 C	35 A	

UNIT 3 ECONOMICS

PART A: LISTENING

1 A	6 A	11 C	16 B	21 B	26 B	31 B
2 C	7 D	12 D	17 C	22C	27 A	32 A
3 D	8 D	13 A	18 A	23 C	28 C	
4 B	9 B	14 C	19 C	24 A	29 B	
5 A	10 A	15 A	20 B	25 D	30 C	

PART B: READING

1 A	6 C	11 A	16 B	21 C	26 A	31 B	36 A
2 D	7 B	12 C	17 A	22 A	27 D	32 C	
3 A	8 B	13 B	18 C	23 C	28 A	33 D	
4 C	9 D	14 A	19 D	24 B	29 C	34 B	
5 A	10 D	15 D	20 B	25 C	30 D	35 B	

UNIT 4 EDUCATION

PART A: LISTENING

1 C	6 B	11 D	16 B	21 C	26 C	31 A
2 B	7 C	12 A	17 C	22 C	27 B	32 D
3 D	8 B	13 D	18 A	23 D	28 D	
4 A	9 B	14 B	19 D	24 C	29 C	
5 B	10 B	15 D	20 B	25 B	30 C	

PART B: READING

1 D	6 C	11 B	16 C	21 D	26 A	31 A	36 C
2 A	7 C	12 B	17 B	22 C	27 B	32 B	
3 A	8 A	13 A	18 D	23 D	28 D	33 C	
4 B	9 A	14 C	19 A	24 A	29 D	34 A	
5 C	10 A	15 B	20 C	25 C	30 B	35 D	

UNIT 5 ENTERTAINMENT

PART A: LISTENING

1 A 6 B 11 B 16 C 21 D 26 D 31 C

2 B 7 D 12 D 17B 22 C 27 C 32 B

3 B 8 A 13 D 18 A 23 A 28 B

4 D 9 D 14 B 19 B 24 A 29 A

5 D 10 C 15 C 20 C 25 B 30 B

PART B: READING

1 B 6 C 11 D 16 D 21 B 26 D 31 D 36 B

2 C 7 D 12 C 17 C 22 D 27 B 32 A

3 D 8 D 13 D 18 C 23 D 28 C 33 A

4 C 9 B 14 B 19 A 24 A 29 C 34 A

5 B 10 A 15 B 20 D 25 B 30 A 35 C

UNIT 6 FAMILY

PART A: LISTENING

1 C 6 B 11 C 16 C 21 B 26 D 31 D

2 A 7 B 12 A 17 B 22 D 27 A 32 A

3 B 8 A 13 A 18 A 23 D 28 B

4 A 9 C 14 B 19 D 24 C 29 C

5 C 10 D 15 D 20 C 25 A 30 B

PART B: READING

1 C 6 B 11 A 16 D 21 B 26 C 31 C 36 C

2 D 7 A 12 B 17 B 22 C 27 B 32 D

3 A 8 D 13 B 18 B 23 D 28 D 33 C

4 D 9 C 14 C 19 C 24 A 29 B 34 A

5 C 10 B 15 A 20 A 25 D 30 D 35 B

UNIT 7 GEOGRAPHY

PART A: LISTENING

1 A 6 C 11 B 16 B 21 A 26 C 31 C

2 C 7 A 12 C 17 D 22 B 27 C 32 B

3 B 8 D 13 B 18 C 23 D 28 D

4 A 9 A 14 D 19 A 24 C 29 C

5 D 10 A 15 B 20 D 25 C 30 A

PART B: READING

1 C 6 D 11 D 16 D 21 A 26 A 31 C 36 C

2 A 7 B 12 C 17 C 22 D 27 D 32 D 37 A

3 C 8 D 13 A 18 A 23 D 28 A 33 D

4 A 9 C 14 B 19 C 24 C 29 C 34 B

5 B 10 D 15 A 20 B 25 A 30 A 35 C

UNIT 8 MIXED THEME

PART A: LISTENING

1 B 6 B 11 D 16 A 21 C 26 B 31 D

2 A 7 A 12 C 17 B 22 D 27 A 32 A

3 B 8 B 13 A 18 C 23 A 28 D 33 C

4 D 9 B 14 D 19 A 24 C 29 A 34 B

5 D 10 C 15 D 20 B 25 B 30 D

PART B: READING

1 C 6 C 11 C 16 A 21 B 26 B 31 B

2 B 7 B 12 D 17 C 22 A 27 A 32 A

3 B 8 D 13 A 18 B 23 B 28 C 33 C

4 C 9 A 14 C 19 C 24 C 29 B 34 D

5 D 10 B 15 D 20 B 25 C 30 D 35 A

APPENDIX I

LISTENING AND CONVERSATION SCRIPTS

UNIT 1. CUSTOMS

Listening Part A: Rejoinders

	(Simplified Characters)	(Traditional Characters)
1.		
(Woman)	爸爸请等一下，妈妈让您把这个"一帆风顺"的同心结挂在车上。祝您一路顺风！	爸爸請等一下，媽媽讓您把這個"一帆風順"的同心結掛在車上。祝您一路順風！
(Man)	(A) 我找到车钥匙了，旅途会顺利的。	(A) 我找到車鑰匙了，旅途會順利的。
	(B) 好啊！ 我这就挂上，图个吉祥。	(B) 好啊！ 我這就掛上，圖個吉祥。
	(C) 外边的风很大，同心结会被吹走的。	(C) 外邊的風很大，同心結會被吹走的。
	(D) 心情好，车开起来就顺当多了。	(D) 心情好，車開起來就順當多了。
2.		
(Woman)	今天是正月十五，我得赶紧抽空买些元宵给我妈送去，不然就太晚了。	今天是正月十五，我得趕緊抽空買些元宵給我媽送去，不然就太晚了。
(Man)	(A) 真的！ 我都忘了明天是正月十五了。你妈妈好吗？	(A) 真的！ 我都忘了明天是正月十五了。你媽媽好嗎？
	(B) 是的，今天吃元宵有点儿晚了。	(B) 是的，今天吃元宵有點兒晚了。
	(C) 你真孝顺，快去买吧！ 祝你们元宵节快乐！	(C) 你真孝順，快去買吧！ 祝你們元宵節快樂！
	(D) 你买的元宵都是什么馅儿的？	(D) 你買的元宵都是什麼餡兒的？

	(Simplified Characters)	(Traditional Characters)
3.		
(Woman)	昨天的灯谜晚会上，我中奖了！	昨天的燈謎晚會上，我中獎了！
(Man)	(A) 好主意，提着灯笼来我家玩吧。	(A) 好主意，提著燈籠來我家玩吧。
	(B) 我对谜语可是一窍不通。	(B) 我對謎語可是一竅不通。
	(C) 老实说，我不知道你对灯笼这么着迷。	(C) 老實說，我不知道你對燈籠這麼着迷。
	(D) 你运气真好！ 快给我看看你的奖品。	(D) 你運氣真好！ 快給我看看你的獎品。
4.		
(Woman)	我天天都在盼着过年，大年初一我会收到很多压岁钱。	我天天都在盼著過年，大年初一我會收到很多壓歲錢。
(Man)	(A) 我也是。我爸妈也会给我红包。	(A) 我也是。我爸媽也會給我紅包。
	(B) 是吗？ 我不知道你的生日是大年初一。	(B) 是嗎？ 我不知道你的生日是大年初一。
	(C) 你说得对，元旦放假最好玩儿了。	(C) 你說得對，元旦放假最好玩兒了。
	(D) 耐心点，寄钱总得花些时间嘛。	(D) 耐心點，寄錢總得花些時間嘛。
5.		
(Woman)	我们北方人过年吃饺子，你们呢？	我們北方人過年吃餃子，你們呢？
(Man)	(A) 我们东方人爱吃粽子。	(A) 我們東方人愛吃粽子。
	(B) 我们南方人通常吃年糕。	(B) 我們南方人通常吃年糕。
	(C) 我们西方人喜欢吃蛋糕。	(C) 我們西方人喜歡要吃蛋糕。
	(D) 我们过节有时吃月饼。	(D) 我們過節有時吃月餅。

	(Simplified Characters)	(Traditional Characters)
6.		
(Woman)	这次去北京开会觉得中国的变化太大了。	這次去北京開會覺得中國的變化太大了。
(Man)	(A) 我去过北京很多次，但记不清都是开什么会了。	(A) 我去過北京很多次，但記不清都是開什麼會了。
	(B) 我也有同感！ 中国队进步真是很大。	(B) 我也有同感！ 中國隊進步真是很大。
	(C) 这次奥运会办得的确不错。	(C) 這次奧運會辦得的確不錯。
	(D) 是呀，到处是高楼大厦，都快认不出来了。	(D) 是呀，到處是高樓大廈，都快認不出來了。
7.		
(Woman)	爸爸看京剧看得那么津津有味儿，等会儿再吃饭吧。	爸爸看京劇看得那麼津津有味兒，等會兒再吃飯吧。
(Man)	(A) 那我们赶紧吃饭吧，可别错过了时间。	(A) 那我們趕緊吃飯吧，可別錯過了時間。
	(B) 可是，再等，饭就要凉了。	(B) 可是，再等，飯就要涼了。
	(C) 可是，我不知道他喜欢吃什么味道的菜。	(C) 可是，我不知道他喜歡吃什麼味道的菜。
	(D) 京剧是得慢慢地看才有味儿。	(D) 京劇是得慢慢地看才有味兒。
8.		
(Woman)	快过年了，明天我们去红桥市场逛街，你去吗？	快過年了，明天我們去紅橋市場逛街，你去嗎？
(Man)	(A) 我们为什么要到红桥市场那儿去过年？	(A) 我們為什麼要到紅橋市場那兒去過年？
	(B) 我今天有些不舒服，明天就不去了。	(B) 我今天有些不舒服，明天就不去了。
	(C) 好的，谢谢你请我去红桥市场过年。	(C) 好的，謝謝你請我去紅橋市場過年。
	(D) 不去了，年都过完了。	(D) 不去了，年都過完了。

	(Simplified Characters)	(Traditional Characters)
9.		
(Woman)	今年唐装风靡上海滩，真是风水轮流转。	今年唐裝風靡上海灘，真是風水輪流轉。
(Man)	可不，我今天在街上还看到一群外国人，个个穿着唐装。	可不，我今天在街上還看到一群外國人，個個穿著唐裝。
(Woman)	(A) 外滩风大，穿唐装不合适。	(A) 外灘風大，穿唐裝不合適。
	(B) 真的？连外国人都赶时髦穿唐装啦。	(B) 真的？ 連外國人都趕時髦穿唐裝啦。
	(C) 在上海见到外国模特儿是再普通不过的事了。	(C) 在上海見到外國模特兒是再普通不過的事了。
	(D) 传统的上海人是很讲究风水的。	(D) 傳統的上海人是很講究風水的。
10.		
(Woman)	我做了些粽子来庆祝端午节。	我做了些粽子來慶祝端午節。
(Man)	端午节除了吃粽子以外，还有什么习俗？	端午節除了吃粽子以外，還有什麼習俗？
(Woman)	(A) 吃元宵	(A) 吃元宵
	(B) 赛龙舟	(B) 賽龍舟
	(C) 赏月	(C) 賞月
	(D) 扫墓	(D) 掃墓
11.		
(Woman)	爸妈金婚纪念日那天，我们一起给他们庆祝一下吧。	爸媽金婚紀念日那天，我們一起給他們慶祝一下吧。
(Man)	好主意，我们还可以一起拍张全家福。	好主意，我們還可以一起拍張全家福。
(Woman)	(A) 好啊，我早就想尝尝全家福这道名菜了。	(A) 好啊，我早就想嘗嘗全家福這道名菜了。
	(B) 是的，爸妈很高兴有那么多人来给他们过生日。	(B) 是的，爸媽很高興有那麼多人來給他們過生日。
	(C) 吃完饭后，我们全家又去照相馆照了相。	(C) 吃完飯後，我們全家又去照相館照了相。
	(D) 可不是，爸妈一定会很开心。	(D) 可不是，爸媽一定會很開心。

	(Simplified Characters)	**(Traditional Characters)**
12.		
(Woman)	这是什么乐器，这么大，还有这么多琴弦？	這是什麼樂器，這麼大，還有這麼多琴弦？
(Man)	这是古筝，声音非常好听。	這是古箏，聲音非常好聽。
(Woman)	(A) 我知道，古筝是很好听。	(A) 我知道，古箏是很好聽。
	(B) 是吗？这我还是第一次见到，容易学吗？	(B) 是嗎？這我還是第一次見到，容易學嗎？
	(C) 是吗？古代的风筝怎么会发出声音呢？	(C) 是嗎？古代的風箏怎麼會發出聲音呢？
	(D) 这么多弦的乐器，只有古代人才会弹的。	(D) 這麼多弦的樂器，只有古代人才會彈的。
13.		
(Woman)	就要过年了，你看看这年夜饭的菜谱还缺点什么？	就要過年了，你看看這年夜飯的菜譜還缺點什麼？
(Man)	哦，要再加一道鱼就好了，年年有余嘛。	哦，要再加一道魚就好了，年年有餘嘛。
(Woman)	(A) 这就对了，我怎么把这么重要的菜给忘了！	(A) 這就對了，我怎麼把這麼重要的菜給忘了！
	(B) 没想到，你的烹调手艺还真是蛮高的呢！	(B) 沒想到，你的烹調手藝還真是蠻高的呢！
	(C) 都这么晚了，烧鱼恐怕来不及了。	(C) 都這麼晚了，燒魚恐怕來不及了。
	(D) 刀鱼那么贵，还是换条别的鱼吧。	(D) 刀魚那麼貴，還是換條別的魚吧。
14.		
(Woman)	我这次去美国探亲，带些什么礼物比较好？	我這次去美國探親，帶些什麼禮物比較好？
(Man)	听说中国丝绸在西方国家挺受欢迎的。	聽說中國絲綢在西方國家挺受歡迎的。
(Woman)	(A) 可是我这次去的是美国东部呀。	(A) 可是我這次去的是美國東部呀。
	(B) 怪不得你的丝绸生意做得这么好。	(B) 怪不得你的絲綢生意做得這麼好。
	(C) 太好了，那我就买些丝绸制品送礼吧。	(C) 太好了，那我就買些絲綢製品送禮吧。
	(D) 西方国家的礼物的确比较受欢迎。	(D) 西方國家的禮物的確比較受歡迎。

	(Simplified Characters)	(Traditional Characters)
15.		
(Woman)	我最喜欢齐白石的国画，特别是他画的虾。	我最喜歡齊白石的國畫，特別是他畫的蝦。
(Man)	他画的虾有什么特色呢？	他畫的蝦有什麼特色呢？
	(A) 他的虾画得很鲜艳。	(A) 他的蝦畫得很鮮艷。
	(B) 他的虾画得很呆板。	(B) 他的蝦畫得很呆板。
	(C) 他的虾画得很抽象。	(C) 他的蝦畫得很抽象。
	(D) 他的虾画得活灵活现。	(D) 他的蝦畫得活靈活現。

Listening Part B: Listening Selections

SELECTION 1

(Narrator) Now you will listen **twice** to an announcement.

	(Simplified Characters)	(Traditional Characters)
(Woman)	各位来宾们，欢迎你们前来参观中华民俗工艺展。本工艺展内容丰富，展品众多，从剪纸、风筝、灯笼、刺绣到地方乐器，应有尽有。展馆按类别排列。详情请参阅展览指南。如果大家有任何问题，请随时向工作人员询问。	各位來賓們，歡迎你們前來參觀中華民俗工藝展。本工藝展內容豐富，展品眾多，從剪紙、風箏、燈籠、刺繡到地方樂器，應有盡有。展館按類別排列。詳情請參閱展覽指南。如果大家有任何問題，請隨時向工作人員詢問。

(Narrator) Now listen again.
(Woman) (Same announcement)
(Narrator) Now answer the questions for this selection.

SELECTION 2

(Narrator) Now you will listen **twice** to this recording.

	(Simplified Characters)	**(Traditional Characters)**
(Man)	乐乐，下星期我们就要回中国了。虽说这已经是你第二次去中国了，可上次回去的时候你年纪还小，记事不多，所以我还得再教你一些礼节。第一，见了长辈一定要主动打招呼，要叫叔叔阿姨或公公婆婆，不能直呼其名。第二，吃饭时要等大家都到齐了，长辈们开始吃了，你才能动筷子。记住了吗？	樂樂，下星期我們就要回中國了。雖說這已經是你第二次去中國了，可上次回去的時候你年紀還小，記事不多，所以我還得再教你一些禮節。第一，見了長輩一定要主動打招呼，要叫叔叔阿姨或公公婆婆，不能直呼其名。第二，吃飯時要等大家都到齊了，長輩們開始吃了，你才能動筷子。記住了嗎？

(Narrator) Now listen again.
(Man) (Same recording)
(Narrator) Now answer the questions for this selection.

SELECTION 3

(Narrator) Now you will listen **twice** to a voice message.

	(Simplified Characters)	**(Traditional Characters)**
(Woman)	Wendy，我是 Annie，我刚从中国回来，才下飞机。你要的旗袍我帮你带来了，怕你急，所以马上告诉你。旗袍是你妈妈替你选的，我们都非常喜欢。等你在民族文化节上做主持人的时候，就可以穿了。我甚至能想象你穿着它，站在台上，美丽动人的样子。明天我在家，有空你可以随时来拿。	Wendy，我是 Annie，我剛從中國回來，才下飛機。你要的旗袍我幫你帶來了，怕你急，所以馬上告訴你。旗袍是你媽媽替你選的，我們都非常喜歡。等你在民族文化節上做主持人的時候，就可以穿了。我甚至能想像你穿著它，站在台上，美麗動人的樣子。明天我在家，有空你可以隨時來拿。

(Narrator) Now listen again.
(Woman) (Same voice message)
(Narrator) Now answer the questions for this selection.

SELECTION 4

(Narrator) Now you will listen **once** to a conversation between two friends.

(Woman)	海明，下星期是端午节，想请你帮个忙，行吗？	海明，下星期是端午節，想請你幫個忙，行嗎？
(Man)	什么事呀？	什麼事呀？
(Woman)	我正在上中国历史课，老师想利用端午节介绍一下中国的食品文化。	我正在上中國歷史課，老師想利用端午節介紹一下中國的食品文化。
(Man)	呵呵，要我来帮着吃一定没问题。	呵呵，要我來幫着吃一定沒問題。
(Woman)	不是要你吃，是想请你妈妈帮我包几个粽子。	不是要你吃，是想請你媽媽幫我包幾個粽子。

(Narrator) Now answer the questions for this selection.

SELECTION 5

(Narrator) Now you will listen **once** to a news report.

	(Simplified Characters)	**(Traditional Characters)**
(Man)	春节是中国的第一大传统节日。每逢春节，出门在外的男男女女，老老少少都会想方设法地赶回家，过个团圆年。经历了去年的那场百年不遇的风雪，不少人今年早早地就开始了返乡的旅程。你看，离春节还有好几个星期呢，火车站已经是人山人海，熙熙攘攘了。	春節是中國的第一大傳統節日。每逢春節，出門在外的男男女女，老老少少都會想方設法地趕回家，過個團圓年。經歷了去年的那場百年不遇的風雪，不少人今年早早地就開始了返鄉的旅程。你看，離春節還有好幾個星期呢，火車站已經是人山人海，熙熙攘攘了。

(Narrator) Now answer the questions for this selection.

Speaking Part A: Conversation

You have a conversation with David, a friend that you have just met, about the Chinese zodiac at a Chinese New Year party.

	(Simplified Characters)	**(Traditional Characters)**
David:	春节快乐！ 你知道今年的生肖是十二生肖中的哪一个吗？	春節快樂！你知道今年的生肖是十二生肖中的哪一個嗎？
David:	你是属什么的？ 你的爸爸妈妈又是属什么的呢？	你是屬什麼的？你的爸爸媽媽又是屬什麼的呢？
David:	你还能说出其他哪些生肖呢？	你還能說出其他哪些生肖呢？
David:	在十二个生肖中，你最喜欢哪一个？为什么？	在十二個生肖中，你最喜歡哪一個？為什麼？
David:	如果有两个人属同一个生肖，他们一定是在同一年出生的吗？ 为什么？	如果有兩個人屬同一個生肖，他們一定是在同一年出生的嗎？為什麼？
David:	很多人认为一个人的性格和他所属的生肖有关系，你觉得是这样吗？为什么？	很多人認為一個人的性格和他所屬的生肖有關系，你覺得是這樣嗎？為什麼？

UNIT 2. DAILY LIFE

Listening Part A: Rejoinders

	(Simplified Characters)	(Traditional Characters)
1.		
(Woman)	哎哟，我的皮包不见了！	哎喲，我的皮包不見了！
(Man)	(A) 一定是小狗把面包吃了！	(A) 一定是小狗把面包吃了！
	(B) 里面有钱吗？	(B) 裡面有錢嗎？
	(C) 你的皮肤怎么啦？	(C) 你的皮膚怎麼啦？
	(D) 你没戴眼镜当然看不见了。	(D) 你沒戴眼鏡當然看不見了。
2.		
(Woman)	父母年纪大了，我给他们买了些补品。	父母年紀大了，我給他們買了些補品。
(Man)	(A) 那就请你把父母送到我家来。	(A) 那就請你把父母送到我家來。
	(B) 为什么？年纪大小对他们来说不是个问题。	(B) 為什麼？年紀大小對他們來說不是個問題。
	(C) 是啊，很多老人都喜欢用化妆品。	(C) 是啊，很多老人都喜歡用化妝品。
	(D) 你真是个孝顺的女儿。	(D) 你真是個孝順的女兒。
3.		
(Woman)	我脸上突然长了青春痘，真难看，你有什么办法吗？	我臉上突然長了青春痘，真難看，你有什麼辦法嗎？
(Man)	(A) 我有个好方子，网上找到的，回头寄给你。	(A) 我有個好方子，網上找到的，回頭寄給你。
	(B) 我有不少强身健体的好办法。	(B) 我有不少強身健體的好辦法。
	(C) 我还想问你保持青春的好办法呢。	(C) 我還想問你保持青春的好辦法呢。
	(D) 别动，我帮你重新画一下就好看了。	(D) 別動，我幫你重新畫一下就好看了。

	(Simplified Characters)	(Traditional Characters)
4.		
(Woman)	天气太热了，外公总是觉得头痛，我挺担心的。	天氣太熱了，外公總是覺得頭痛，我挺擔心的。
(Man)	(A) 也许得带他去看看医生。	(A) 也許得帶他去看看醫生。
	(B) 你说得对，天气太热，外公会担心的。	(B) 你說得對，天氣太熱，外公會擔心的。
	(C) 是呀，外面太热了，我们就待在家里吧。	(C) 是呀，外面太熱了，我們就待在家裡吧。
	(D) 外公肚子痛要赶快去看医生。	(D) 外公肚子痛要趕快去看醫生。
5.		
(Woman)	不好，他伤得挺厉害的，快去叫救护车！	不好，他傷得挺厲害的，快去叫救護車！
(Man)	(A) 我叫了，护士马上就来。	(A) 我叫了，護士馬上就來。
	(B) 大家让一让，救火车马上就到。	(B) 大家讓一讓，救火車馬上就到。
	(C) 不能随便叫救火车，屋子着火了才能叫。	(C) 不能隨便叫救火車，屋子着火了才能叫。
	(D) 我叫了，救护车已经上路了。	(D) 我叫了，救護車已經上路了。
6.		
(Woman)	我真后悔出门没带把伞，淋了个落汤鸡。	我真後悔出門沒帶把傘，淋了個落湯雞。
(Man)	(A) 我的记性不好，忘了煮鸡汤。	(A) 我的記性不好，忘了煮雞湯。
	(B) 太好啦！我最喜欢喝你做的鸡汤了。	(B) 太好啦！ 我最喜歡喝你做的雞湯了。
	(C) 那你提醒她一下，不要忘了带伞。	(C) 那你提醒她一下，不要忘了帶傘。
	(D) 啊呀，赶紧换上干衣服，可不要着凉了。	(D) 啊呀，趕緊換上乾衣服，可不要着涼了。

	(Simplified Characters)	(Traditional Characters)
7.		
(Woman)	这本小说很吸引人，我一口气就看完了，你为什么不喜欢呢？	這本小說很吸引人，我一口氣就看完了，你為什麼不喜歡呢？
(Man)	(A) 我很喜欢呼吸新鲜空气。	(A) 我很喜歡呼吸新鮮空氣。
	(B) 这本小说生词太多了，我看不下去了。	(B) 這本小說生詞太多了，我看不下去了。
	(C) 你喜欢不喜欢这本小说？	(C) 你喜歡不喜歡這本小說？
	(D) 别着急，慢慢地读下去，你就会喜欢的。	(D) 別着急，慢慢地讀下去，你就會喜歡的。
8.		
(Woman)	明天我们去北京度假一周，你能帮我看小狗吗？	明天我們去北京度假一週，你能幫我看小狗嗎？
(Man)	没问题，你把小狗的生活习惯告诉我就行了。	沒問題，你把小狗的生活習慣告訴我就行了。
(Woman)	(A) 没办法，小狗不喜欢度假。	(A) 沒辦法，小狗不喜歡度假。
	(B) 谢谢，我会给你留个条儿交代清楚的。	(B) 謝謝，我會給你留個條兒交代清楚的。
	(C) 好的，谢谢你带小狗去度假。	(C) 好的，謝謝你帶小狗去度假。
	(D) 度假村里有各种各样的狗，我会拍些照片回来。	(D) 度假村裡有各種各樣的狗，我會拍些照片回來。
9.		
(Woman)	这星期我每天干通宵，连喘口气的机会都没有。	這星期我每天幹通宵，連喘口氣的機會都沒有。
(Man)	公司上市前都是忙得累死人，没什么稀奇的。	公司上市前都是忙得累死人，沒什麼稀奇的。
(Woman)	(A) 这么说，我们公司已经上市啦？	(A) 這麼說，我們公司已經上市啦？
	(B) 我只是没想到连星期天也不例外。	(B) 我只是沒想到連星期天也不例外。
	(C) 那也不能天天吃夜宵啊。	(C) 那也不能天天吃夜宵啊。
	(D) 早知道以前累死过人，我才不做这份工作呢。	(D) 早知道以前累死過人，我才不做這份工作呢。

10.

	(Simplified Characters)	(Traditional Characters)
(Woman)	儿子现在迷上电子游戏了，连吃饭都叫不动，真让人心烦。	兒子現在迷上電子遊戲了，連吃飯都叫不動，真讓人心煩。
(Man)	嗨，现在孩子都这样，别太操心了。	嗨，現在孩子都這樣，別太操心了。
(Woman)	(A) 不吃饭，怎么有力气玩电子游戏？	(A) 不吃飯，怎麼有力氣玩電子遊戲？
	(B) 说是这么说，可做妈妈的哪能不为儿子操心呢。	(B) 說是這麼說，可做媽媽的哪能不為兒子操心呢。
	(C) 叫来叫去的，能不把孩子搞烦吗？	(C) 叫來叫去的，能不把孩子搞煩嗎？
	(D) 是啊，我早就不为他吃饭的事儿操心了。	(D) 是啊，我早就不為他吃飯的事兒操心了。

11.

	(Simplified Characters)	(Traditional Characters)
(Woman)	马上就是圣诞节了，我们班有什么活动吗？	馬上就是聖誕節了，我們班有什麼活動嗎？
(Man)	办个聚会怎样？再加上交换礼物，一定很热闹。	辦個聚會怎樣？再加上交換禮物，一定很熱鬧。
(Woman)	(A) 你要给大家送礼物？ 想得真周到！	(A) 你要給大家送禮物？ 想得真周到！
	(B) 真不好意思，总是在你家办聚会。	(B) 真不好意思，總是在你家辦聚會。
	(C) 圣诞节以前的确是办礼品交易会的好时机。	(C) 聖誕節以前的確是辦禮品交易會的好時機。
	(D) 好主意！ 我得想想应该准备什么样的礼物。	(D) 好主意！ 我得想想應該準備什麼樣的禮物。

12.

	(Simplified Characters)	(Traditional Characters)
(Woman)	我的电脑有病毒了，怎么办？	我的電腦有病毒了，怎麼辦？
(Man)	我有反病毒软件，可以帮你清理一下。	我有反病毒軟件，可以幫你清理一下。
(Woman)	(A) 谢谢你帮我清理垃圾。	(A) 謝謝你幫我清理垃圾。
	(B) 你的软件也有病毒吗？	(B) 你的軟件也有病毒嗎？
	(C) 我的脑子没有问题。	(C) 我的腦子沒有問題。
	(D) 太好了，现在就开始吧！	(D) 太好了，現在就開始吧！

	(Simplified Characters)	(Traditional Characters)
13.		
(Woman)	我想去商店买点东西。	我想去商店買點東西。
(Man)	天气很冷，让我开车送你去吧。	天氣很冷，讓我開車送你去吧。
(Woman)	(A) 你的车有冷气吗?	(A) 你的車有冷氣嗎?
	(B) 我没有车，还是走路去吧。	(B) 我沒有車，還是走路去吧。
	(C) 不用啦，走路去还可以运动运动。	(C) 不用啦，走路去還可以運動運動。
	(D) 谢谢你帮我买东西。	(D) 謝謝你幫我買東西。
14.		
(Woman)	周末我给你打手机，没人接。	週末我給你打手機，沒人接。
(Man)	对不起，我去海边了，那儿收不到信号。	對不起，我去海邊了，那兒收不到信號。
(Woman)	(A) 海边怎么会收不到信呢？	(A) 海邊怎麼會收不到信呢？
	(B) 手机丢了会很麻烦的。	(B) 手機丢了會很麻煩的。
	(C) 难怪找不到人。	(C) 難怪找不到人。
	(D) 为什么要去那儿修手机？	(D) 為什麼要去那兒修手機？
15.		
(Woman)	今年公司生意兴隆，老板决定给大家多放几天假。	今年公司生意興隆，老板決定給大家多放幾天假。
(Man)	太好了！这下我就有时间去西安旅游了。	太好了！這下我就有時間去西安旅遊了。
(Woman)	(A) 可不是嘛，老板在西安工作，我们大家都沾光！	(A) 可不是嘛，老板在西安工作，我們大家都沾光！
	(B) 我真羡慕你，每年都有时间去西安旅游。	(B) 我真羡慕你，每年都有時間去西安旅遊。
	(C) 谢天谢地公司上市了，老板总算给我们加工资了。	(C) 謝天謝地公司上市了，老板總算給我們加工資了。
	(D) 真不敢想象，你很快就能亲眼看到兵马俑了。	(D) 真不敢想像，你很快就能親眼看到兵馬俑了。

Listening Part B: Listening Selections

SELECTION 1

(Narrator) Now you will listen **twice** to an announcement.

(Man)

(Simplified Characters)

<通告>

由于经费削减，经图书馆委员会决定，从三月一日起，图书馆开放时间每天缩短两个小时。

新的开馆时间为：

星期一、三、五

早上九点到下午三点

星期二、四、六

下午三点到晚上九点

星期天休息

不便之处，敬请见谅。

(Traditional Characters)

<通告>

由於經費削減，經圖書館委員會決定，從三月一日起，圖書館開放時間每天縮短兩個小時。

新的開馆時間為：

星期一、三、五

早上九點到下午三點

星期二、四、六

下午三點到晚上九點

星期天休息

不便之處，敬請見諒。

(Narrator) Now listen again.
(Man) (Same announcement)
(Narrator) Now answer the questions for this selection.

SELECTION 2

(Narrator) Now you will listen **twice** to the following instructions.

(Simplified Characters)

(Woman) 蛋炒饭的做法：

1. 开大火把空锅子烧热
2. 放一茶匙油，把油在锅内转动
3. 把打散的蛋液倒入锅内，用锅铲快速地把蛋炒均匀
4. 放入白饭，用锅铲背一边轻压、一边混合拌炒

一盘美味可口的蛋炒饭就做好了。

(Traditional Characters)

蛋炒飯的做法：

1. 開大火把空鍋子燒熱
2. 放一茶匙油，把油在鍋內轉動
3. 把打散的蛋液倒入鍋內，用鍋鏟快速地把蛋炒均勻
4. 放入白飯，用鍋鏟背一邊輕壓、一 邊混合拌炒

一盤美味可口的蛋炒飯就做好了。

(Narrator) Now listen again.
(Woman) (Same instructions)
(Narrator) Now answer the questions for this selection.

SELECTION 3

(Narrator) Now you will listen **twice** to a voice message.

(Simplified Characters)

(Man) 张明，我是陈大伟。我的车坏了，不能用了。现在我在车站，准备坐公共汽车到你家，不过两点恐怕到不了，我估计会晚到半个小时。你和玛丽先开始讨论下星期的春节活动吧，等我到了以后，我们再一起作最后的决定。我会帶些点心，到时候你泡一壶茶，我们可以一边开会一边喝下午茶。等会儿见。

(Traditional Characters)

張明，我是陳大偉。我的車壞了，不能用了。現在我在車站，準備坐公共汽車到你家，不過兩點恐怕到不了，我估計會晚到半個小時。你和瑪麗先開始討論下星期的春節活動吧，等我到了以後，我們再一起作最後的決定。我會帶些點心，到時候你泡一壺茶，我們可以一邊開會一邊喝下午茶。等會兒見。

(Narrator) Now listen again.
(Man) (Same voice message)
(Narrator) Now answer the questions for this selection.

SELECTION 4

(Narrator) Now you will listen **once** to a conversation between two friends.

	(Simplified Characters)	**(Traditional Characters)**
(Woman)	喂，请问大伟在吗？	喂，請問大偉在嗎？
(Man)	我就是，你是玛丽吧！有什么事吗？	我就是，你是瑪麗吧！有什麼事嗎？
(Woman)	我星期五要考英文，你可以帮我练习英文会话吗？	我星期五要考英文，你可以幫我練習英文會話嗎？
(Man)	没问题，但是你得请我喝咖啡。	沒問題，但是你得請我喝咖啡。
(Woman)	好！我们可以一边喝咖啡，一边练习。	好！我們可以一邊喝咖啡，一邊練習。

(Narrator) Now answer the questions for this selection.

SELECTION 5

(Narrator) Now you will listen **once** to a weather report.

	(Simplified Characters)	**(Traditional Characters)**
(Man)	天气预报：今晚有雷雨。明天多云转晴，风速十到十五英里，最高气温华氏八十度，最低六十五度。后天的天气预测是阴天，局部地区有阵雨，最高七十五度，最低五十度。	天氣預報：今晚有雷雨。明天多雲轉晴，風速十到十五英哩，最高氣溫華氏八十度，最低六十五度。後天的天氣預測是陰天，局部地區有陣雨，最高七十五度，最低五十度。

(Narrator) Now answer the questions for this selection.

Speaking Part A: Conversation

You are having a conversation with your mother about your father's upcoming birthday celebration.

	(Simplified Characters)	(Traditional Characters)
Mom:	下个月你爸爸要过生日了！我想给他开个生日会，你觉得我们应该邀请哪些客人呢？	下個月你爸爸要過生日了！我想給他開個生日會，你覺得我們應該邀請哪些客人呢？
Mom:	如果我们想给他一个惊喜，我们在哪里开生日会比较好？为什么？	如果我們想給他一個驚喜，我們在哪裡開生日會比較好？為什麼？
Mom:	我们该选哪天开生日会，星期六还是星期天？为什么？	我們該選哪天開生日會，星期六還是星期天？為什麼？
Mom:	你说说爸爸最喜欢吃些什么？我们给他买一个什么样的蛋糕呢？	你說說爸爸最喜歡吃些什麼？我們給他買一個什麼樣的蛋糕呢？
Mom:	我想给爸爸买件礼物，你给我出出主意好吗？	我想給爸爸買件禮物，你給我出出主意好嗎？
Mom:	你打算送什么礼物给爸爸？需要我帮忙吗？	你打算送什麼禮物給爸爸？需要我幫忙嗎？

UNIT 3. ECONOMICS

Listening Part A: Rejoinders

	(Simplified Characters)	(Traditional Characters)
1.		
(Woman)	听说你买房子了，贷款手续麻烦吗？	聽說你買房子了，貸款手續麻煩嗎？
(Man)	(A) 还可以，你不妨也去银行试试。	(A) 還可以，你不妨也去銀行試試。
	(B) 我不买房。	(B) 我不買房。
	(C) 我正在装修。	(C) 我正在裝修。
	(D) 很容易，用提款机的人不多。	(D) 很容易，用提款機的人不多。
2.		
(Woman)	柜台前排队的人太多了，我还是到银行门口用提款机取钱吧。	櫃台前排隊的人太多了，我還是到銀行門口用提款機取錢吧。
(Man)	(A) 我取钱向来都用网上银行，挺方便的。	(A) 我取錢向來都用網上銀行，挺方便的。
	(B) 都十点半了，银行怎么还不开门呢？	(B) 都十點半了，銀行怎麼還不開門呢？
	(C) 提款机坏了，所以大家都只好在这里排队。	(C) 提款機壞了，所以大家都只好在這裡排隊。
	(D) 那不好吧，别人会以为我不排队呢。	(D) 那不好吧，別人會以為我不排隊呢。
3.		
(Woman)	这本杂志介绍很多金融知识，也许对你有帮助。	這本雜誌介紹很多金融知識，也許對你有幫助。
(Man)	(A) 谢谢，不过我对金银珠宝兴趣不大。	(A) 謝謝，不過我對金銀珠寶興趣不大。
	(B) 我的确需要认识一些金融界的朋友。	(B) 我的確需要認識一些金融界的朋友。
	(C) 好啊，我们去听金融知识讲座吧。	(C) 好啊，我們去聽金融知識講座吧。
	(D) 太好了，谢谢你的推荐。	(D) 太好了，謝謝你的推薦。

	(Simplified Characters)	(Traditional Characters)
4.		
(Woman)	昨天你有没有看新闻？股市大跌，好几个人昏倒了呢。	昨天你有沒有看新聞？股市大跌，好幾個人昏倒了呢。
(Man)	(A) 我很少注意看名人结婚的新闻。	(A) 我很少注意看名人結婚的新聞。
	(B) 唉，他们一定是因为损失太重，无法承受吧。	(B) 唉，他們一定是因為損失太重，無法承受吧。
	(C) 又发生意外了，安全措施不健全啊。	(C) 又發生意外了，安全措施不健全啊。
	(D) 超市里那么滑，太危险了！	(D) 超市裡那麼滑，太危險了！
5.		
(Woman)	听说那片新区不错，周末要不要一起去看样品房？	聽說那片新區不錯，週末要不要一起去看樣品房？
(Man)	(A) 这个周末不行，我们要去郊游。	(A) 這個週末不行，我們要去郊遊。
	(B) 好啊，我们一起去拿样品。	(B) 好啊，我們一起去拿樣品。
	(C) 新区商店里有很多样品。	(C) 新區商店裡有很多樣品。
	(D) 你怎么知道我们正想买二手房。	(D) 你怎麼知道我們正想買二手房。
6.		
(Woman)	我想请钟点工，一小时十元，你有合适的人选吗？	我想請鐘點工，一小時十元，你有合適的人選嗎？
(Man)	(A) 我的钟点工不错，可以介绍给你。	(A) 我的鐘點工不錯，可以介紹給你。
	(B) 对不起，我没带表，不知道时间。	(B) 對不起，我沒帶錶，不知道時間。
	(C) 我的朋友那儿正在招人，你要不要去试试看？	(C) 我的朋友那兒正在招人，你要不要去試試看？
	(D) 对不起，我钱带得不够，不能买。	(D) 對不起，我錢帶得不夠，不能買。

	(Simplified Characters)	**(Traditional Characters)**
7.		
(Woman)	美元贬值，中国持有的美国债券也跟着缩水了。	美元貶值，中國持有的美國債券也跟着縮水了。
(Man)	(A) 真糟糕，中国欠了美国这么多债。	(A) 真糟糕，中國欠了美國這麼多債。
	(B) 那人民币的购买力不就下降了嘛。	(B) 那人民幣的購買力不就下降了嘛。
	(C) 那美国人去中国旅游就便宜了。	(C) 那美國人去中國旅遊就便宜了。
	(D) 是啊，美元价值下降，中国也受连累。	(D) 是啊，美元價值下降，中國也受連累。
8.		
(Woman)	听说你在校期间就已经开始工作了，会不会耽误学习？	聽說你在校期間就已經開始工作了，會不會耽誤學習？
(Man)	我还是以学习为主，有空才去兼职的。	我還是以學習為主，有空才去兼職的。
(Woman)	(A) 也对，全职工作也是一种学习。	(A) 也對，全職工作也是一種學習。
	(B) 学生会主席的工作一定非常难。	(B) 學生會主席的工作一定非常難。
	(C) 先工作再学习，体会果然不一样。	(C) 先工作再學習，體會果然不一樣。
	(D) 真佩服你，既不耽误功课，又能经济独立了。	(D) 真佩服你，既不耽誤功課，又能經濟獨立了。
9.		
(Woman)	你工作找得怎么样啦？	你工作找得怎麼樣啦？
(Man)	有一家公司已经录用我了，但这家公司比较小，恐怕没有发展前途。	有一家公司已經錄用我了，但這家公司比較小，恐怕沒有發展前途。
(Woman)	(A) 工作先干着，薪水以后可以慢慢加嘛！	(A) 工作先幹著，薪水以後可以慢慢加嘛！
	(B) 公司小有小的好处，你就别挑剔了。	(B) 公司小有小的好處，你就別挑剔了。
	(C) 这是你第一次找工作，难免害怕。	(C) 這是你第一次找工作，難免害怕。
	(D) 不用怕，你已经通过了面试，很有希望被录取！	(D) 不用怕，你已經通過了面試，很有希望被錄取！

(Simplified Characters)

10.

(Woman) 这个长周末我们一起去逛商店好吗？

(Man) 好啊！我看到百货商场的促销广告，家具要打七到八折呢。

(Woman) (A) 我倒不需要家具。我想买些衣服。

(B) 广告降价这么多，这是我们促销的好机会！

(C) 天哪，逛七八家商店，你想累死我啊？

(D) 家具减价百分之七十到八十很少见，一定得去看看。

11.

(Woman) 一年一度的科技博览会就要开幕了，你想不想去参观一下？

(Man) 我早就等不及了。你知道今年的主题吗？

(Woman) (A) 什么猪蹄鸭脚的，我都吃不惯。

(B) 我猜今年的主席跟去年的不一样。

(C) 听说是能源技术。我最感兴趣的是太阳能。

(D) 等不及？那你就先去吧。

12.

(Woman) 李经理，我这个星期要考试。我想请韩冰帮我一起做这项工作，可以吗？

(Man) 只要韩冰没意见，就请他能者多劳吧！但你考完试还得把工作做完。

(Woman) (A) 太好了。韩冰完成了我的工作。

(B) 韩冰对我的工作没有任何意见。

(C) 考试是多劳多得的美差。

(D) 谢谢您。等考完试，我一定会加倍努力地工作。

(Traditional Characters)

10.

(Woman) 這個長週末我們一起去逛商店好嗎？

(Man) 好啊！我看到百貨商場的促銷廣告，家俱要打七到八折呢。

(Woman) (A) 我倒不需要家俱。我想買些衣服。

(B) 廣告降價這麼多，這是我們促銷的好機會！

(C) 天哪，逛七八家商店，你想累死我啊？

(D) 家俱減價百分之七十到八十很少見，一定得去看看。

11.

(Woman) 一年一度的科技博覽會就要開幕了，你想不想去參觀一下？

(Man) 我早就等不及了。你知道今年的主題嗎？

(Woman) (A) 什麼豬蹄鴨腳的，我都吃不慣。

(B) 我猜今年的主席跟去年的不一樣。

(C) 聽說是能源技術。我最感興趣的是太陽能。

(D) 等不及？ 那你就先去吧。

12.

(Woman) 李經理，我這個星期要考試。我想請韓冰幫我一起做這項工作，可以嗎？

(Man) 只要韓冰沒意見，就請他能者多勞吧！但你考完試還得把工作做完。

(Woman) (A) 太好了。韓冰完成了我的工作。

(B) 韓冰對我的工作沒有任何意見。

(C) 考試是多勞多得的美差。

(D) 謝謝您。等考完試，我一定會加倍努力地工作。

	(Simplified Characters)	**(Traditional Characters)**
13.		
(Woman)	先生，这些书买一送一，多买多送。	先生，這些書買一送一，多買多送。
(Man)	我只买一本，不要那本送的，可以打折吗？	我只買一本，不要那本送的，可以打折嗎？
(Woman)	(A) 我也许可以给你打七折。	(A) 我也許可以給你打七折。
	(B) 对不起。书页折过以后就不能卖了。	(B) 對不起。書頁折過以後就不能賣了。
	(C) 一本太少了，一般我们是不替客人打包的。	(C) 一本太少了，一般我們是不替客人打包的。
	(D) 这本书不能送。	(D) 這本書不能送。
14.		
(Woman)	你的手机看上去很时髦，在什么地方买的？	你的手機看上去很時髦，在什麼地方買的？
(Man)	我的手机是在网上订购的，很便宜。	我的手機是在網上訂購的，很便宜。
(Woman)	(A) 巧了，我也有一位朋友在做网上销售。	(A) 巧了，我也有一位朋友在做網上銷售。
	(B) 用手机也能上网订票啊，真是太方便了。	(B) 用手機也能上網訂票啊，真是太方便了。
	(C) 网上订购手机大概要多少天才能收到？	(C) 網上訂購手機大概要多少天才能收到？
	(D) 送给你的手机一般都是便宜货。	(D) 送給你的手機一般都是便宜貨。
15.		
(Woman)	周末我在快餐店兼职赚零用钱。	週末我在快餐店兼職賺零用錢。
(Man)	你要零用钱做什么？	你要零用錢做什麼？
(Woman)	(A) 我把零用钱存起来买游戏机。	(A) 我把零用錢存起來買遊戲機。
	(B) 零用钱是客人给的小费。	(B) 零用錢是客人給的小費。
	(C) 我用零用钱买快餐店。	(C) 我用零用錢買快餐店。
	(D) 快餐店的零钱是用来找还给顾客的。	(D) 快餐店的零錢是用來找還給顧客的。

Listening Part B: Listening Selections

SELECTION 1

(Narrator) Now you will listen **twice** to an announcement.

(Simplified Characters)

(Man) <迁址公告>

首都人才服务中心已于 2009 年 4 月 7 日迁至复兴门外，办公时间和联系电话不变。

新地址： 海淀区复兴路八号二楼

办公时间：周一至周五
上午 9:00－12:00
下午 2:00－6:00

联系电话：6868-6688

特此公告。不便之处，请见谅。

(Traditional Characters)

<遷址公告>

首都人才服務中心已於 2009 年 4 月 7 日遷至復興門外，辦公時間和聯系電話不變。

新地址： 海淀區復興路八號二樓

辦公時間：週一至週五
上午 9:00－12:00
下午 2:00－6:00

聯系電話：6868-6688

特此公告。不便之處，請見諒。

(Narrator) Now listen again.
(Man) (Same announcement)
(Narrator) Now answer the questions for this selection.

SELECTION 2

(Narrator) Now you will listen **twice** to the following instructions.

(Simplified Characters)

(Woman) 谢谢您使用自动电话系统来启动您的新卡。为了确认您是信用卡的持有人，首先请您用电话输入信用卡正面的十六位数字。接着请输入您的社会安全卡的最后四位数。然后请输入您在申请表格上填写的十位数的电话号码。谢谢您的合作。

(Traditional Characters)

謝謝您使用自動電話系統來啟動您的新卡。為了確認您是信用卡的持有人，首先請您用電話輸入信用卡正面的十六位數字。接著請輸入您的社會安全卡的最後四位數。然後請輸入您在申請表格上填寫的十位數的電話號碼。謝謝您的合作。

(Narrator) Now listen again.
(Woman) (Same instructions)
(Narrator) Now answer the questions for this selection.

SELECTION 3

(Narrator) Now you will listen **twice** to a voice message.

	(Simplified Characters)	**(Traditional Characters)**
(Man)	喂，Anna，我是张池。明天上午九点，我陪同的商务代表团要去参观中国银行。可是公司里这一大堆有关保险业务的资料等着我翻译，我实在走不开。我知道你对中国银行了如指掌，你明天能不能替我去陪团？报酬很不错！请尽快给我回个电话！	喂，Anna，我是張池。明天上午九點，我陪同的商務代表團要去參觀中國銀行。可是公司裡這一大堆有關保險業務的資料等着我翻譯，我實在走不開。我知道你對中國銀行瞭如指掌，你明天能不能替我去陪團？報酬很不錯！請盡快給我回個電話！

(Narrator) Now listen again.
(Man) (Same voice message)
(Narrator) Now answer the questions for this selection.

SELECTION 4

(Narrator) Now you will listen **once** to a commercial.

	(Simplified Characters)	**(Traditional Characters)**
(Woman)	今年的健康保险费又涨了！ 怎么办?	今年的健康保險費又漲了！ 怎麼辦?
(Man)	不用担心，我们太平公司代理多家保险公司，最佳服务，最低收费。	不用擔心，我們太平公司代理多家保險公司，最佳服務，最低收費。
(Woman)	太好了！ 那太平公司除了代理健康保险以外还代理其他保险吗?	太好了！ 那太平公司除了代理健康保險以外還代理其他保險嗎?
(Man)	我们还代理汽车及房屋保险。电话是：(888) 925-6868，有任何关于保险的问题，随时打电话给我。	我們還代理汽車及房屋保險。電話是：(888) 925-6868，有任何關於保險的問題，隨時打電話給我。
(Woman)	一定会的。	一定會的。

(Narrator) Now answer the questions for this selection.

SELECTION 5

(Narrator) Now you will listen **once** to a news report.

	(Simplified Characters)	**(Traditional Characters)**
(Woman)	根据香港特区政府统计署公布的人口普查结果， 从 1996 年到 2006 年，香港六十五岁以上的老年人口增长迅速。到 2006 年，老年人口已经超过了八十五万，达总人口的百分之十二。按照国际标准，香港已经成为一个老年化社会了。	根據香港特區政府統計署公佈的人口普查結果， 從 1996 年到 2006 年，香港六十五歲以上的老年人口增長迅速。到 2006 年，老年人口已經超過了八十五萬，達總人口的百分之十二。按照國際標準，香港已經成為一個老年化社會了。

(Narrator) Now answer the questions for this selection.

Speaking Part A: Conversation

You have a conversation with Mary, a reporter for your school's student-run newspaper.

	(Simplified Characters)	**(Traditional Characters)**
Mary:	很多高中生在暑期里打工，你今年准备打工吗？为什么？	很多高中生在暑期裡打工，你今年準備打工嗎？為什麼？
Mary:	你觉得现在的高中生打工的主要目的是什么？	你覺得現在的高中生打工的主要目的是什麼？
Mary:	有人觉得打工会耽误暑期修课，不值得，请谈谈你的看法。	有人覺得打工會耽誤暑期修課，不值得，請談談你的看法。
Mary:	你认为去打工对申请大学有什么帮助吗？	你認為去打工對申請大學有什麼幫助嗎？
Mary:	暑期打工还有哪些好处和坏处？	暑假打工還有哪些好處和壞處？
Mary:	假如你想打工，你最希望能找到什么样的工作呢？为什么？	假如你想打工，你最希望能找到什麼樣的工作呢？ 為什麼？

UNIT 4. EDUCATION

Listing Part A: Rejoinders

	(Simplified Characters)	(Traditional Characters)
1.		
(Woman)	老师表扬你听力考得很好，祝贺你！	老師表揚你聽力考得很好，祝賀你！
(Man)	(A) 听说你听力考得很好，是吗？	(A) 聽說你聽力考得很好，是嗎？
	(B) 是啊，同学们学习都很努力。	(B) 是啊，同學們學習都很努力。
	(C) 的确比我预期的结果好多了。	(C) 的確比我預期的結果好多了。
	(D) 你知道我的听力考得怎么样吗？	(D) 你知道我的聽力考得怎麼樣嗎？
2.		
(Woman)	大卫，你的中国话说得很标准。	大衛，你的中國話說得很標準。
(Man)	(A) 谢谢，其实我的标准并不高。	(A) 謝謝，其實我的標準並不高。
	(B) 哪里，还差得远呢！	(B) 哪裡，還差得遠呢！
	(C) 不客气，很高兴你喜欢听中国话。	(C) 不客氣，很高興你喜歡聽中國話。
	(D) 是啊，你在哪里学中文学得这么好？	(D) 是啊，你在哪裡學中文學得這麼好？
3.		
(Woman)	这个学期，除了五门必修课以外，我还选了两门选修课。	這個學期，除了五門必修課以外，我還選了兩門選修課。
(Man)	(A) 你怎么可以不选必修课呢？	(A) 你怎麼可以不選必修課呢？
	(B) 你为什么只选五门课呢？	(B) 你為什麼只選五門課呢？
	(C) 那你一共选了几门选修课呢？	(C) 那你一共選了幾門選修課呢？
	(D) 这么多的课！这学期可真够你忙的啦！	(D) 這麼多的課！ 這學期可真夠你忙的啦！

	(Simplified Characters)	(Traditional Characters)
4.		
(Woman)	杰克，你的西班牙语那么好。希望你多多指教。	傑克，你的西班牙語那麼好。希望你多多指教。
(Man)	(A) 说不上指教，你需要帮助的话，我会尽力而为的。	(A) 說不上指教，你需要幫助的話，我會盡力而為的。
	(B) 我没去过西班牙，是在这儿学的。	(B) 我沒去過西班牙，是在這兒學的。
	(C) 西班牙好玩的地方很多，你想先去哪里？	(C) 西班牙好玩的地方很多，你想先去哪裡？
	(D) 我刚刚开始教西班牙语，还没有经验。	(D) 我剛剛開始教西班牙語，還沒有經驗。
5.		
(Woman)	你这么喜欢生物工程，那你将来打算上医学院还是工学院呢？	你這麼喜歡生物工程，那你將來打算上醫學院還是工學院呢？
(Man)	(A) 这个暑假，我打算申请参加一个生物夏令营。	(A) 這個暑假，我打算申請參加一個生物夏令營。
	(B) 很难说，但是我肯定要选跟生物学有关的专业。	(B) 很難說，但是我肯定要選跟生物學有關的專業。
	(C) 就是因为喜欢生物，我才上了医学院的。	(C) 就是因為喜歡生物，我才上了醫學院的。
	(D) 医学院课程很重，你要慎重考虑。	(D) 醫學院課程很重，你要慎重考慮。
6.		
(Woman)	想不到你们的校园这么漂亮，校舍也别具风格 。	想不到你們的校園這麼漂亮，校舍也別具風格 。
(Man)	(A) 我也没有想到你这么爱漂亮！	(A) 我也沒有想到你這麼愛漂亮！
	(B) 我们校园之美是相当出名的，你从来没听说过？	(B) 我們校園之美是相當出名的，你從來沒聽說過？
	(C) 是啊，我也注意到校园里的风特别大。	(C) 是啊，我也注意到校園裡的風特別大。
	(D) 谢谢你带我看这么漂亮的校园！	(D) 謝謝你帶我看這麼漂亮的校園！

	(Simplified Characters)	**(Traditional Characters)**
7.		
(Woman)	中国的父母们都希望孩子长大后能知书达理。	中國的父母們都希望孩子長大後能知書達理。
(Man)	(A) 我知道，光有书本知识还不够，还要懂送礼的规矩。	(A) 我知道，光有書本知識還不夠，還要懂送禮的規矩。
	(B) 怪不得到中国人家去做客，一定要讲究礼仪。	(B) 怪不得到中國人家去做客，一定要講究禮儀。
	(C) 是啊，孩子们不但要学习好，还应该懂得做人的道理。	(C) 是啊，孩子們不但要學習好，還應該懂得做人的道理。
	(D) 是的，中国的孩子们都很喜欢读书。	(D) 是的，中國的孩子們都很喜歡讀書。
8.		
(Woman)	老师，请问在选中国哲学课以前，应该先修什么课？	老師，請問在選中國哲學課以前，應該先修什麼課？
(Man)	中国文学或者中国历史。	中國文學或者中國歷史。
(Woman)	(A) 我就是要选中国文学专业。	(A) 我就是要選中國文學專業。
	(B) 真巧，我正在修中国历史。	(B) 真巧，我正在修中國歷史。
	(C) 那我修了哲学课以后，马上就选中国历史课。	(C) 那我修了哲學課以後，馬上就選中國歷史課。
	(D) 我正在修中国哲学。	(D) 我正在修中國哲學。
9.		
(Woman)	大卫，你们的辩论比赛结果怎么样？	大衛，你們的辯論比賽結果怎麼樣？
(Man)	第一轮比赛的结果马马虎虎，我们争取下一轮能有进步。	第一輪比賽的結果馬馬虎虎，我們爭取下一輪能有進步。
(Woman)	(A) 你们马马虎虎的，怎么能有进步呢？	(A) 你們馬馬虎虎的，怎麼能有進步呢？
	(B) 有信心最重要，下一轮你们一定会发挥得更好。	(B) 有信心最重要，下一輪你們一定會發揮得更好。
	(C) 那我们一起去庆祝你们得冠军吧！	(C) 那我們一起去慶祝你們得冠軍吧！
	(D) 比赛可不能有一丝一毫的马虎。	(D) 比賽可不能有一絲一毫的馬虎。

	(Simplified Characters)	(Traditional Characters)
10.		
(Woman)	学校快要放春假了，我打算去旅行。	學校快要放春假了，我打算去旅行。
(Man)	你计划去哪儿旅行呢？	你計劃去哪兒旅行呢？
(Woman)	(A) 我打算在家陪陪我父母。	(A) 我打算在家陪陪我父母。
	(B) 我打算去几个欧洲国家看看。	(B) 我打算去幾個歐洲國家看看。
	(C) 我打算看春节联欢会。	(C) 我打算看春節聯歡會。
	(D) 我打算去旅行社买票。	(D) 我打算去旅行社買票。
11.		
(Woman)	要考试了，下午我们一起复习功课，好不好？	要考試了，下午我們一起複習功課，好不好？
(Man)	好啊，可是我下午三点半才下课呢。	好啊，可是我下午三點半才下課呢。
(Woman)	(A) 噢，那我就自己先去考试吧。	(A) 噢，那我就自己先去考試吧。
	(B) 没关系，那我们就改考试时间吧。	(B) 沒關系，那我們就改考試時間吧。
	(C) 那你就自己去上课吧。	(C) 那你就自己去上課吧。
	(D) 那你下课以后到图书馆来找我吧。	(D) 那你下課以後到圖書館來找我吧。
12.		
(Woman)	中美两国的教学方式很不同，你认为哪一种方式比较有效？	中美兩國的教學方式很不同，你認為哪一種方式比較有效？
(Man)	各有所长，再说，效果好坏也因人而异。	各有所長，再說，效果好壞也因人而異。
(Woman)	(A) 有道理，那么哪一种方式比较适合你呢？	(A) 有道理，那麼哪一種方式比較適合你呢？
	(B) 是啊，多多交流才能取长补短嘛。	(B) 是啊，多多交流才能取長補短嘛。
	(C) 你为什么不大喜欢中国的教学方式呢？	(C) 你為什麼不大喜歡中國的教學方式呢？
	(D) 你为什么认为两种教学方式的效果都不好呢？	(D) 你為什麼認為兩種教學方式的效果都不好呢？

	(Simplified Characters)	**(Traditional Characters)**
13.		
(Woman)	我的指导教授总是没完没了地跟我强调数学的重要性。	我的指導教授總是沒完沒了地跟我強調數學的重要性。
(Man)	他这是为你好啊，数学的用途的确很广泛。	他這是為你好啊，數學的用途的確很廣泛。
(Woman)	(A) 真的？ 你怎么会认识我的指导教授呢？	(A) 真的？ 你怎麼會認識我的指導教授呢？
	(B) 是吗，数学成绩好就能找到好工作？	(B) 是嗎，數學成績好就能找到好工作？
	(C) 其实，教授并不常到我的办公室来。	(C) 其實，教授並不常到我的辦公室來。
	(D) 我知道，可是说多了就成了耳边风了。	(D) 我知道，可是說多了就成了耳邊風了。
14.		
(Woman)	萧雨，你今天的作业做完了吗？	蕭雨，你今天的作業做完了嗎？
(Man)	还没有，正在做。今天的功课有点难。	還沒有，正在做。今天的功課有點難。
(Woman)	(A) 你家有困难的话，我可以想办法帮你。	(A) 你家有困難的話，我可以想辦法幫你。
	(B) 我也觉得有几道题挺难的，所以想问问你。	(B) 我也覺得有幾道題挺難的，所以想問問你。
	(C) 我不知道你今天有这么多的功课！	(C) 我不知道你今天有這麼多的功課！
	(D) 都已经这么晚了，你应该赶快去做功课了。	(D) 都已經這麼晚了，你應該趕快去做功課了。
15.		
(Woman)	张帆，你怎么搬到校外去住了？	張帆，你怎麼搬到校外去住了？
(Man)	唉，跟别人合住一个宿舍的生活，我实在不习惯。	唉，跟別人合住一個宿舍的生活，我實在不習慣。
(Woman)	(A) 那你可以和你的室友一起搬嘛。	(A) 那你可以和你的室友一起搬嘛。
	(B) 真的？搬到校外住可以省这么多钱啊！	(B) 真的？ 搬到校外住可以省這麼多錢啊！
	(C) 我也很不适应在校外住的生活。	(C) 我也很不適應在校外住的生活。
	(D) 是吗？我倒是挺喜欢宿舍生活的。	(D) 是嗎？我倒是挺喜歡宿舍生活的。

Listening Part B: Listening Selections

SELECTION 1

(Narrator) Now you will listen **once** to a conversation.

	(Simplified Characters)	(Traditional Characters)
(Woman)	今天是选课的第一天，你下学期的课都选好了吗？	今天是選課的第一天，你下學期的課都選好了嗎？
(Man)	还没有，排队注册的人太多了，要等两个多小时呢，过几天再去吧！	還沒有，排隊註冊的人太多了，要等兩個多小時呢，過幾天再去吧！
(Woman)	过几天就太晚了！热门课都会爆满的。	過幾天就太晚了！ 熱門課都會爆滿的。
(Man)	有这么严重吗？ 会选不上课吗？	有這麼嚴重嗎？ 會選不上課嗎？
(Woman)	当然会，尤其是大家都想上的课。不过，你可以上网选课啊。	當然會，尤其是大家都想上的課。不過，你可以上網選課啊。
(Man)	好主意，我现在就去上网选课。	好主意，我現在就去上網選課。

(Narrator) Now answer the questions for this selection.

SELECTION 2

(Narrator) Now you will listen **twice** to an announcement.

	(Simplified Characters)	(Traditional Characters)
(Woman)	各位家长，各位同学，下午好！ 欢迎大家来我们学校参观。我是工程学院二年级的学生。今天由我做大家的校园导游。从这里出发，我们先去生物系教学实验楼，然后参观旁边的音乐系和演出厅，再去看看社会科学系的教室。最后，我们去学校的餐厅和学生宿舍转一转。参观过程中如果有任何问题，请尽管问我。	各位家長，各位同學，下午好！ 歡迎大家來我們學校參觀。我是工程學院二年級的學生。今天由我做大家的校園導遊。從這裡出發，我們先去生物系教學實驗樓，然後參觀旁邊的音樂系和演出廳，再去看看社會科學系的教室。最後，我們去學校的餐廳和學生宿舍轉一轉。參觀過程中如果有任何問題，請盡管問我。

(Narrator) Now listen again.
(Woman) (Same announcement)
(Narrator) Now answer the questions for this selection.

SELECTION 3

(Narrator) Now you will listen **twice** to the following instructions.

	(Simplified Characters)	**(Traditional Characters)**
(Man)	各位同学，数学比赛再有五分钟就开始了，现在宣布比赛规则和注意事项：	各位同學，數學比賽再有五分鐘就開始了，現在宣佈比賽規則和注意事項：
	1. 比赛分个人赛和团体赛两个部分。	1. 比賽分個人賽和團體賽兩個部分。
	2. 个人赛时间是三十分钟，五道题，大家不能相互讨论。	2. 個人賽時間是三十分鐘，五道題，大家不能相互討論。
	3. 团体赛时间是四十分钟，三人一组，共六道题，团体赛时，组员之间允许讨论。	3. 團體賽時間是四十分鐘，三人一組，共六道題，團體賽時，組員之間允許討論。
	4. 不遵守以上规则的同学或团体，将被取消比赛资格。	4. 不遵守以上規則的同學或團體，將被取消比賽資格。

(Narrator) Now listen again.
(Man) (Same instructions)
(Narrator) Now answer the questions for this selection.

SELECTION 4

(Narrator) Now you will listen **once** to a commercial.

	(Simplified Characters)	(Traditional Characters)
(Woman)	听说你的女儿考上了一流大学，有什么诀窍吗？	聽說你的女兒考上了一流大學，有什麼訣竅嗎？
(Man)	当然有！诀窍就是参加新时代的 SAT 补习班。	當然有！ 訣竅就是參加新時代的 SAT 補習班。
(Woman)	我也听说过新时代，真的很有帮助吗？	我也聽說過新時代，真的很有幫助嗎？
(Man)	帮助非常大，我女儿的 SAT 总分提高了三百分。	幫助非常大，我女兒的 SAT 總分提高了三百分。
(Woman)	明天我就带我儿子去新时代看看。	明天我就帶我兒子去新時代看看。

(Narrator) Now answer the questions for this selection.

SELECTION 5

(Narrator) Now you will listen **once** to a voice message.

	(Simplified Characters)	(Traditional Characters)
(Man)	Lily，我是王园。今天的数学功课做好了吗？有一道题，我左思右想都解不出来，明天就要交了，真急人，能帮帮我吗？听到我的留言后，请尽快给我回电，谢谢！	Lily，我是王園。今天的數學功課做好了嗎？有一道題，我左思右想都解不出來，明天就要交了，真急人，能幫幫我嗎？聽到我的留言後，請盡快給我回電，謝謝！

(Narrator) Now answer the questions for this selection.

Speaking Part A: Conversation

Anna has just moved to the United States from China with her family and enrolled in your high school. She wants to ask you some questions about the life of high school students in the United States.

	(Simplified Characters)	**(Traditional Characters)**
Anna:	你好！ 谢谢你抽空来帮助我。你上几年级了？你喜欢你的学校吗？为什么？	你好！ 謝謝你抽空來幫助我。你上幾年級了？你喜歡你的學校嗎？為什麼？
Anna:	你这学期都在上些什么课呢？你比较喜欢哪些课？	你這學期都在上些什麼課呢？你比較喜歡哪些課？
Anna:	你们中午都在哪儿吃饭？学校有餐厅吗？可以自己带饭吗？	你們中午都在哪兒吃飯？學校有餐廳嗎？可以自己帶飯嗎？
Anna:	学校都有哪些体育队和文艺团体？怎么申请参加呢？	學校都有哪些體育隊和文藝團體？怎麼申請參加呢？
Anna:	听说美国高中生都得做义工，是吗？都做些什么呢？	聽說美國高中生都得做義工，是嗎？都做些什麼呢？
Anna:	你都参加些什么课外和校外活动呢？你最喜欢的活动是什么？	你都參加些什麼課外和校外活動呢？你最喜歡的活動是什麼？

UNIT 5. ENTERTAINMENT

Listening Part A: Rejoinders

(Simplified Characters)

1.

(Woman) 今年旧金山芭蕾舞团的节目不错，我买了年票，你呢？

(Man) (A) 我也有年票，常常去看。

(B) 我也有，我的歌剧年票的座位还不错呢。

(C) 我没有年票，我不喜欢旧金山歌剧团的节目。

(D) 今年的节目不好啊？真扫兴！

2.

(Woman) 中国很多年轻人打乒乓球，而且打得很好，你的看法呢？

(Man) (A) 我认为打网球比打乒乓球更有意思。

(B) 我认为中国年轻人的乒乓球没有老一代人打得好。

(C) 我认为美国年轻人并不怎么爱打乒乓球。

(D) 我认为提高乒乓球水平不一定非要打比赛。

3.

(Woman) 她唱歌唱得太难听了，她常去卡拉OK歌厅吗？

(Man) (A) 常去，不过你唱的歌我听不懂。

(B) 她常去，不过她的歌唱得的确不好听。

(C) 他们常去卡拉OK歌厅玩。

(D) 她常去卡拉OK歌厅练习跳舞。

(Traditional Characters)

1.

(Woman) 今年舊金山芭蕾舞團的節目不錯，我買了年票，你呢？

(Man) (A) 我也有年票，常常去看。

(B) 我也有，我的歌劇年票的座位還不錯呢。

(C) 我沒有年票，我不喜歡舊金山歌劇團的節目。

(D) 今年的節目不好啊？ 真掃興！

2.

(Woman) 中國很多年輕人打乒乓球，而且打得很好，你的看法呢？

(Man) (A) 我認為打網球比打乒乓球更有意思。

(B) 我認為中國年輕人的乒乓球沒有老一代人打得好。

(C) 我認為美國年輕人並不怎麼愛打乒乓球。

(D) 我認為提高乒乓球水平不一定非要打比賽。

3.

(Woman) 她唱歌唱得太難聽了，她常去卡拉OK歌廳嗎？

(Man) (A) 常去，不過你唱的歌我聽不懂。

(B) 她常去，不過她的歌唱得的確不好聽。

(C) 他們常去卡拉OK歌廳玩。

(D) 她常去卡拉OK歌廳練習跳舞。

	(Simplified Characters)	**(Traditional Characters)**
4.		
(Woman)	今晚电视上有女子网球决赛转播，你会看吗？	今晚電視上有女子網球決賽轉播，你會看嗎？
(Man)	(A) 很可惜，我没有票，不能去。	(A) 很可惜，我沒有票，不能去。
	(B) 我不喜欢看篮球比赛。	(B) 我不喜歡看籃球比賽。
	(C) 当然会看，我最喜欢看男子网球比赛了。	(C) 當然會看，我最喜歡看男子網球比賽了。
	(D) 真不巧，我要准备考试，恐怕没有时间看了。	(D) 真不巧，我要準備考試，恐怕沒有時間看了。
5.		
(Woman)	你看过的电影里，哪些有描述中西文化差异的？	你看過的電影裡，哪些有描述中西文化差異的？
(Man)	(A) 只要是电影，我都喜欢看。	(A) 只要是電影，我都喜歡看。
	(B) 中国电影的对话太难懂了。	(B) 中國電影的對話太難懂了。
	(C) 我看中国电影不一定比西方电影差。	(C) 我看中國電影不一定比西方電影差。
	(D) 电影“喜宴”里就有不少这样的描写。	(D) 電影“喜宴”裡就有不少這樣的描寫。
6.		
(Woman)	你在北京时有没有去看过京剧？	你在北京時有沒有去看過京劇？
(Man)	(A) 我在北京看了歌剧，很不错。	(A) 我在北京看了歌劇，很不錯。
	(B) 真不巧，我在北京时，没有一个剧场上演京剧。	(B) 真不巧，我在北京時，沒有一個劇場上演京劇。
	(C) 你在北京看到京剧了，运气真好！	(C) 你在北京看到京劇了，運氣真好！
	(D) 我在旧金山看过一场京剧，特棒！	(D) 我在舊金山看過一場京劇，特棒！

(Simplified Characters)

7.

(Woman) 你有没有看昨天电视转播的排球比赛？中国队险胜古巴队。

(Man) (A) 真没劲，中国队又输了。

(B) 没看成，体育馆里的气氛热烈吗？谁赢了？

(C) 看了。中国队输是输了，球赛还是蛮精彩的！

(D) 古巴队虽然输了，打得还是很棒的。

8.

(Woman) 下午我和大伟去看电影，你也一起去，好吗？

(Man) 今天不行，我表弟一家从美国回来，我要去机场接他们。

(Woman) (A) 那就下次吧。

(B) 可是机场里没有电影院啊。

(C) 那你不送大伟去美国了？

(D) 这个电影不好看吗？

9.

(Woman) 城市广场今天晚上有免费音乐会，你知道吗？

(Man) 是吗？那我今天晚上就不去健身房了。

(Woman) (A) 跟老板请假去听音乐会可不太容易。

(B) 你有城市广场音乐会的票吗？

(C) 你在健身房也能看见转播吗？

(D) 太好了！这样我们就能一起去听音乐会了。

(Traditional Characters)

7.

(Woman) 你有沒有看昨天電視轉播的排球比賽？中國隊險勝古巴隊。

(Man) (A) 真沒勁，中國隊又輸了。

(B) 沒看成，體育館裡的氣氛熱烈嗎？ 誰贏了？

(C) 看了。中國隊輸是輸了，球賽還是蠻精彩的！

(D) 古巴隊雖然輸了，打得還是很棒的。

8.

(Woman) 下午我和大偉去看電影，你也一起去，好嗎？

(Man) 今天不行，我表弟一家從美國回來，我要去機場接他們。

(Woman) (A) 那就下次吧。

(B) 可是機場裡沒有電影院啊。

(C) 那你不送大偉去美國了？

(D) 這個電影不好看嗎？

9.

(Woman) 今天晚上城市廣場有免費音樂會，你知道嗎？

(Man) 是嗎？那我今天晚上就不去健身房了。

(Woman) (A) 跟老板請假去聽音樂會可不太容易。

(B) 你有城市廣場音樂會的票嗎？

(C) 你在健身房也能看見轉播嗎？

(D) 太好了！這樣我們就能一起去聽音樂會了。

(Simplified Characters)

10.

(Woman) 这么晚才回来，都干什么去了？放学了也不回家。

(Man) 妈妈，对不起，我们球队放学后有场比赛，临时通知的，来不及告诉你。

(Woman) (A) 没关系，我可以帮你通知别人。

(B) 哦，能在学校就把作业做完也不错。

(C) 看你一身的汗，快去洗个澡吧。

(D) 你应该告诉我你是跑着回家的嘛。

11.

(Woman) 张婷从小能歌善舞，只要有文艺演出，她都一马当先。

(Man) 她在中国可是个大名鼎鼎的电影明星呢！

(Woman) (A) 怪不得她骑马的水平那么高。

(B) 她真是多才多艺。

(C) 真厉害，她竟然敢冒名顶替演电影。

(D) 她居然成了电影导演啦。

12.

(Woman) 还记得小丽第一次上台时为大家演奏的样子吗？

(Man) 记得，战战兢兢的。可你看她现在多老练啊！

(Woman) (A) 是啊，小丽溜冰溜得多了，变老练了。

(B) 是啊，想不到她变得这么老。

(C) 也难怪，这是她第一次为大家演出啊！

(D) 可不是嘛，她现在一点也不怯场了。

(Traditional Characters)

10.

這麼晚才回來，都幹什麼去了？放學了也不回家。

媽媽，對不起，我們球隊放學後有場比賽，臨時通知的，來不及告訴你。

(A) 沒關系，我可以幫你通知別人。

(B) 哦，能在學校就把作業做完也不錯。

(C) 看你一身的汗，快去洗個澡吧。

(D) 你應該告訴我你是跑着回家的嘛。

11.

張婷從小能歌善舞，只要有文藝演出，她都一馬當先。

她在中國可是個大名鼎鼎的電影明星呢！

(A) 怪不得她騎馬的水平那麼高。

(B) 她真是多才多藝！

(C) 真厲害，她竟然敢冒名頂替演電影。

(D) 她居然成了電影導演啦。

12.

還記得小麗第一次上台時為大家演奏的樣子嗎？

記得，戰戰兢兢的。可你看她現在多老練啊！

(A) 是啊，小麗溜冰溜得多了，變老練了。

(B) 是啊，想不到她變得這麼老。

(C) 也難怪，這是她第一次為大家演出啊！

(D) 可不是嘛，她現在一點也不怯場了。

	(Simplified Characters)	(Traditional Characters)
13.		
(Woman)	我烦躁的时候，戴上耳机，听听音乐，心情就会变得平静多了。	我煩躁的時候，戴上耳機，聽聽音樂，心情就會變得平靜多了。
(Man)	音乐真的有那么灵吗？那我也得试试。	音樂真的有那麼靈嗎？那我也得試試。
(Woman)	(A) 不过真有病的话还是要去看医生。	(A) 不過真有病的話還是要去看醫生。
	(B) 如果你要买，一定要找正版的，质量不一样。	(B) 如果你要買，一定要找正版的，質量不一樣。
	(C) 不过听音乐会就不用耳机了。	(C) 不過聽音樂會就不用耳機了。
	(D) 你试一试就会明白我说的意思了。	(D) 你試一試就會明白我說的意思了。
14.		
(Woman)	安妮的演唱会刚上演了第一场，就已经是好评如潮了。	安妮的演唱會剛上演了第一場，就已是經好評如潮了。
(Man)	真的吗？怪不得我周围的朋友们都在想办法弄演唱会的票呢。	真的嗎？怪不得我周圍的朋友們都在想辦法弄演唱會的票呢。
(Woman)	(A) 我知道，安妮一向都很会做评论的。	(A) 我知道，安妮一向都很會做評論的。
	(B) 你能弄到票吗？ 我也想去看看。	(B) 你能弄到票嗎？ 我也想去看看。
	(C) 朋友们一起办个演唱会也是情理中的事。	(C) 朋友們一起辦個演唱會也是情理中的事。
	(D) 是啊，这下她就不用去电视台了。	(D) 是啊，這下她就不用去電視台了。
15.		
(Woman)	今晚电视里有相声晚会，约几位朋友一起到我家来看吧。	今晚電視裡有相聲晚會，約幾位朋友一起到我家來看吧。
(Man)	咱们想到一块儿去了，我这就去打电话叫他们。	咱們想到一塊兒去了，我這就去打電話叫他們。
(Woman)	(A) 快去，电话号码可千万不能丢了。	(A) 快去，電話號碼可千萬不能丟了。
	(B) 这下大家就能一起看我家乐乐上电视了。	(B) 這下大家就能一起看我家樂樂上電視了。
	(C) 看你高兴的样子，别忘了，节目七点开始哦。	(C) 看你高興的樣子，別忘了，節目七點開始哦。
	(D) 你搞错了，我可没说请他们吃饭噢。	(D) 你搞錯了，我可沒說請他們吃飯噢。

Listening Part B: Listening Selections

SELECTION 1

(Narrator) Now you will listen **twice** to a voice message.

	(Simplified Characters)	**(Traditional Characters)**
(Woman)	小李，我是刘云，你今晚有空吗？我有两张电影票，是中国电影"红高粱"。我的室友临时有事不能去看了，不知道你能不能去？是晚上七点的。如果你能去，尽快给我回音，要不然的话，我可以问问别的朋友。等你的电话。再见！	小李，我是劉雲，你今晚有空嗎？我有兩張電影票，是中國電影"紅高粱"。我的室友臨時有事不能去看了，不知道你能不能去？是晚上七點的。如果你能去，盡快給我回音，要不然的話，我可以問問別的朋友。等你的電話。再見！

(Narrator) Now listen again.
(Woman) (Same voice message)
(Narrator) Now answer the questions for this selection.

SELECTION 2

(Narrator) Now you will listen **twice** to an announcement.

	(Simplified Characters)	**(Traditional Characters)**
(Man)	各位参加网球比赛的选手们注意了，由于昨晚下雨，场地未干，原定的赛程和场地都有所变动，女子和男子单打的比赛将顺延三小时，女子和男子的双打比赛时间不变，但地点换到附近华盛顿高中的网球场。如果你需要去华盛顿高中的路线图，请到报到处索取。谢谢合作！	各位參加網球比賽的選手們注意了，由於昨晚下雨，場地未乾，原定的賽程和場地都有所變動，女子和男子單打的比賽將順延三小時，女子和男子的雙打比賽時間不變，但地點換到附近華盛頓高中的網球場。如果你需要去華盛頓高中的路線圖，請到報到處索取。謝謝合作！

(Narrator) Now listen again.
(Man) (Same announcement)
(Narrator) Now answer the questions for this selection.

SELECTION 3

(Narrator) Now you will listen **once** to an announcement.

	(Simplified Characters)	**(Traditional Characters)**
(Woman)	各位排队买票的观众请注意，现在公布音乐会门票购买规则：	各位排隊買票的觀眾請注意，現在公佈音樂會門票購買規則：
	1. 由于门票供不应求，为了尽量让排队的观众们都能买到票，每人限购两张门票。	1. 由於門票供不應求，為了盡量讓排隊的觀眾們都能買到票，每人限購兩張門票。
	2. 成人票每张二十元，儿童票半价。	2. 成人票每張二十元，兒童票半價。
	3. 十二岁或十二岁以下的儿童凭儿童票入场。	3. 十二歲或十二歲以下的兒童憑兒童票入場。

(Narrator) Now answer the questions for this selection.

SELECTION 4

(Narrator) Now you will listen **once** to a conversation between two friends.

	(Simplified Characters)	**(Traditional Characters)**
(Woman)	最近见到过李梅吗？	最近見到過李梅嗎？
(Man)	两个星期前在她的摄影棚见到过，她刚接了一个新片子。	兩個星期前在她的攝影棚見到過，她剛接了一個新片子。
(Woman)	是吗？ 我想约她喝咖啡，聊聊她正在拍的电影。	是嗎？ 我想約她喝咖啡，聊聊她正在拍的電影。
(Man)	上星期她就坐火车离开北京了。导演说，演谁就得象谁，所以叫她到农村体验生活去了。	上星期她就坐火車離開北京了。導演說，演誰就得像誰，所以叫她到農村體驗生活去了。
(Woman)	做个好演员也不容易啊。	做個好演員也不容易啊。

(Narrator) Now answer the questions for this selection.

SELECTION 5

(Narrator) Now you will listen **twice** to a TV report.

	(Simplified Characters)	**(Traditional Characters)**
(Man)	各位观众，今天是 NBA 火箭队在中国的最后一场访问比赛。球赛票早在一个月前就被抢购一空，今天球迷们早早就来到了赛场，观众席上已经是座无虚席了。比赛还有五分钟就要开始了，球员们正在场上热身，球迷们正在兴奋地等待着一场精彩的比赛。	各位觀眾，今天是 NBA 火箭隊在中國的最後一場訪問比賽。球賽票早在一個月前就被搶購一空，今天球迷們早早就來到了賽場，觀眾席上已經是座無虛席了。比賽還有五分鐘就要開始了，球員們正在場上熱身，球迷們正在興奮地等待著一場精彩的比賽。

(Narrator) Now listen again.
(Man) (Same TV report)
(Narrator) Now answer the questions for this selection.

Speaking Part A: Conversation

You are having a conversation with a college student named David, who is conducting a survey about people's opinions regarding the Internet and its usage.

	(Simplified Characters)	**(Traditional Characters)**
David:	你平常上互联网都做些什么呢？ 最喜欢的网上娱乐是什么？	你平常上互聯網都做些什麼呢？ 最喜歡的網上娛樂是什麼？
David:	你认为在网上交朋友或者聊天有哪些好处和坏处呢？	你認為在網上交朋友或者聊天有哪些好處和壞處呢？
David:	有人觉得在网上打游戏会耽误学习，请说说你的看法。	有人覺得在網上打遊戲會耽誤學習，請說說你的看法。
David:	现在很流行从网上免费下载音乐，你对此有什么看法？	現在很流行從網上免費下載音樂，你對此有什麼看法？
David:	你认为在网上购物，都应该注意什么呢？	你認為在網上購物，都應該注意什麼呢？
David:	你能不能谈一谈互联网在你日常生活中的重要性。	你能不能談一談互聯網在你日常生活中的重要性。

UNIT 6. FAMILY

Listing Part A: Rejoinders

	(Simplified Characters)	(Traditional Characters)
1.		
(Woman)	过几天就是感恩节了，今年你家准备怎么庆祝？	過幾天就是感恩節了，今年你家準備怎麼慶祝？
(Man)	(A) 去年我们去朋友家过感恩节。	(A) 去年我們去朋友家過感恩節。
	(B) 圣诞节期间我们全家要去旅行。	(B) 聖誕節期間我們全家要去旅行。
	(C) 朋友请我们一块儿吃火鸡。	(C) 朋友請我們一塊兒吃火雞。
	(D) 我的朋友准备在餐馆过感恩节。	(D) 我的朋友準備在餐館過感恩節。
2.		
(Woman)	我要去中国探亲，需要帮你带东西回来吗？	我要去中國探親，需要幫你帶東西回來嗎？
(Man)	(A) 不用了，祝你一路顺风！	(A) 不用了，祝你一路順風！
	(B) 你已经从中国回来了？	(B) 你已經從中國回來了？
	(C) 探亲访友嘛，总得带些礼品才好。	(C) 探親訪友嘛，總得帶些禮品才好。
	(D) 我没有东西要带给我妈妈。	(D) 我沒有東西要帶給我媽媽。
3.		
(Woman)	我弟弟太调皮了，真让我妈妈操心。	我弟弟太調皮了，真讓我媽媽操心。
(Man)	(A) 能让你妈妈开心，不好吗？	(A) 能讓你媽媽開心，不好嗎？
	(B) 你不能帮你妈妈管管他吗？	(B) 你不能幫你媽媽管管他嗎？
	(C) 我才不为他操心呢！	(C) 我才不為他操心呢！
	(D) 妈妈管多了，孩子就容易调皮。	(D) 媽媽管多了，孩子就容易調皮。

	(Simplified Characters)	**(Traditional Characters)**
4.		
(Woman)	我爷爷奶奶下星期来美国，要在我们家住一阵子。	我爺爺奶奶下星期來美國，要在我們家住一陣子。
(Man)	(A) 这下你们家该热闹了！	(A) 這下你們家該熱鬧了！
	(B) 他们在你家住了多久了？	(B) 他們在你家住了多久了？
	(C) 那我昨天在你家怎么没有见到他们？	(C) 那我昨天在你家怎麼沒有見到他們？
	(D) 你爷爷奶奶真是太喜欢你了！	(D) 你爺爺奶奶真是太喜歡你了！
5.		
(Woman)	我姑姑一家住得离我不远，我常常有机会和两个表弟玩。	我姑姑一家住得離我不遠，我常常有機會和兩個表弟玩。
(Man)	(A) 你的姨妈不是还有个女儿吗？	(A) 你的姨媽不是還有個女兒嗎？
	(B) 我不大喜欢和女孩玩儿。	(B) 我不大喜歡和女孩玩兒。
	(C) 你真幸运！我的表兄妹们住得很远。	(C) 你真幸運！我的表兄妹們住得很遠。
	(D) 就是，远亲不如近邻嘛。	(D) 就是，遠親不如近鄰嘛。
6.		
(Woman)	我们家的水管又出问题了！你有好的水暖工推荐吗？	我們家的水管又出問題了！你有好的水暖工推薦嗎？
(Man)	(A) 你在电话簿上找的水暖工，不一定可靠。	(A) 你在電話簿上找的水暖工，不一定可靠。
	(B) 我用过一个不错的水暖工，这是他的电话号码。	(B) 我用過一個不錯的水暖工，這是他的電話號碼。
	(C) 冬天快到了，暖气坏了可要赶紧修。	(C) 冬天快到了，暖氣壞了可要趕緊修。
	(D) 对不起，我对电工这个行业不熟悉。	(D) 對不起，我對電工這個行業不熟悉。

	(Simplified Characters)	(Traditional Characters)
7.		
(Woman)	我妈妈的厨艺远近闻名，亲朋好友都喜欢上我们家聚会。	我媽媽的廚藝遠近聞名，親朋好友都喜歡上我們家聚會。
(Man)	(A) 是吗，那我可得去你们家厨房参观参观。	(A) 是嗎，那我可得去你們家廚房參觀參觀。
(Woman)	(B) 家里总有好吃好喝的，你可真有福气。	(B) 家裡總有好吃好喝的，你可真有福氣。
	(C) 你妈妈总是那么好客，谢谢你的邀请。	(C) 你媽媽總是那麼好客，謝謝你的邀請。
	(D) 真不知道，你妈妈的亲朋好友都那么有名。	(D) 真不知道，你媽媽的親朋好友都那麼有名。
8.		
(Woman)	中秋节快到了，爷爷从中国订购了几盒月饼寄给我们。	中秋節快到了，爺爺從中國訂購了幾盒月餅寄給我們。
(Man)	真的！每逢佳节倍思亲，你们一定很想他吧？	真的！每逢佳節倍思親，你們一定很想他吧？
(Woman)	(A) 可不是，要是他能和我们一起过中秋就好了。	(A) 可不是，要是他能和我們一起過中秋就好了。
	(B) 我爷爷可能干了，会钉盒子。	(B) 我爺爺可能幹了，會釘盒子。
	(C) 那还用说，我当然想吃月饼啦。	(C) 那還用說，我當然想吃月餅啦。
	(D) 是啊，我爷爷做的月饼别提多好吃了。	(D) 是啊，我爺爺做的月餅別提多好吃了。
9.		
(Woman)	我整个周末都在帮爸爸、妈妈在后院种花。	我整個週末都在幫爸爸、媽媽在後院種花。
(Man)	真看不出来，你还会干这些活儿啊。	真看不出來，你還會幹這些活兒啊。
(Woman)	(A) 是啊，谁在周末干这种活儿啊。	(A) 是啊，誰在週末幹這種活兒啊。
	(B) 我爸妈的确很会整理后花园。	(B) 我爸媽的確很會整理後花園。
	(C) 那当然，我从小就喜欢花草树木。	(C) 那當然，我從小就喜歡花草樹木。
	(D) 没办法，花园里的野草都长疯了。	(D) 沒辦法，花園裡的野草都長瘋了。

	(Simplified Characters)	**(Traditional Characters)**
10.		
(Woman)	迈克被耶鲁大学录取了，这个周末他们全家都送他去报到。	邁克被耶魯大學錄取了，這個週末他們全家都送他去報到。
(Man)	他父母一定很舍不得他离开家。	他父母一定很捨不得他離開家。
(Woman)	(A) 不会吧，迈克小时候就离家出走过呢。	(A) 不會吧，邁克小時候就離家出走過呢。
	(B) 迈克聪明乖巧，就是太恋家了。	(B) 邁克聰明乖巧，就是太戀家了。
	(C) 是啊，所以他们全家都搬到大学附近去了。	(C) 是啊，所以他們全家都搬到大學附近去了。
	(D) 的确很舍不得，同时又很为他骄傲。	(D) 的確很捨不得，同時又很為他驕傲。
11.		
(Woman)	以前我很害羞，妈妈建议我上表演课，现在我迷上了表演。	以前我很害羞，媽媽建議我上表演課，現在我迷上了表演。
(Man)	那你可得好好感谢你妈妈。	那你可得好好感謝你媽媽。
(Woman)	(A) 是啊，我从前很害怕上表演课。	(A) 是啊，我從前很害怕上表演課。
	(B) 是啊，多亏妈妈教我学表演。	(B) 是啊，多虧媽媽教我學表演。
	(C) 是啊，从小到大，妈妈都是我的良师益友。	(C) 是啊，從小到大，媽媽都是我的良師益友。
	(D) 是啊，妈妈常说太害羞就当不了演员了。	(D) 是啊，媽媽常說太害羞就當不了演員了。
12.		
(Woman)	小明想要领养一条小狗，你看怎么样？	小明想要領養一條小狗，你看怎麼樣？
(Man)	如果他自己能把小狗照顾好，我又何乐而不为呢？	如果他自己能把小狗照顧好，我又何樂而不為呢？
(Woman)	(A) 那就算你答应啦？	(A) 那就算你答應啦？
	(B) 领养哪用自己照顾啊！	(B) 領養哪用自己照顧啊！
	(C) 谁说我不能把狗照顾好？	(C) 誰說我不能把狗照顧好？
	(D) 你真是的，狗哪能自己照顾自己！	(D) 你真是的，狗哪能自己照顧自己！

	(Simplified Characters)	(Traditional Characters)
13.		
(Woman)	现在给孩子办护照要父母和孩子集体出马，都快成为家庭活动了。	現在給孩子辦護照要父母和孩子集體出馬，都快成為家庭活動了。
(Man)	那还不是为了保护儿童吗？你就别埋怨了。	那還不是為了保護兒童嗎？你就別埋怨了。
(Woman)	(A) 家长们都很忙，他们应该采用更简捷的办法。	(A) 家長們都很忙，他們應該採用更簡捷的辦法。
	(B) 还是你懂得怎么保护儿童。	(B) 還是你懂得怎麼保護兒童。
	(C) 骑马为什么要父母也一起去？	(C) 騎馬為什麼要父母也一起去？
	(D) 既然是家庭活动，就多带点吃的吧。	(D) 既然是家庭活動，就多帶點吃的吧。
14.		
(Woman)	你中文讲得真好，我还以为你是刚从中国来的呢。	你中文講得真好，我還以為你是剛從中國來的呢。
(Man)	那是因为我妈妈天天和我一起读中文书，从不间断。	那是因為我媽媽天天和我一起讀中文書，從不間斷。
(Woman)	(A) 原来你妈妈是中文老师啊。	(A) 原來你媽媽是中文老師啊。
	(B) 真佩服你妈妈那么有恒心。	(B) 真佩服你媽媽那麼有恆心。
	(C) 刚从中国来，中文说得就是不一样。	(C) 剛從中國來，中文說得就是不一樣。
	(D) 怪不得你妈妈的中文讲得那么流利。	(D) 怪不得你媽媽的中文講得那麼流利。
15.		
(Woman)	丽莎这孩子最近丢三落四的，也不知道是怎么回事。	麗莎這孩子最近丟三落四的，也不知道是怎麼回事。
(Man)	也许，孩子刚进入青春期，有些逆反心理吧。	也許，孩子剛進入青春期，有些逆反心理吧。
(Woman)	(A) 嗨，怎么说也不该老丢东西啊。	(A) 嗨，怎麼說也不該老丟東西啊。
	(B) 可丽莎不认识什么张三李四的呀？	(B) 可麗莎不認識什麼張三李四的呀？
	(C) 其实丽莎青春痘长得倒不多。	(C) 其實麗莎青春痘長得倒不多。
	(D) 有可能，我得尽量理解她才是。	(D) 有可能，我得盡量理解她才是。

Listening Part B: Listening Selections

SELECTION 1

(Narrator) Now you will listen **twice** to a voice message.

	(Simplified Characters)	**(Traditional Characters)**
(Woman)	喂，Lily，是我，Jasmine。我现在正在机场等我表妹。她上个月刚结婚，今天她和先生从上海来美国度蜜月。可是飞机晚点了，我怕来不及去学校接女儿，你能不能帮我接一下？请你听到留言后尽快给我回个话， 请打手机。谢谢。	喂，Lily，是我，Jasmine。我現在正在機場等我表妹。她上個月剛結婚，今天她和先生從上海來美國度蜜月。可是飛機晚點了，我怕來不及去學校接女兒，你能不能幫我接一下？請你聽到留言後盡快給我回個話， 請打手機。謝謝。

(Narrator) Now listen again.
(Woman) (Same voice message)
(Narrator) Now answer the questions for this selection.

SELECTION 2

(Narrator) Now you will listen **twice** to a recording.

	(Simplified Characters)	**(Traditional Characters)**
(Man)	这个周末我原来打算和朋友一起去滑雪的。可是一早起来，发现天气不好。上网一查，才知道大雪封山。雪滑不成了，于是，大家商量着去打保龄球，没想到球道已经占满了，可能需要等很久，我们又没耐性，只好作罢。最后大家一起去看了场电影，总算没白跑一趟。	這個週末我原來打算和朋友一起去滑雪的。可是一早起來，發現天氣不好。上網一查，才知道大雪封山。雪滑不成了，於是，大家商量着去打保齡球，沒想到球道已經佔滿了，可能需要等很久，我們又沒耐性，只好作罷。最後大家一起去看了場電影，總算沒白跑一趟。

(Narrator) Now listen again.
(Man) (Same recording)
(Narrator) Now answer the questions for this selection.

SELECTION 3

(Narrator) Now you will listen **twice** to a recording.

	(Simplified Characters)	**(Traditional Characters)**
(Woman)	今天天气这么好，你们兄弟俩又没有其他活动，那就来帮我们一起把花园收拾一下吧。宝宝，你先来扫落叶，再和我一起拔草。贝贝，你去帮爸爸粉刷围墙，如果有空能把树枝修剪一下就更好了。这些活儿大概得要几个小时才能干完，晚上我们就出去吃饭吧。	今天天氣這麼好，你們兄弟倆又沒有其他活動，那就來幫我們一起把花園收拾一下吧。寶寶，你先來掃落葉，再和我一起拔草。貝貝，你去幫爸爸粉刷圍牆，如果有空能把樹枝修剪一下就更好了。這些活兒大概得要幾個小時才能幹完，晚上我們就出去吃飯吧。

(Narrator) Now listen again.
(Woman) (Same recording)
(Narrator) Now answer the questions for this selection.

SELECTION 4

(Narrator) Now you will listen **once** to a conversation between two people.

	(Simplified Characters)	**(Traditional Characters)**
(Woman)	感恩节快到了，学校要放一周的假，我们是不是找个地方去度假？	感恩節快到了，學校要放一週的假，我們是不是找個地方去度假？
(Man)	太好了，可是去哪儿呢？ 我非常想去纽约。	太好了，可是去哪兒呢？ 我非常想去紐約。
(Woman)	那我们再问问你哥哥，看他想去哪儿。	那我們再問問你哥哥，看他想去哪兒。
(Man)	哥哥大概会选夏威夷，他既喜欢游泳，又喜欢海滩，更不用说那儿的好天气了。	哥哥大概會選夏威夷，他既喜歡游泳，又喜歡海灘，更不用說那兒的好天氣了。
(Woman)	还是你最了解你哥哥。	還是你最瞭解你哥哥。

(Narrator) Now answer the questions for this selection.

SELECTION 5

(Narrator) Now you will listen **once** to an announcement.

	(Simplified Characters)	**(Traditional Characters)**
(Woman)	亲爱的观众朋友们，这个星期是我们剧院的家庭周。所有在本周与父母一同前来观看演出的小朋友，都可以享用一份免费快餐。凡是与子女们一起来看演出、七十岁以上的老人，都可以得到一张免费电影票。符合上述条件的观众，请到一号窗口领取餐券或电影票。	親愛的觀眾朋友們，這個星期是我們劇院的家庭週。所有在本週與父母一同前來觀看演出的小朋友，都可以享用一份免費快餐。凡是與子女們一起來看演出、七十歲以上的老人，都可以得到一張免費電影票。符合上述條件的觀眾，請到一號窗口領取餐券或電影票。

(Narrator) Now answer the questions for this selection.

Speaking Part A: Conversation

You are having a conversation with your mother about your summer plans.

	(Simplified Characters)	**(Traditional Characters)**
Mom:	就要放暑假了，今年夏天你打算选课吗？ 为什么？	就要放暑假了，今年夏天你打算選課嗎？ 為什麼？
Mom:	你打算什么时候考 SAT？ 要不要去上个补习班？	你打算什麼時候考 SAT？ 要不要去上個補習班？
Mom:	你想不想趁这个暑假去看看大学？ 你最想看的有哪几所大学呢？	你想不想趁這個暑假去看看大學？你最想看的有哪幾所大學呢？
Mom:	如果我们八月份去度假，你想去旅游还是去露营？ 为什么？	如果我們八月份去度假，你想去旅遊還是去露營？ 為什麼？
Mom:	除了学习和旅游之外，这个暑假你还想做些什么？	除了學習和旅遊之外，這個暑假你還想做些什麼？
Mom:	还有，你表妹要来这里过暑假，我们给她安排些什么活动呢？ 给我说说你的想法。	還有，你的表妹要來這裡過暑假，我們給她安排些什麼活動呢？給我說說你的想法。

UNIT 7. GEOGRAPHY

Listing Part A: Rejoinders

	(Simplified Characters)	(Traditional Characters)
1.		
(Man)	我想在送你上飞机时，顺便去机场免税商店买点东西。	我想在送你上飛機時，順便去機場免稅商店買點東西。
(Woman)	(A) 不行啊，只有搭乘国际航班的旅客才能在那儿购物。	(A) 不行啊，只有搭乘國際航班的旅客才能在那兒購物。
	(B) 时间太紧，我来不及去机场的免税商店。	(B) 時間太緊，我來不及去機場的免稅商店。
	(C) 我看你还是先上飞机，再买东西吧。	(C) 我看你還是先上飛機，再買東西吧。
	(D) 我已经有很多行李了，再买东西就没地方装了。	(D) 我已經有很多行李了，再買東西就沒地方裝了。
2.		
(Man)	最近的油价越来越贵，我们租一辆小型车去旅行好吗？	最近的油價越來越貴，我們租一輛小型車去旅行好嗎？
(Woman)	(A) 让我们再想想还有什么办法能降低油价吧。	(A) 讓我們再想想還有什麼辦法能降低油價吧。
	(B) 是太贵了，我们去别的加油站看看。	(B) 是太貴了，我們去別的加油站看看。
	(C) 小型车倒是又省油又省钱，可是坐得下这么多人吗？	(C) 小型車倒是又省油又省錢，可是坐得下這麼多人嗎？
	(D) 恐怕太晚了，旅行社可能关门了。	(D) 恐怕太晚了，旅行社可能關門了。
3.		
(Man)	你在台湾旅游时，有没有去著名的日月潭？	你在台灣旅遊時，有沒有去著名的日月潭？
(Woman)	(A) 日月潭那么出名，我怎么会没听说过呢？	(A) 日月潭那麼出名，我怎麼會沒聽說過呢？
	(B) 我当时水土不服，所以什么地方也没去。	(B) 我當時水土不服，所以什麼地方也沒去。
	(C) 我这次去台湾出差，时间会很紧。	(C) 我這次去台灣出差，時間會很緊。
	(D) 五龙潭的风景的确很美，在台湾吗？	(D) 五龍潭的風景的確很美，在台灣嗎？

	(Simplified Characters)	(Traditional Characters)
4.		
(Man)	这家旅馆的设施真不错，不但有健身房还有游泳池。	這家旅館的設施真不錯，不但有健身房還有游泳池。
(Woman)	(A) 好是好，可惜太贵了。	(A) 好是好，可惜太貴了。
	(B) 其实，我最喜欢的运动是打篮球。	(B) 其實，我最喜歡的運動是打籃球。
	(C) 我介绍过好几位朋友加入这个健身俱乐部。	(C) 我介紹過好幾位朋友加入這個健身俱樂部。
	(D) 餐馆怎么会有健身房？	(D) 餐館怎麼會有健身房？
5.		
(Man)	出国旅游，不但能散心还可以长见识，真是一举两得。	出國旅遊，不但能散心還可以長見識，真是一舉兩得。
(Woman)	(A) 嗬，到底是练举重的，一只手就能举起两样重东西！	(A) 嗬，到底是練舉重的，一隻手就能舉起兩樣重東西！
	(B) 就是嘛，凡事都会有得必有失。	(B) 就是嘛，凡事都會有得必有失。
	(C) 是啊，这就是为什么我们不喜欢出国旅游。	(C) 是啊，這就是為什麼我們不喜歡出國旅遊。
	(D) 一点不错，所以我们经常带孩子出国旅游。	(D) 一點不錯，所以我們經常帶孩子出國旅遊。
6.		
(Man)	你知道南太平洋上漂浮着一座巨大的垃圾山吗？	你知道南太平洋上漂浮著一座巨大的垃圾山嗎？
(Woman)	(A) 南极有冰山又不是什么新闻。	(A) 南極有冰山又不是什麼新聞。
	(B) 太平洋上是有一些活火山，怎么啦？	(B) 太平洋上是有一些活火山，怎麼啦？
	(C) 太不应该了，真希望能马上把它清除掉。	(C) 太不應該了，真希望能馬上把它清除掉。
	(D) 洛基山在美洲，怎么会到太平洋里去了？	(D) 洛基山在美洲，怎麼會到太平洋裡去了？

	(Simplified Characters)	(Traditional Characters)
7.		
(Man)	航空公司规定，每件托运的行李不能超过五十磅，否则就要另收费。	航空公司規定，每件托運的行李不能超過五十磅，否則就要另收費。
(Woman)	(A) 真的？那我得把两个箱子的东西匀一匀，争取不超重。	(A) 真的？ 那我得把兩個箱子的東西匀一匀，爭取不超重。
	(B) 超重的行李还要交额外的保险费？太过分了！	(B) 超重的行李還要交額外的保險費？太過分了！
	(C) 超重的行李要收五十元一磅？那么贵！	(C) 超重的行李要收五十元一磅？ 那麼貴！
	(D) 真巧，我们的随身行李刚好五十磅。	(D) 真巧，我們的隨身行李剛好五十磅。
8.		
(Woman)	我准备下个月从纽约去上海旅行。	我準備下個月從紐約去上海旅行。
(Man)	你的护照和入境签证都办好了吗？	你的護照和入境簽証都辦好了嗎？
(Woman)	(A) 我的行李已经收拾得差不多了。	(A) 我的行李已經收拾得差不多了。
	(B) 我的护照和美国签证都已经办好了。	(B) 我的護照和美國簽証都已經辦好了。
	(C) 你真会开玩笑，去纽约不要签证。	(C) 你真會開玩笑，去紐約不要簽証。
	(D) 护照有了，但签证还没办呢。	(D) 護照有了，但簽証還沒辦呢。
9.		
(Woman)	先生，请问你要托运行李吗？	先生，請問你要托運行李嗎？
(Man)	只托运这一件大的，另外一件小的随身带。	只托運這一件大的，另外一件小的隨身帶。
(Woman)	(A) 没问题。这是你的收据。	(A) 沒問題。這是你的收據。
	(B) 你拿定主意了，我才能帮你办。	(B) 你拿定主意了，我才能幫你辦。
	(C) 你不能随身携带这么多的行李。	(C) 你不能隨身攜帶這麼多的行李。
	(D) 你这两件托运行李都超重，要额外收费。	(D) 你這兩件托運行李都超重，要額外收費。

	(Simplified Characters)	**(Traditional Characters)**
10.		
(Woman)	请问，国庆节期间，你们酒店还有空房间吗？	請問，國慶節期間，你們酒店還有空房間嗎？
(Man)	有，你们几个人？要住几天？怎么付款？	有，你們幾個人？要住幾天？怎麼付款？
(Woman)	(A) 两个人，住两天。用信用卡付款。	(A) 兩個人，住兩天。用信用卡付款。
	(B) 两个人，住两天。收现金。	(B) 兩個人，住兩天。收現金。
	(C) 两个人，住两天。付不付都可以。	(C) 兩個人，住兩天。付不付都可以。
	(D) 两个人，住两天。付零钱。	(D) 兩個人，住兩天。付零錢。
11.		
(Woman)	张导游，我们今天去什么地方参观？	張導遊，我們今天去什麼地方參觀？
(Man)	上午去长城，下午自由活动。	上午去長城，下午自由活動。
(Woman)	(A) 长城上那么多人， 大概没法自由活动吧。	(A) 長城上那麼多人，大概沒法自由活動吧。
	(B) 太好了，我一直盼着去长城呢！	(B) 太好了，我一直盼著去長城呢！
	(C) 这样安排好，我最喜欢自由自在地游览名胜古迹了。	(C) 這樣安排好，我最喜歡自由自在地遊覽名勝古跡了。
	(D) 好极了，上午跟导游去自由活动一定很有意思！	(D) 好極了，上午跟導遊去自由活動一定很有意思！
12.		
(Woman)	从上海到北京，是坐飞机好呢，还是坐火车好？	從上海到北京，是坐飛機好呢，還是坐火車好？
(Man)	我喜欢坐火车，特别是夜车的卧铺，睡一觉，早上一睁眼就到了。	我喜歡坐火車，特別是夜車的臥鋪，睡一覺，早上一睜眼就到了。
(Woman)	(A) 可是飞机上没有卧铺啊？	(A) 可是飛機上沒有臥鋪啊？
	(B) 坐在飞机上一夜睡不好觉！	(B) 坐在飛機上一夜睡不好覺！
	(C) 看来坐夜车的卧铺挺不错。	(C) 看來坐夜車的臥鋪挺不錯。
	(D) 可是晚上到北京多不方便。	(D) 可是晚上到北京多不方便。

	(Simplified Characters)	(Traditional Characters)
13.		
(Woman)	我们星期六去海滩游泳好不好？	我們星期六去海灘游泳好不好？
(Man)	可是天气预报说周末又刮风又下雨。	可是天氣預報說週末又刮風又下雨。
(Woman)	(A) 那我们就改到星期天去吧。	(A) 那我們就改到星期天去吧。
	(B) 那我们去看电影吧。	(B) 那我們去看電影吧。
	(C) 我们听完天气预报再去游泳吧。	(C) 我們聽完天氣預報再去游泳吧。
	(D) 天气预报员周末不休息吗？	(D) 天氣預報員週末不休息嗎？
14.		
(Woman)	加州的天气真好，好像总是阳光明媚的。	加州的天氣真好，好像總是陽光明媚的。
(Man)	好是好，可是我常常担心地震。	好是好，可是我常常擔心地震。
(Woman)	(A) 那倒是，老是不下雨容易引起山火。	(A) 那倒是，老是不下雨容易引起山火。
	(B) 是很令人担心，可你怎么知道要地震了？	(B) 是很令人擔心，可你怎麼知道要地震了？
	(C) 太阳是蛮厉害的，所以出门要擦防晒霜。	(C) 太陽是蠻厲害的，所以出門要擦防晒霜。
	(D) 地震的确让人担忧，但是毕竟难得发生。	(D) 地震的確令人擔憂，但是畢竟難得發生。
15.		
(Woman)	我有了全球定位系统后，开车即使没有地图，也不怕迷路了。	我有了全球定位系统後，开车即使没有地图，也不怕迷路了。
(Man)	全球定位系统真的那么有用吗？	全球定位系统真的那么有用吗？
(Woman)	(A) 可不是，有了地图就不会迷路了。	(A) 可不是，有了地图就不会迷路了。
	(B) 对我来说，开车不能没有它。	(B) 对我来说，开车不能没有它。
	(C) 可不是，每年都有新款式。	(C) 可不是，每年都有新款式。
	(D) 自动订票系统还能确认坐位，特别方便。	(D) 自动订票系统还能确认座位，特别方便。

Listening Part B: Listening Selections

SELECTION 1

(Narrator) Now you will listen **twice** to an announcement.

	(Simplified Characters)	**(Traditional Characters)**
(Woman)	各位旅客，欢迎乘坐 D32 次由上海开往北京的列车！本次列车全程对号入座，并设有餐车，我们为您准备了美味可口的炒菜、米饭和饮料，欢迎大家光临！下一站是南京站，到南京站下车的旅客，请提前做好准备。祝您旅途愉快！	各位旅客，歡迎乘坐 D32 次由上海開往北京的列車！本次列車全程對號入座，並設有餐車，我們為您準備了美味可口的炒菜、米飯和飲料，歡迎大家光臨！下一站是南京站，到南京站下車的旅客，請提前做好準備。祝您旅途愉快！

(Narrator) Now listen again.
(Woman) (Same announcement)
(Narrator) Now answer the questions for this selection.

SELECTION 2

(Narrator) Now you will listen **once** to a commercial..

	(Simplified Characters)	**(Traditional Characters)**
(Man)	听说你去中国旅游了，好玩吗？自己去的还是参加旅游团去的？	聽說你去中國旅遊了，好玩嗎？ 自己去的還是參加旅遊團去的？
(Woman)	很好玩。我们参加的是平安旅行社主办的中国旅行团。导游热情周到，团费又便宜。	很好玩。我們參加的是平安旅行社主辦的中國旅行團。導遊熱情周到，團費又便宜。
(Man)	团费都包括些什么呢？	團費都包括些什麼呢？
(Woman)	团费包括机票，五星级豪华酒店，一日三餐，景点门票以及旅行保险。	團費包括機票，五星級豪華酒店，一日三餐，景點門票以及旅行保險。
(Man)	去中国旅游一定要找平安旅行社。服务好，价钱低。	去中國旅遊一定要找平安旅行社。服務好，價錢低。
(Woman)	电话号码 1-(800) 123-4567。	電話號碼 1-(800) 123-4567。

(Narrator) Now answer the questions for this selection.

SELECTION 3

(Narrator) Now you will listen **twice** to a voice message.

	(Simplified Characters)	**(Traditional Characters)**
(Man)	喂，妈妈，我是小明。我现在还在纽约的肯尼迪机场。纽约市正在下大雪，所有的航班都暂停起飞。我搭乘的班机要推迟三个小时起飞。对不起，我赶不回去跟您和爸爸一起吃晚饭了。你们先吃吧，千万别等我。我的班机是 A123，请爸爸先上网确认一下飞机到达时间，然后再来接我。晚上见。	喂，媽媽，我是小明。我現在還在紐約的肯尼迪機場。紐約市正在下大雪，所有的航班都暫停起飛。我搭乘的班機要推遲三個小時起飛。對不起，我趕不回去跟您和爸爸一起吃晚飯了。你們先吃吧，千萬別等我。我的班機是 A123，請爸爸先上網確認一下飛機到達時間，然後再來接我。晚上見。

(Narrator) Now listen again.
(Man) (Same voice message)
(Narrator) Now answer the questions for this selection.

SELECTION 4

(Narrator) Now you will listen **once** to a conversation between two friends.

	(Simplified Characters)	**(Traditional Characters)**
(Man)	你春节回家吗？	你春節回家嗎？
(Woman)	当然回家。我已经买了下星期六的机票。	當然回家。我已經買了下星期六的機票。
(Man)	几点的飞机？你怎么去机场？	幾點的飛機？ 你怎麼去機場？
(Woman)	是早上六点钟的飞机。我打算坐地铁去机场。	是早上六點鐘的飛機。我打算坐地鐵去機場。
(Man)	可是，早上六点以后才有去机场的地铁。那天我有空，我可以开车送你去机场。	可是，早上六點以後才有去機場的地鐵。那天我有空，我可以開車送你去機場。
(Woman)	太好了！谢谢你！	太好了！ 謝謝你！

(Narrator) Now answer the questions for this selection.

SELECTION 5

(Narrator) Now you will listen **once** to a news report.

	(Simplified Characters)	**(Traditional Characters)**
(Woman)	三藩市的金山酒店将于十二月七日下午五点至七点，在美丽的酒店大草坪上举行圣诞树点灯仪式。届时，酒店将向公众免费提供节日饮料、糖果点心和风味小吃，现场音乐表演更是锦上添花，欢迎大家前往同享浓厚的节日气氛。	三藩市的金山酒店將於十二月七日下午五點至七點，在美麗的酒店大草坪上舉行聖誕樹點燈儀式。屆時，酒店將向公眾免費提供節日飲料、糖果點心和風味小吃，現場音樂表演更是錦上添花，歡迎大家前往同享濃厚的節日氣氛。

(Narrator) Now answer the questions for this selection.

Speaking Part A: Conversation

Your friend David plans to visit China this summer. He wants to get some ideas about China and its cities from you.

	(Simplified Characters)	**(Traditional Characters)**
David:	今年夏天我要去中国旅行，先到北京。你能不能说一说北京在中国大致的地理位置？	今年夏天我要去中國旅行，先到北京。你能不能說一說北京在中國大致的地理位置？
David:	在北京除了游览长城外，还有什么其他的名胜古迹一定要去看？ 为什么？	在北京除了遊覽長城外，還有什麼其他的名勝古跡一定要去看？ 為什麼？
David:	旅行团安排我们去西安，西安为什么很有名？ 有什么非常特别的景点？能给我简单介绍一下吗？	旅行團安排我們去西安，西安為什麼很有名？ 有什麼非常特別的景點？能給我簡單介紹一下嗎？
David:	我们还要去桂林，听说桂林的风景很美，你来说说它美在什么地方？	我們還要去桂林，聽說桂林的風景很美，你來說說它美在什麼地方？
David:	我们的最后一站是上海，上海有什么特色呢？	我們的最後一站是上海，上海有什麼特色呢？
David:	如果你去中国游玩，你最想去哪些地方？ 为什么？	如果你去中國遊玩，你最想去哪些地方？ 為什麼？

UNIT 8. MIXED THEME

Listing Part A: Rejoinders

	(Simplified Characters)	(Traditional Characters)
1.		
(Woman)	你最近在博客上读过些什么精彩的文章？	你最近在博客上讀過些什麼精彩的文章？
(Man)	(A) 没有，我没听说她开博客啊。	(A) 沒有，我沒聽說她開博客啊。
	(B) 没有，最近很忙，没有时间上网。	(B) 沒有，最近很忙，沒有時間上網。
	(C) 当然啦，我最近写了很多文章。	(C) 當然啦，我最近寫了很多文章。
	(D) 当然读过，博士写的文章肯定很精彩。	(D) 當然讀過，博士寫的文章肯定很精彩。
2.		
(Woman)	现在买东西真方便，不用出门，上网就可以了。	現在買東西真方便，不用出門，上網就可以了。
(Man)	(A) 方便是方便，不过，要看买什么东西了。	(A) 方便是方便，不過，要看買什麼東西了。
	(B) 一出门就能买东西，真方便。	(B) 一出門就能買東西，真方便。
	(C) 网路断了，就没法出去买东西了。	(C) 網路斷了，就沒法出門買東西了。
	(D) 是啊，上网买东西还不如出门方便。	(D) 是啊，上網買東西還不如出門方便。
3.		
(Man)	你明天上午有课吗？	你明天上午有課嗎？
(Woman)	(A) 我昨天上午没有课。	(A) 我昨天上午沒有課。
	(B) 我上午没有课，但是下午有两节。	(B) 我上午沒有課，但是下午有兩節。
	(C) 你明天也没有课吗？	(C) 你明天也沒有課嗎？
	(D) 今天上午我只有一节课，下午和晚上都有空。	(D) 今天上午我只有一節課，下午和晚上都有空。

	(Simplified Characters)	(Traditional Characters)
4.		
(Man)	我每天发很多短信，妈妈看到账单后很不高兴。	我每天發很多短信，媽媽看到賬單後很不高興。
(Woman)	(A) 你妈妈每天都记账吗？	(A) 你媽媽每天都記賬嗎？
	(B) 不会吧，在电脑上发电子邮件又不要钱。	(B) 不會吧，在電腦上發電子郵件又不要錢。
	(C) 你现在还寄信啊？太落后了！	(C) 你現在還寄信啊？ 太落後了！
	(D) 那你今后该收敛一些了！	(D) 那你今後該收斂一些了！
5.		
(Man)	我是姚明的超级球迷！他的球赛，我每场必看。	我是姚明的超級球迷！他的球賽，我每場必看。
(Woman)	(A) 我也喜欢看现场比赛。	(A) 我也喜歡看現場比賽。
	(B) 看球也是姚明训练的一种方式。	(B) 看球也是姚明訓練的一種方式。
	(C) 姚明的球赛真好看，你居然不看！	(C) 姚明的球賽真好看，你居然不看！
	(D) 我也喜欢看姚明打球，但我还算不上他的球迷。	(D) 我也喜歡看姚明打球，但我還算不上他的球迷。
6.		
(Man)	这个季度的垃圾费又涨了。	這個季度的垃圾費又漲了。
(Woman)	(A) 能换大的垃圾桶，太好了。	(A) 能換大的垃圾桶，太好了。
	(B) 不是半年前刚涨过吗？	(B) 不是半年前剛漲過嗎？
	(C) 下个季度的事，到时候再说吧。	(C) 下個季度的事，到時候再說吧。
	(D) 太好了，我们可以少交垃圾费了。	(D) 太好了，我們可以少交垃圾費了。

	(Simplified Characters)	(Traditional Characters)
7.		
(Man)	新的一季"与星共舞"电视节目昨天首播了，你有没有看？	新的一季"與星共舞"電視節目昨天首播了，你有沒有看？
(Woman)	(A) 看了，很喜欢，我几乎每季都看。	(A) 看了，很喜歡，我幾乎每季都看。
	(B) 还没有，"与星共舞"在哪些电影院上演？	(B) 還沒有，"與星共舞"在哪些電影院上演？
	(C) 没有看，昨天是不是最后一集了？	(C) 沒有看，昨天是不是最後一集了？
	(D) 没有看到。不过"与星共舞"去年已经放过了。	(D) 沒有看到。不過"與星共舞"去年已經放過了。
8.		
(Woman)	这就是青海湖吗？	這就是青海湖嗎？
(Man)	是啊，你知道吗，它刚被评为中国最美的湖。	是啊，你知道嗎，它剛被評為中國最美的湖。
(Woman)	(A) 那东北虎被评为第几啊？	(A) 那東北虎被評為第幾啊？
	(B) 确实是美不胜收啊。	(B) 確實是美不勝收啊。
	(C) 我倒觉得可爱的小雪狐更漂亮。	(C) 我倒覺得可愛的小雪狐更漂亮。
	(D) 不过，我还是最喜欢紫砂壶。	(D) 不過，我還是最喜歡紫砂壺。
9.		
(Woman)	外面鞭炮放得那么热闹，是不是有人在举行婚礼？	外面鞭炮放得那麼熱鬧，是不是有人在舉行婚禮？
(Man)	一定是小波，你没看见他家门上贴着红双喜吗？	一定是小波，你沒看見他家門上貼著紅雙喜嗎？
(Woman)	(A) 我看不像，年还没过完呢。	(A) 我看不像，年還沒過完呢。
	(B) 那我得赶紧去讨喜糖吃。	(B) 那我得趕緊去討喜糖吃。
	(C) 放鞭炮我赞成，红双喜就别贴了。	(C) 放鞭炮我贊成，紅雙喜就別貼了。
	(D) 你还别说，贴红双喜就是不如放鞭炮热闹。	(D) 你還別說，貼紅雙喜就是不如放鞭炮熱鬧。

	(Simplified Characters)	**(Traditional Characters)**
10.		
(Woman)	真香啊！你这是什么茶？	真香啊！你這是什麼茶？
(Man)	就知道你会喜欢，这可是上好的乌龙茶。	就知道你會喜歡，這可是上好的烏龍茶。
(Woman)	(A) 你为什么总是喜欢碧螺春？	(A) 你為什麼總是喜歡碧螺春？
	(B) 原来里面有菊花，难怪这么香。	(B) 原來裡面有菊花，難怪這麼香。
	(C) 谢谢你想到我，那我可得好好享用。	(C) 謝謝你想到我，那我可得好好享用。
	(D) 我一闻就知道是龙井茶。	(D) 我一聞就知道是龍井茶。
11.		
(Woman)	这个花园可真漂亮，都快赶上拙政园了。	這個花園可真漂亮，都快趕上拙政園了。
(Man)	还是你有眼光，这是请设计师模仿苏州园林设计的。	還是你有眼光，這是請設計師模仿蘇州園林設計的。
(Woman)	(A) 苏州园林的设计可不能你说了算。	(A) 蘇州園林的設計可不能你說了算。
	(B) 苏州的产品就是不一样。	(B) 蘇州的產品就是不一樣。
	(C) 苏州没有园林设计师吗？	(C) 蘇州沒有園林設計師嗎？
	(D) 那你可得介绍我认识这位设计师。	(D) 那你可得介紹我認識這位設計師。
12.		
(Woman)	这个周末，我要去中国大剧院看歌剧“秦始皇”。	這個週末，我要去中國大劇院看歌劇“秦始皇”。
(Man)	真的？听说是西班牙歌唱家多明戈主演的。	真的？聽說是西班牙歌唱家多明戈主演的。
(Woman)	(A) 不会吧？多明戈没有秦始皇有名。	(A) 不會吧？多明戈沒有秦始皇有名。
	(B) 可是，西班牙歌唱家听不懂中国歌剧呀。	(B) 可是，西班牙歌唱家聽不懂中國歌劇呀。
	(C) 对，就是因为多明戈演中国皇帝，所以我非去看不可！	(C) 對，就是因為多明戈演中國皇帝，所以我非去看不可！
	(D) 你搞错啦，秦始皇是中国皇帝，不是西班牙人！	(D) 你搞錯啦，秦始皇是中國皇帝，不是西班牙人！

	(Simplified Characters)	**(Traditional Characters)**
13.		
(Woman)	今晚六点，我在学校有场演出，你能来看吗？	今晚六點，我在學校有場演出，你能來看嗎？
(Man)	我争取早点儿下班，赶过去看看。	我爭取早點兒下班，趕過去看看。
(Woman)	(A) 太好了，谢谢你答应来看。	(A) 太好了，謝謝你答應來看。
	(B) 谢谢你答应参加我们的演出。	(B) 謝謝你答應參加我們的演出。
	(C) 你要不来，我们就没法演出了！	(C) 你要不來，我們就沒法演出了！
	(D) 等你下班再来送我就来不及了。	(D) 等你下班再來送我就來不及了。
14.		
(Man)	这条裙子挺适合你的，买吗？	這條裙子挺適合你的，買嗎？
(Woman)	多少钱啊？还有别的颜色吗?	多少錢啊？還有別的顏色嗎?
(Man)	(A) 对不起，我们只有小号的了。	(A) 對不起，我們只有小號的了。
	(B) 不要紧，裙子颜色多一点才好看。	(B) 不要緊，裙子顏色多一點才好看。
	(C) 五十二元，太贵了，颜色也都差不多。	(C) 五十二元，太貴了，顏色也都差不多。
	(D) 五十二块。还有红色和蓝色的。	(D) 五十二塊。還有紅色和藍色的。
15.		
(Woman)	你去过四川成都吗？	你去過四川成都嗎？
(Man)	天府之国，当然去过。	天府之國，當然去過。
(Woman)	(A) 我问你的是成都，不是天府。	(A) 我問你的是成都，不是天府。
	(B) 真的？杜甫的故居你都去过了。	(B) 真的？杜甫的故居你都去過了。
	(C) 成都的确是四川省的省会。	(C) 成都的確是四川省的省會。
	(D) 能给我介绍介绍吗？	(D) 能給我介紹介紹嗎？

Listening Part B: Listening Selections

SELECTION 1

(Narrator) Now you will listen **once** to a conversation between two people.

	(Simplified Characters)	**(Traditional Characters)**
(Woman)	请问哪一位是李大夫？	請問哪一位是李大夫？
(Man)	我就是，你是来作入学身体检查的吧？	我就是，你是來作入學身體檢查的吧？
(Woman)	是的，我是刚从美国来这儿的留学生。	是的，我是剛從美國來這兒的留學生。
(Man)	你最近在美国做过身体检查吗？	你最近在美國做過身體檢查嗎？
(Woman)	最近没有，我最后一次身体检查大约是一年以前了。	最近沒有，我最後一次身體檢查大約是一年以前了。
(Man)	那你先填一下体检表，然后去验血。	那你先填一下體檢表，然後去驗血。

(Narrator) Now answer the questions for this selection.

SELECTION 2

(Narrator) Now you will listen **once** to a conversation between two people.

	(Simplified Characters)	**(Traditional Characters)**
(Woman)	旺旺，瞧你，拿着人参，急急忙忙地去见谁呢？	旺旺，瞧你，拿著人蔘，急急忙忙地去見誰呢？
(Man)	你不知道，今天是我外婆的生日，我赶着去见她老人家。	你不知道，今天是我外婆的生日，我趕着去見她老人家。
(Woman)	那人参是你给外婆的礼物喽？	那人蔘是你給外婆的禮物嘍？
(Man)	那当然，我外婆都快一百岁了，还是那么硬朗，人参立了大功，这是我每年都要给外婆的礼物。	那當然，我外婆都快一百歲了，還是那麼硬朗，人蔘立了大功，這是我每年都要給外婆的禮物。
(Woman)	怪不得你外婆那么长寿。	怪不得你外婆那麼長壽。

(Narrator) Now answer the questions for this selection.

SELECTION 3

(Narrator) Now you will listen **twice** to a commercial.

	(Simplified Characters)	**(Traditional Characters)**
(Woman)	金桥翻译公司为客户提供八国文字翻译，各类场合口译，法律、科技以及其他类型文件的翻译。此外，还办理公证。本公司所有专家都持有专业执照，经验丰富。多年来的客户包括各级政府部门和多国大使馆、领事馆。我们的各项服务都受到很高的评价。联系电话：415-123-4567。	金橋翻譯公司為客戶提供八國文字翻譯，各類場合口譯，法律、科技以及其他類型文件的翻譯。此外，還辦理公証。本公司所有專家都持有專業執照，經驗豐富。多年來的客戶包括各級政府部門和多國大使館、領事館。我們的各項服務都受到很高的評價。聯系電話：415-123-4567。

(Narrator) Now listen again.
(Women) (Same commercial)
(Narrator) Now answer the questions for this selection.

SELECTION 4

(Narrator) Now you will listen **once** to a conversation between two friends.

	(Simplified Characters)	**(Traditional Characters)**
(Woman)	今晚学校有舞会，和我一起去吧？	今晚學校有舞會，和我一起去吧？
(Man)	对不起，我不去了，看看小张能不能和你一块儿去。	對不起，我不去了，看看小張能不能和你一塊兒去。
(Woman)	你真是的，星期六也不放松放松？	你真是的，星期六也不放鬆放鬆？
(Man)	我觉得舞会上的音乐太响了，受不了！我宁愿去看电影。	我覺得舞會上的音樂太響了，受不了！ 我寧願去看電影。
(Woman)	音乐是响了点儿，但跳舞还是很好玩的。	音樂是響了點兒，但跳舞還是很好玩的。

(Narrator) Now answer the questions for this selection.

SELECTION 5

(Narrator) Now you will listen **once** to a conversation between two people.

	(Simplified Characters)	**(Traditional Characters)**
(Woman)	爸爸，我今天的作业需要你帮忙。	爸爸，我今天的作業需要你幫忙。
(Man)	是什么作业把你都给难住了？你怎么没去问妈妈呢？	是什麼作業把你都給難住了？ 你怎麼沒去問媽媽呢？
(Woman)	老师特意要求爸爸们来做这件事。	老師特意要求爸爸們來做這件事。
(Man)	那我可得认真对待，做个称职的好爸爸。你说吧。	那我可得認真對待，做個稱職的好爸爸。你說吧。
(Woman)	作业是"听爸爸讲他小时候的故事"。	作業是"聽爸爸講他小時候的故事"。

(Narrator) Now answer the questions for this selection.

SELECTION 6

(Narrator) Now you will listen **twice** to the following instructions.

	(Simplified Characters)	**(Traditional Characters)**
(Woman)	美国公民到中国旅游必须申请旅游签证。	美國公民到中國旅遊必須申請旅遊簽証。
	申请签证需要提供：	申請簽証需要提供：
	(1) 有效期六个月以上的美国护照	(1) 有效期六個月以上的美國護照
	(2) 签证申请表一份	(2) 簽証申請表一份
	(3) 2 x 2 英寸近照一张	(3) 2 x 2 英吋近照一張
	办理地点：中国领事馆或大使馆	辦理地點：中國領事館或大使館
	办理时间：四个工作日	辦理時間：四個工作日
	办理费用：一百三十美元。接受现金、银行支票或信用卡，但不接受私人支票。	辦理費用：一百三十美元。接受現金、銀行支票或信用卡，但不接受私人支票。

(Narrator) Now listen again.
(Woman) (Same instructions)
(Narrator) Now answer the questions for this selection.

Speaking Part A: Conversation

Imagine you are having a conversation with David, a friend of yours who has been to China many times, about your very first trip to China this summer.

	(Simplified Characters)	**(Traditional Characters)**
David:	听说你决定今年夏天去中国旅游，你为什么想去中国呢？	聽說你決定今年夏天去中國旅遊，你為什麼想去中國呢？
David:	你是跟团去旅游，还是自助游？为什么？	你是跟團去旅遊，還是自助遊？為什麼？
David:	你做了什么准备呢？有没有办好护照和签证？	你做了什麼準備呢？有没有辦好護照和簽証？
David:	到了中国，你都会去哪些地方玩？	到了中國，你都會去哪些地方玩？
David:	你将要在中国待多久？	你將要在中國待多久？
David:	除了游览名胜古迹以外，你还想在中国做些什么呢？	除了遊覽名勝古跡以外，你還想在中國做些什麼呢？

APPENDIX II

ADDITIONAL RESOURCES [1]

Official College Board Links

AP Chinese Language and Culture Course Home Page
http://apcentral.collegeboard.com/apc/public/courses/teachers_corner/37221.html

AP Chinese Language and Culture Course Description
http://www.collegeboard.com/student/testing/ap/sub_chineselang.html

AP Chinese Language and Culture Sample Questions & Scoring Guidelines
http://www.collegeboard.com/student/testing/ap/chinese/samp.html?chineselang

AP Central Teachers' Resources Search
http://apcentral.collegeboard.com/apc/Pageflows/TeachersResource/TeachersResourceController.jpf

Online News Resources

Sing Tao Chinese Radio 星岛中文电台（星島中文電台）
http://www.chineseradio.com

Sinovision Television 美国中文电视（美國中文電視）
http://www.sinovision.net/index_tv.php

BBC News BBC 中文网（BBC 中文網）
http://www.bbc.co.uk/zhongwen

Voice of America 美国之音中文网（美國之音中文網）
http://www.voanews.com/chinese

Sing Tao Daily 星岛日报（星島日報）
http://www.singtaousa.com

World Journal 世界日报（世界日報）
http://www.worldjournal.com

[1] For a clickable list of links in this appendix, please visit the *AP Chinese Practice Tests* companion page on PeerSource (my.cheng-tsui.com).

Caijing Magazine 财经网（財經網）
http://www.caijing.com.cn

Sinovision 美国中文网（美國中文網）
http://www.sinovision.net

Chinese Learning Tools

Online Dictionaries

http://www.dict.cn

http://usa.mdbg.net/chindict/chindict.php

http://www.chinese-tools.com/tools/dictionary.html

Online Language Translators

http://babelfish.yahoo.com

http://translate.google.com

http://www.microsofttranslator.com

Websites Designed Specifically for Language Learners

ChinesePod
http://www.chinesepod.com

Learning Chinese Online
http://learningchineseonline.net

Sexy Beijing
http://www.sexybeijing.tv

Chinese Video Exercises
http://www.conncoll.edu/academics/departments/chinese/mhu/videos2/home.html

Read Chinese!
http://readchinese.nflc.org

Chinese Learn Online
http://www.chineselearnonline.com

Chinese Reading World
http://www.uiowa.edu/~chnsrdng

Progressive Reading
http://www.usc.edu/dept/ealc/chinese/Level/1.htm

A Chinese Text Sampler
http://www-personal.umich.edu/~dporter/sampler/sampler.html

Chinese Voices Project
http://www.clavisinica.com/voices.html

BBC Language Learning Site
http://www.bbc.co.uk/languages/chinese

Chinese Art, Culture and Literature

China the Beautiful 锦绣中华（錦繡中華）
http://www.chinapage.org/china.html

Classical Chinese art, calligraphy, poetry, history, literature, and more

WenGu 温故（温故）
http://afpc.asso.fr/wengu/wg/wengu.php?l=bienvenue

Chinese classics and translations

The Art of Chinese Culture
http://www.chineseart.com/

Chinese art, food and drink, festivals

My China Start
http://literature.mychinastart.com/

Literature, legends, poetry

Bookstores and Publishers

Cheng & Tsui Company 剑桥出版社（劍橋出版社）

http://www.cheng-tsui.com

VOCABULARY INDEX

D

E

F

G

H

J

K

L

M

N

O

P

Q

T

W

X

Y

Z

Notes: